BACK FIRED

A nation founded on
religious tolerance
no longer tolerates
its founders' religion

William J. Federer

*The faith
that gave birth
to tolerance
is no longer tolerated.*

BACKFIRED
*- A nation founded for religious tolerance
no longer tolerates its founders' religion*
by William J. Federer

Library of Congress
HISTORY / EDUCATION   ISBN 0-9753455-4-0
ISBN13 978-0-9753455-4-2

Picture: *Battle of Lake Erie* by William Henry Powell, 1873.
Ronald Reagan photograph - Library of Congress.

Cover design by: Dustin Myers
dustinmyersdesign.com
573-308-6060, info@dustinmyersdesign.com

A limited-time offer, as owner of this book, you may
receive a **free *ebook*** of this title by visiting
www.AmericanMinute.com
click "Contact"and send an email with the subject line
Backfired ebook

Amerisearch, Inc., P.O. Box 20163, St. Louis, MO 63123,
1-888-USA-WORD, 314-487-4395
www.amerisearch.net, wjfederer@gmail.com

To

my

sons,

Will   and   Michael

"Mr. Speaker,
One of
the first
things we,
our parents before us,
and our children after us,
learned in school was that
the settlement of America came about
because of the desire of oppressed peoples
to have the freedom to worship as they please."

- U.S. Rep. Nick Joe Rahall, II, (WV)
United States Congress, Aug. 11, 1992 [1]

CONTENTS

CONTENTS

INTRODUCTION

Afraid of expensive ACLU lawsuits, Los Angeles removed the cross off its city seal, even though the city was founded as a Spanish Mission; a San Francisco teacher was not allowed to show students the Declaration of Independence because it mentioned the "Creator"; a Senior Center in Balch Springs, Texas, told seniors they could no longer pray over their meals; a school in Plano, Texas, changed its "Christmas" party to "winter" and told parents not to bring red and green paper plates because it might remind the children of Christmas.

The ACLU sued in Louisiana to stop student prayer; sued in California to ban "under God" from Pledge; sued in New Orleans to remove a "Jesus is Lord" billboard; sued in Alabama, Kentucky, Texas, Tennessee and Pennsylvania to remove the Ten Commandments; sued in San Diego to kick the Boy Scouts off Balboa Park because of their oath: "Do my duty to God and my country."

The ACLU demanded a "God Bless America" sign in Rocklin, California, taken down after 911; opposed the posting of the National Motto "In God We Trust"; rejected the Bible as history and literature in Florida schools; and censored nativity scenes, Christmas carols, religious art and music.

From de-funding the Salvation Army to the Bible being called "hate speech," the question begs to be asked:

"How did America go from Pilgrims seeking freedom to express their Judeo-Christian beliefs to today's discrimination against those very beliefs in the name of tolerance?"

While I was interviewed by a radio station in Madison, Wisconsin, the host remarked that he thought Christians were intolerant.

I commented that his view was interesting, given that it was the Judeo-Christian beliefs of America's founders that gave birth to the modern concept of tolerance.

Though hesitating, he agreed that tolerance did not originate in Saudi Arabia, where it is still the death penalty if one converts from Islam to another faith.

Nor did it originate in India's caste-system, where the lowest caste was considered "untouchable"; nor from the former atheistic Soviet Union, where for seventy years thousands were persecuted for their faith; nor from atheistic Communist China, where illegal house church leaders and Falun Gong members are still arrested;

Nor did tolerance originate with Robespierre's Reign of Terror, where thousands accused of not supporting the bloody atheistic French Revolution lost their heads in the guillotine.

I explained to the radio host that tolerance, as we know it, was an American Judeo-Christian contribution to the world.

But as to the question of who is intolerant, in strict Islamic countries Shari'a Courts prohibit public Judeo-Christian expression, and in the United States, activist Courts prohibit public Judeo-Christian expression. It is as if secular fundamentalists are on a fanatical jihad to establish an oppressive, intolerant state religion of secularism - a secular Taliban - right here on American soil.

President of the American Legion, Thomas P. Cadmus, called the ACLU a legal terrorist organization, as activist judges order communities to pay millions of dollars to the ACLU. They are, in effect, establishing a State Religion of Atheistic Secular Humanism.

President Reagan, Feb. 25, 1984, stated: "We're told our children have no right to pray in school. Nonsense. The pendulum has swung too far toward intolerance against genuine religious freedom. It is time to redress the balance."

Tolerance. What is its origin? How did it evolve? What has it become? This book uncovers the answers.

TOLERANCE
THE JOURNEY BEGINS

America is known around the world for freedom. People have come from virtually every nation, culture, racial background, economic class, and religion.

They know that in America they will have the freedom to pursue opportunities to better their lives. They come because of the deep desire in the human heart to be accepted, to be free, to be tolerated.

There are many great people of all faiths in America, as well as kind, considerate individuals who are atheists or agnostics. This book is not intended to depict any group in a less favorable light, but to discover the true origins of tolerance so it can be preserved for everyone.

So what is tolerance? Where did it originate and how has it evolved? What has tolerance transformed into today? To gain a proper perspective, one must understand how its journey began. Today's *Webster's Dictionary* defines "tolerance" as: "to put up with, bear, forbear," but Noah Webster's original 1828 *Dictionary of the English Language*, defined "tolerance" as:

> Allowance of religious opinions and modes of worship in a state, when contrary to or different from those of the established church or belief....The Protestant religion is tolerated in France, and the Roman Catholic in Great Britain.[2]

Why was this definition so important?

In the 1500-1700's in Europe, whatever the king believed, the kingdom had to believe. In general, England was Anglican; Scotland was Presbyterian; Holland was Dutch Reformed; Switzerland was Calvinist; Germany and Scandinavia were Lutheran; Greece and Russia were Eastern Orthodox; Italy, Spain, France, Hungary, Poland and Belgium were Roman Catholic.

If someone believed differently than their king, they were persecuted and fled, such as Anabaptists, Huguenots or Puritans. Various refugees migrated to America where the concept of tolerance evolved at different rates in different regions, proportional to the arrival of immigrants of any particular faith. Calvin Coolidge, May 3, 1925, commented:

> A common spiritual inspiration was potent to bring and mold and weld together into a national unity, the many and scattered colonial communities that had been planted along the Atlantic seaboard....
>
> There were well-nigh as many divergencies of religious faith as there were of origin, politics and geography....From its beginning, the new continent had seemed destined to be the home of religious tolerance. Those who claimed the right of individual choice for themselves finally had to grant it to others.
>
> One of the factors which I think weighed heaviest on the side of unity-the Bible was the one work of literature that was common to all of them. The Scriptures were read and studied everywhere. There are many testimonies that their teachings became the most important intellectual and spiritual force for unification....The sturdy old divines of those days found the Bible a chief source of illumination for their arguments in support of the patriot cause. They knew the Book.[3]

In the next chapters, you will discover the fascinating journey of tolerance through the centuries.

TOLERANCE FOR PURITANS

Henry VIII brought the Reformation to England in the 1530's, not because he had a spiritual experience, but because he wanted another wife.

He was married to Catherine of Aragon, daughter of King Ferdinand and Queen Isabella of Spain, who sent Columbus to America. After eighteen years, Catherine did not produce a male heir, so Henry decided to divorce her.

The Pope would not recognize the divorce, so Henry remedied the situation by declaring himself the head of the Church of England and granting himself permission to divorce. Henry eventually had six wives, and their fates were: divorced, beheaded, died, divorced, beheaded, survived.

During this time, Henry's advisors suggested that to finalize his break with Rome, England should stop using the Latin Bible, and instead use an English Bible, thereby leading the people to look to England for their spiritual heritage.

Henry liked the idea and circulated the English Bible, but something unexpected happened - people read it and compared the actions of King Henry to what was in the book.

This group desired to "purify" the Church of England, thus they were nicknamed the "Puritans." The King obviously did not think he needed "purifying," so he persecuted them.

A number of years later, Anglican Archbishop William Laud shared King Charles I's passion for uniformity.

Laud published a New Prayer book to standardize worship in England, and even inspected churches to enforce the observance of the liturgy. He purged academia of all Puritans and in 1625 compiled a list of churchmen, placing an "O" for Orthodox beside the names of those to be promoted, and a "P" for Puritan of those not to be.

The Test Act of 1673 effectively barred non-Anglicans from office by requiring public office holders to receive the sacraments in the Church of England. Voltaire later wrote in his *Letters Concerning the English Nation*, 1733: "No one can hold office in England or in Ireland unless he is a faithful Anglican."

Another group in England gave up hope of trying to "purify" the Church of England. They were called "Separatists" because they met in secret, at night, by candlelight, in barns and basements, similar to illegal Chinese house churches.

These Separatists were punished by being put in stocks, whipped, imprisoned or even branded as heretics.

In 1607, these Separatists, who came to be called "Pilgrims," fled to Holland, where they lived twelve years. Seeing their children assimilating into the Dutch culture, they realized they would be a short-lived movement unless they did something - so they sailed to America in 1620.

Governor William Bradford, in his *History of the Plymouth Settlement,* 1650, wrote:

> They shook off this yoke of antichristian bondage, and as the Lord's free people, joined themselves by a covenant of the Lord into a church estate in the fellowship of the gospel, to walk in all His ways, made known unto them, according to their best endeavours, whatsoever it should cost them, the Lord assisting them.[4]

Of the Pilgrims, President Ronald Reagan stated in his National Day of Prayer Proclamation, March 19, 1981:

The earliest settlers of this land came in search of religious freedom. Landing on a desolate shoreline, they established a spiritual foundation that has served us ever since.

It was the hard work of our people, the freedom they enjoyed and their faith in God that built this country and made it the envy of the world.[5]

These Pilgrims, through much hardship, built a successful colony in America, which encouraged the Puritans back in England, who were experiencing increased persecution, to also come to America's shores. It is difficult for us to imagine the abuse of power that took place with the King of England as the head of the Anglican Church and all the Anglican ministers controlled by his government.

This scenario was the only frame of reference that America's settlers had - that of European monarchs controlling every aspect of the church within their countries.

When this background is properly understood, then the quotations of some founders, which to the unlearned appear to be critical of biblical faith, were in reality critical of the corruptions resulting from churches being regulated by the government.

In 1630, the Great Migration began, where in just sixteen years 20,000 Puritans fled England and settled in Massachusetts. In 1702, Cotton Mather published a history of the first 50 years of New England, titled *Magnalia Christi Americana* (The Great Achievement of Christ in America):

From the beginning of the Reformation in the English nation, there had always been a generation of godly men, desirous to pursue the reformation of religion, according to the Word of God,..[though resisted by individuals with] power in their hands...not only to stop the progress of the desired reformation but also, with innumerable vexation, to persecute those that heartily wish well unto it....

The **Puritans** were driven to seek a place for the exercise of the Protestant religion, according to the light of conscience, in the deserts of America. [6]

Puritan John Higginson (1616-1708) gave his *Election Sermon-The Cause of God & His People in New England, 1663:*

My Fathers and Brethren, this is never to be forgotten - that New England is originally a plantation of religion, not a plantation of trade.[7]

Henry Wilson (1812-75), U.S. Senator and Vice-President under Ulysses Grant, told the Young Men's Christian Association, Natick, Massachusetts, December 23, 1866:

God has given us an existence in this Christian republic, founded by men who proclaim as their living faith, amid persecution and exile:

"We give ourselves to the Lord Jesus Christ and the Word of His Grace, for the teaching, ruling and sanctifying of us in matters of worship and conversation."

Privileged to live in an age when the selectest influences of the religion of our fathers seem to be visibly descending upon our land, we too often hear the Providence of God, the religion of our Lord and Saviour Jesus Christ, the inspiration of the Holy Bible doubted, questioned, denied with an air of gracious condescension.

Remember ever, and always, that your country was founded, not by the "most superficial, the lightest, the most irreflective of all European races," but by the stern old **Puritans** who made the deck of the Mayflower an altar of the living God, and whose first act on touching the soil of the new world was to offer on bended knees thanksgiving to Almighty God. [8]

George Bancroft (1800-91) was Secretary of Navy under President James Polk. He established the U.S. Naval Academy at Annapolis and Naval Observatory in Washington, D.C. In his *History of the United States,* 1834-76, Bancroft wrote:

> **Puritanism** had exalted the laity....For him the wonderful counsels of the Almighty had appointed a Saviour; for him the laws of nature had been compelled and consulted, the heavens had opened, the earth had quaked, the Sun had veiled his face, and Christ had died and risen again. [9]

James Russell Lowell (1819-91), a Harvard Professor and U.S. Minister to Spain, was editor of the *Atlantic Monthly* and *North American Review*. In his *Literary Essays,* 1810-90, James Russell Lowell wrote *New England Two Centuries Ago*:

> **Puritanism**, believing itself quick with the seed of religious liberty, laid, without knowing it, the egg of democracy. [10]

After Puritans settled in Massachusetts, they extended religious toleration to only Puritans. In a kind of "us or them" mentality, a fear was that if other denominations were tolerated, they may gain ascendancy, take control and begin again the persecution of Puritans, which were still fresh in their memory from England. In his *Election Sermon*, 1672, Rev. Thomas Shepherd described tolerance as "having its origin with the devil." President Urian Oakes, in his *Election Sermon*, 1673, described tolerance as "The first of all abominations."[11]

Those not tolerated in Puritan Massachusetts fled. Roger Williams fled and founded Providence, Rhode Island, and the first Baptist Church in the America. Thomas Hooker fled and founded Hartford, Connecticut, and the first Congregationalist Church in America. John Wheelwright, a preacher banished from Boston for his religious opinions, fled with some adherents and founded Exeter, New Hampshire, and when the Puritans assumed control over New Hampshire, he fled again to Maine.

Considered heretics by the Puritans, the Quakers were not tolerated in Massachusetts, being fined, jailed, banished, whipped, beaten and four were hung, including Mary Dyer, for whom there is a statue on the Boston Commons. Puritan leader Cotton Mather wrote of the Quakers on September 15, 1682:

> To ye Aged and Beloved Mr. John Higginson:
>
> There is now a ship at sea called the Welcome, which has on board a hundred or more of the heretics and malignants called Quakers, with W. Penn, who is the chief scamp, at the head of them.
>
> The General Court has accordingly given secret orders to master Malachi Huscott, of the brig Porpoise, to **waylay the said Welcome**, slyly as near the Cape of Cod as may be, **and make captive the said Penn and his ungodly crew, so the Lord may be glorified, and not mocked on the soil of this new country with the heathen worship of this people.**
>
> Much spoil can be made by **selling the whole lot to Barbados, where slaves fetch good prices** in rum and sugar, and we shall not only do the Lord great service by punishing the wicked, but we shall make great good for his minister and people. Master Huscott feels hopeful and I will set down the news when the ship comes back.[12]

TOLERANCE
FOR
PROTESTANTS

Post-Reformation religious tensions in the countries of Europe between the state-favored denominations and rival denominations resulted in displaced religious-ethnic groups leaving to start colonies in America.

Upon arrival, each colony initially favored only one denomination, providing them, in many cases, with state tax support, special privileges and requiring mandatory church membership of its citizens. This caused rival denominations to leave and start new settlements favoring their denomination.

The original denominations in the Colonies were: NEW ENGLAND COLONIES: Massachusetts 1630-**Puritan**; Rhode Island 1636-**Baptist**; Connecticut 1636-**Congregational**; New Hampshire 1638-**Congregational** MIDDLE COLONIES: New York 1626-**Dutch Reformed**; Delaware 1638-**Lutheran & Dutch Reformed**; Pennsylvania 1682-**Quaker & Lutheran**; New Jersey 1664-**Lutheran & Dutch Reformed** SOUTHERN COLONIES: Virginia 1607-**Anglican**; Maryland 1633-**Catholic**; North Carolina 1653-**Anglican**; South Carolina 1663-**Anglican**; Georgia 1732-**Protestant**

Puritans in Massachusetts were intolerant of Baptists, Congregationalists and Quakers. Anglicans in Virginia expelled Puritans. Dutch Reformed in New York (originally New Amsterdam) drove out Lutherans and Quakers. Quakers in Pennsylvania conflicted with Scotch-Irish Presbyterians.

The American phenomenon of different denominations tolerating each other *within* the same colony took place first in the Middle Colonies which received the most immigrants. Due to the relatively sparse population in America, it was found by working together all groups could benefit economically, as well as receive needed support in times of distress such as famines, smallpox epidemics, Indian attacks or wars.

Having several denominations in one colony made it difficult to enforce mandatory church membership, so membership gradually became voluntary. Time eventually brought an end to each colonies' mandatory tax support and special privileges for the state-sanctioned denominations.

In following generations, Protestant denominations in New England grew to tolerate each other, giving birth to a new kind of liberty which other groups later benefited from, such as Roman Catholics, Spanish-Portuguese Jews (Sephardic), German Jews (Ashkenazic), and others.

The Protestant denominations populating colonial America included: Anglican-Church of England, Puritan, Congregationalist, Scotch-Irish Presbyterian, Lutheran, German Reformed, German Baptist, Anabaptist, Welsh Baptist, Quaker, Dutch Reformed, Dutch Mennonite, Dutch Lutheran, Scandinavian Lutheran, French Huguenot, Methodist, Baptist, Evangelical, Calvinist Reformed, Moravian, Seventh Day Baptist, Amish, Dunker, Mennonite, Church of the Brethren and Schwenkfelder.

Patricia U. Bonomi, Professor Emeritus of New York University, wrote an article titled *The Middle Colonies as the Birthplace of American Religious Pluralism.* Citing "the colonists were about 98 percent Protestant," Professor Bonomi stated:

> Early American churchmen and churchwomen soon discovered that if they wanted to practice *their* beliefs unmolested in a diverse society, they had to grant the same right to others. This wisdom did not come easily.

President Calvin Coolidge wrote:

From its beginning, the new continent had seemed destined to be the home of religious tolerance. Those who claimed the right of individual choice for themselves finally had to grant it to others. [13]

The many denominations which fled to America insisting on the "right to worship God according to the dictates of their own consciences" eventually realized that to be intellectually consistent the same rights they were demanding for themselves, they should grant to others.

PROTESTANT CHRISTIANITY IN U.S. HISTORY

During the passage of the *Articles of Association*, Secretary Charles Thomson recorded in the *Journals of the Continental Congress*, September 1774:

Article X. The late Act of Parliament for establishing the French Laws in that extensive country now called Quebec, is dangerous in an extreme degree to the **Protestant** Religion and to the civil rights and liberties of all America; and therefore as men and **Protestant** Christians, we are indispensably obliged to take all proper measures for our security. [14]

British statesman Edmund Burke (1729-97) addressed Parliament during the Revolutionary War, in his *Second Speech on the Conciliation with America,* March 22, 1775:

Religion, always a principle of energy, in this new people is no way worn out or impaired; and their mode of professing it is also one main cause of this free spirit.

The people are **Protestants**; and of that kind which is the most adverse to all implicit submission of mind and opinion. This is a persuasion not only favorable to Liberty, but built upon it....

All **protestantism**, even the most cold and passive, is a sort of dissent. But the religion most prevalent in our Northern Colonies is a refinement on the principle of resistance; it is the dissidence of dissent, and the **protestantism** of the **Protestant** religion. [15]

John Jay (1817-94), grandson of the first Supreme Court Chief Justice, was manager of New York's Young Men's Anti-Slavery Society, 1834, secretary of the Irish Relief Commission during the potato famine, 1847, and member of the Metropolitan Museum of Art & National Academy of Design.

As President of the American Historical Society, John Jay stated in his address titled *National Perils and Opportunities,* delivered in Westchester County, 1887:

This gathering of citizens from distant parts, representing the millions who hold to the Bible, and cherish the institutions founded upon its inspired truths, shows that the nation is awakening to the perils, foreign and domestic, which threatens the purity of its Christian civilization.

Its intellectual and moral strength in our Revolutionary struggle were recognized by the world, and Burke rightly attributed that strength to the character of the emigrants from various lands exhibiting "the dissidence of dissent and the **Protestantism** of the **Protestant** religion."

They brought with them the best and most heroic blood of the peoples of Europe - of the Hollanders, the Waloons of Flanders, the Huguenots of France, the English, Welsh, Scotch, and Irish, of the Norwegians and Swedes, the Germans and the Swiss, of the Bohemian followers of John Hus, of the Albigenses and Waldenses of the Italian Alps, of the Salzbury exiles, the Moravian brothers, with refugees from the Pallatinate, Alsace and southern Germany.

They all brought the Bible, for which they and their ancestors had been ready to suffer and to die; and their devotion to that Book descended to the Continental Congress, which, a week before it was driven from Philadelphia, ordered an importation of twenty thousand Bibles.

At the Centennial celebration, at Philadelphia, of the *Declaration of Independence*, the Acting Vice-President, Ferry, said that the American statesmen who had to choose between the royal authority or popular sovereignty had been inspired by the truth uttered on Mars Hill, and repeated in the opening prayer of the morning, that "God hath made of one blood all nations of men."[16]

Samuel Adams, after signing the *Declaration*, stated to the Continental Congress in Philadelphia, August 1, 1776:

This day, I trust, the reign of political **protestantism** will commence.

We have explored the temple of royalty, and found that the idol we have bowed down to, has eyes which see not, ears that hear not our prayers, and a heart like the nether millstone.

We have this day restored the Sovereign, to whom alone all men ought to be obedient.

He reigns in Heaven, and with a propitious eye beholds his subjects assuming that freedom of thought, and dignity of self-direction which He bestowed on them....

We have fled from the political Sodom; let us not look back, lest we perish and become a monument of infamy and derision to the world!...

Our glorious reformers, when they broke through the fetters of superstition, effected more than could be expected from an age so darkened.

But they left much to be done by their posterity. They lopped off, indeed, some of the branches...but they left the root and stock when they left us under the domination of human systems and decisions, usurping the infallibility which can be attributed to Revelation alone. They dethroned one usurper only to raise up another....

And if we now cast our eyes over the nations of the earth we shall find, that instead of possessing the pure religion of the gospel, they may be divided either into infidels who deny the truth, or politicians who make religion a stalking horse for their ambition, of professors, who walk in the trammels of orthodoxy, and are more attentive to traditions and ordinances of men than to the oracles of truth.

Thus by the beneficence of Providence, we shall behold our empire arising, founded on justice and the voluntary consent of the people, and giving full scope to the exercise of those faculties and rights which most ennoble our species. [17]

Secretary of the Navy George Bancroft wrote that at the time of the Revolution, a full two-thirds of the population of America, estimated at 3,000,000 people, had been trained in the teachings of Protestant Reformer John Calvin:

900,000 were of **Scotch or Scotch-Irish** origin, 600,000 were **Puritan English**, 400,000 were **German or Dutch Reformed**, the **Episcopalians** had a **Calvinistic** confession in their Thirty-nine Articles, in addition to the numerous **French Huguenots** who had come to the western world. [18]

Of Protestant Reformer John Calvin, Bancroft wrote:

He who will not honor the memory and respect the influence of **Calvin** knows little of the origin of American liberty. [19]

James Madison wrote Robert Walsh, March 2, 1819:

The **English church was originally the established religion**...Of other sects there were but few adherents, except the **Presbyterians** who predominated on the west side of the Blue Mountains.

A little time previous to the Revolutionary struggle, the **Baptists** sprang up, and made very rapid progress. Among the early acts of the Republican Legislature, were those abolishing the Religious establishment, and **putting all Sects at full liberty and on a perfect level.**

At present the population is divided, with small exceptions, among the **Protestant Episcopalians, the Presbyterians, the Baptists and the Methodists...**

I conjecture the **Presbyterians** and **Baptists** to form each about a third, and the two other sects together of which the **Methodists** are much the smallest, to make up the remaining third....

Among the other sects, Meeting Houses have multiplied and continue to multiply...

Religious instruction is now diffused throughout the Community by preachers of every sect with almost equal zeal...The qualifications of the Preachers, too among **the new sects**...are understood to be improving.[20]

Gouverneur Morris (1752-1816) was 35 years old when he was a delegate to the Constitutional Convention, speaking more than any delegate, 173 times. Heading the Committee on Style, he penned the final draft of the *U.S. Constitution*, originating the phrase "We the people of the United States."

His Protestant mentality was seen in a mention of priests while serving as the first U.S. Minister to France, in a letter to George Washington shortly before the French Revolution, April 29, 1789:

The materials for a revolution in France are very indifferent. Everybody agrees that there is an utter prostration of morals; but this general proposition can never convey to an American mind the degree of depravity...

A hundred thousand examples are required to show the extreme rottenness of every member...It is however, from such crumbling matter, that the great edifice of freedom is to be erected here....

The great masses of the common people have **no religion but their priests,** no law but their superiors, no morals but their interest.

These are the creatures who, led by drunken curates, are now in the high road a la liberte, and the first use they make of it is to form insurrections everywhere for the want of bread.[21]

EARLY DOCUMENTS

NEW ENGLAND CONFEDERATION 1643:

Whereas we all came to these parts of America with the same end and aim, namely, **to advance the kingdome of our Lord Jesus Christ**, and to **injoy the liberties of the Gospell** thereof with purities and peace, and for preserving and propagating **the truth and liberties of the gospell**.[22]

CHARTER OF COLONY OF GEORGIA 1732:

There shall be a allowed in the worship of God, to all persons inhabiting, or which shall inhabit or be resident within our said provinces and that all such persons, **except papists,** shall have a free exercise of their religion.[23]

NEW JERSEY CONSTITUTION 1776:

Article XVIII. No **Protestant** inhabitant of this Colony shall be denied the enjoyment of any civil right, merely on account of his religious principles;

That all persons, professing a belief in the faith of any **Protestant** sect, and who should demean himself peaceably under the government, should be capable of being elected unto any office of profit or trust.[24]

NORTH CAROLINA CONSTITUTION 1776:

Article XXXII. That no person who shall deny the being of God, or the truth of the **Protestant** religion, or the divine authority of the Old or New Testaments, or who shall hold religious principles incompatible with the freedom and safety of the State, shall be capable of holding any office or place of trust or profit in the civil department within this State. (until 1876)[25]

VERMONT CONSTITUTION 1777:

DECLARATION OF RIGHTS, III. That all men have a natural and Unalienable right to worship Almighty God according to the dictates of their own consciences and understanding, regulated by the word of GOD; and that no man ought, or of right can be compelled to attend any religious worship, or erect, or support any place of worship, or maintain any minister, contrary to the dictates of his conscience;

nor can any man who professes the **Protestant** religion, be justly deprived or abridged of any civil right, as a citizen, on account of his religious sentiment, or peculiar mode of worship, and that no authority can...interfere with, or in any manner control, the rights of conscience, in the free exercise of religious worship.[26]

SOUTH CAROLINA CONSTITUTION 1778:

Article XII. No person shall be eligible to sit in the house of representatives unless he be of the **Protestant** religion. No person shall be eligible to a seat in the said senate unless he be of the **Protestant** religion.

Article XXXVIII. All persons and religious societies, who acknowledge that there is one God, and a future state of rewards and punishments, and that God is publicly to be worshipped, shall be freely tolerated. The Christian **Protestant** religion shall be deemed, and is hereby constituted and declared to be, the established religion, of this State....

Section V...choose...a governor and commander-in-chief, a lieutenant-governor, and privy council, all of the **Protestant** religion; that no person should be eligible to a seat in the Senate unless he be of the **Protestant** religion; that no person should be eligible to sit in the House of Representatives unless he be of the **Protestant** religion.[27]

MASSACHUSETTS CONSTITUTION 1780:

Part I, Article III. Towns, parishes, precincts, and other bodies-politic or religious societies, to make suitable provision, at their own expense, for the institution of the public worship of God and the support and maintenance of public **Protestant** teachers of piety, religion, and morality in all cases where such provision shall not be made voluntary. [28]

NEW HAMPSHIRE CONSTITUTION 1784, 1792:

Representatives and Senators are to be of the **Protestant** religion. (In effect until 1877).

Article I, Section VI. The people of this state...do hereby empower the legislature to authorize...the several towns, parishes, bodies-corporate, or religious societies within this State, to make adequate provision at their own expense, for the support and maintenance of public **Protestant** teachers of piety, religion and morality.[29]

VERMONT CONSTITUTION 1786:

Frame of Government, Section IX. Each [Legislative] member, before he takes his seat, shall make and subscribe the following declaration, viz:

"I do believe in one God, the Creator and Governor of the Universe, the Rewarder of the good and Punisher of the wicked. And I do acknowledge the Scripture of the Old and New Testament to be given by Divine inspiration, and own and profess the **Protestant** religion."

And no further or other religious test shall ever, hereafter, be required of any civil officer or magistrate in this State. [30]

GEORGIA CONSTITUTION 1788:

Article VI. All members of the Legislature shall be of the **Protestant** religion....The representatives shall be chosen out of the residents in each county...and they shall be of the **Protestant** religion. [31]

JEFFERSON & U.S. CONGRESS 1787

President Jefferson extended three times a 1787 act of Congress designating special lands for **Protestant** missionaries:

For the sole use of Christian Indians and the **Moravian Brethren missionaries** for civilizing the Indians and promoting Christianity. [32]

TEXAS INDEPENDENCE DECLARATION 1836

The late changes made in the government by General Antonio Lopez Santa Ana...now offers, as the cruel alternative, either abandon our homes acquired by so many privations, or submit to the most intolerable of all tyranny, the combined despotism of the sword and **the priesthood....**

It denies us the right of worshipping the Almighty according to the dictates of our own conscience, by the support of a National Religion, calculated to promote the temporal interest of its human functionaries, rather than the glory of the true and living God. [33]

These early legislative acts, though narrow-minded by today's standards, were progressive back then, as Protestant countries in Europe only allowed tolerance for the one particular Protestant denomination authorized by the State.

TOLERANCE
FOR
CATHOLICS

The first colony where Catholics were free was Maryland, founded in 1633 as a refuge for persecuted Catholics. Protestants pressured the colony to pass a *Toleration Act* and shortly thereafter took control, being intolerant of Catholics for several generations. The *Toleration Act of 1649* stated:

> Be it therefore... enacted... that no person or persons whatsoever within this province...professing to believe in Jesus Christ shall...from henceforth be any ways troubled, molested (or disapproved of)...in respect of his or her religion nor in the free exercise thereof. [34]

Tolerance was later advanced by William Penn, who had been imprisoned in the Tower of London for his faith.

> He established Pennsylvania in 1682 as a land of religious toleration for every denomination. To emphasize his plan, he named their city "Philadelphia," which is Greek for "City of Brotherly Love." [35]

Soon Quakers, Mennonites, Anglicans, Nonconformists, Lutherans, Calvinists, Dunkards, Church of the Brethren, Evangelical, Moravians, Schwenkfelders, Baptists, Presbyterians, German Reformed, and Catholics from

England, Sweden, Wales, Germany, Scotland and Ireland began arriving in Penn's "holy experiment."

The first Roman Catholic parish in Pennsylvania was St. Joseph's, settled in Philadelphia in 1731. *London's Biographical Review,* 1819, said William Penn:

> Established an absolute toleration; it was his wish that every man who believed in God should partake of the rights of a citizen; and that every man who adored Him as a Christian, of whatever sect he might be, should be a partaker in authority.[36]

As mentioned earlier, though considered narrow-minded by today's standards, back then this was unprecedented in generosity, as other countries in Europe only allowed freedom for the one preferred denomination authorized by the King.

English poet Samuel Johnson (1709-84) organized the London Literary Club and compiled one of the first dictionaries in the English language. Commenting on the emerging tolerance of Catholics, Samuel Johnson wrote in 1763:

> Sir, I think all Christians, whether **Papists** or Protestants, agree in the essential articles and that their differences are trivial, and rather political than religious.[37]

George Washington wrote of toleration to Marquis de Lafayette, who was supporting toleration in France, 1787:

> I am not less ardent in my wish that you may succeed in your plan of toleration in religious matters.
>
> Being no bigot myself to any mode of worship, I am disposed to indulge the **professors of Christianity** in the church with that road to Heaven which to them shall seem the most direct, plainest and easiest, and the least liable to exception.[38]

A prominent Catholic in the 18th century was John Carroll, founder of Georgetown University. He was the brother of U.S. Rep. Daniel Carroll, who signed the U.S. Constitution and gave much of the land where the Capitol is located. He was a cousin of Senator Charles Carroll, the wealthiest man in America, and the only Catholic and longest living signer of the Declaration. John's nephew Robert Brent, was Washington, D.C.'s first mayor, reappointed by Jefferson and Madison.

John Carroll was America's first Catholic bishop, founding the nation's first Catholic seminary and parochial school system. He convinced Elizabeth Seton to start a girls school in Baltimore.

In 1776, the Continental Congress asked John Carroll to be on a commission, with Ben Franklin, to enlist the aid of the French Catholic country of Canada in the Revolution. His influence caused four of the new Thirteen State Constitutions to allow Catholics equality with other citizens.

Bishop John Carroll, who was made the head of the missions in the provinces of the U.S. on June 9, 1784, wrote:

> Thanks to genuine spirit and Christianity, the United States have banished intolerance from their system of government, and many of them have done the justice to **every denomination of Christians, which ought to be done to them in all, of placing them on the same footing of citizenship**, and conferring an equal right of participation in national privileges.
>
> Freedom and independence, acquired by the united efforts, and cemented with the mingled blood of Protestant and **Catholic** fellow-citizens, should be equally enjoyed by all."[39]

President Washington wrote Bishop John Carroll, March 15, 1790:

I presume that your fellow citizens will not forget the patriotic part which you took in the accomplishment of their Revolution...or the important assistance which they received from a nation in which the **Roman Catholic** faith is professed....

May the members of your society in America, animated alone by the pure spirit of Christianity enjoy every temporal and spiritual felicity. [40]

George Washington entered in his diary, May 26, 1787:

Went to the **Romish** Church to high mass.[41]

John Adams wrote to Benjamin Rush, January 21, 1810:

The Christian Religion, as I understand it, is the brightest of the glory and the express portrait of the eternal, self-evident, independent, benevolent, all-powerful and all-merciful Creator, Preserver and Father of the Universe, the first good, first perfect, and first fair. It will last as long as the world.

Neither savage nor civilized man could ever have discovered or invented it. Ask me not then whether I am a **Catholic** or Protestant, Calvinist or Arminian. As far as they are Christians, I wish to be a fellow disciple of them all. [42]

Thomas Jefferson wrote to Miles King, Sept. 26, 1814:

Nay, we have heard it said that there is not a Quaker or a Baptist, a Presbyterian or an Episcopalian, a **Catholic** or a Protestant in heaven; that on entering that gate, we leave those badges of schism behind...

Let us not be uneasy about the different roads we may pursue, as believing them the shortest, to that our last abode; but following the guidance of a good conscience, let us be happy in the hope that by these different paths we shall all meet in the end.

And that you and I may meet and embrace, is my earnest prayer. And with this assurance I salute you with brotherly esteem and respect. [43]

Of the 56 men who signed the *Declaration of Independence*, only one was Catholic, Charles Carroll, who helped finance the Revolution, being one of the richest men in America. His statue was chosen to represent the State of Maryland in the U.S. Capitol's Statuary Hall.

Charles Carroll was a cousin of Bishop John Carroll, founder of Georgetown. He was also a cousin of Daniel Carroll, one of two Catholics to sign the *U.S. Constitution*, the other being Thomas FitzSimmons.

Charles Carroll wrote to Rev. John Stanford, October 9, 1827, that he did not find fault with there being so many denominations, as it was a safeguard of religious freedom:

To obtain religious as well as civil liberty I entered jealously into the Revolution, and **observing the Christian religion divided into many sects, I founded the hope that no one would be so predominant as to become the religion of the State.**

That hope was thus early entertained, because all of them joined in the same cause, with few exceptions of individuals. [44]

Charles Carroll wrote, November 4, 1800, to James McHenry, signer of the Constitution and namesake of Fort McHenry:

"Without morals a republic cannot subsist any length of time; **they therefore who are decrying the Christian religion,** whose morality is so sublime and pure...**are undermining the solid foundation of morals, the best security for the duration of free governments.**"[45]

The U.S. Congress received the report of Mr. Meacham of the House Committee on the Judiciary, March 27, 1854:

Where there is **a spirit of Christianity,** there is a spirit which rises above form, above ceremonies, **independent of sect or creed and the controversies of clashing doctrines.** [46]

On December 3, 1803, it was recommended by President Thomas Jefferson that the U.S. Congress pass a treaty with the Kaskaskia Indians, similar to treaties made with the Wyandots, 1806, and Cherokee, 1807:

And whereas the greater part of the said tribe have been baptized and received into the **Catholic** Church, to which they are much attached, **the United States will give annually, for seven years, one hundred dollars toward the support of a priest** of that religion, who will engage to perform for said tribe the duties of his office, and also to instruct as many of their children as possible, in the rudiments of literature, and **the United States will further give the sum of three hundred dollars, to assist the said tribe in the erection of a church.**[47]

The Library of Congress Exhibition "Religion and the Founding of the Ameircan Republic" (www.loc.gov/exhibits/religion/rel06-2.html) stated:

On January 8, 1826, Bishop John England (1786-1842) of Charleston, SC, became the first Catholic clergyman to preach in the House of Representatives. The overflow audience included President John Quincy Adams, whose July 4, 1821, speech England rebutted in his sermon. Adams had claimed that the Roman Catholic Church was intolerant of other religions and therefore incompatible with republican institutions. England asserted that "we do not believe that God gave to the church any power to interfere with our civil rights, or our civil concerns." "I would not allow to the Pope, or to any bishop of our church," added England, "the smallest interference with the humblest vote at our most insignificant balloting box."

On March 25, 1835, Andrew Jackson wrote in a letter:

I was brought up a rigid Presbyterian, to which I have always adhered. Our excellent *Constitution* guarantees to every one freedom of religion, and charity tells us (and you know Charity is the real basis of all true religion)...judge the tree by its fruit.

All who profess Christianity believe in a Saviour, and that by and through Him we must be saved. We ought, therefore, to consider all good Christians whose walks correspond with their professions, be they Presbyterian, Episcopalian, Baptist, Methodist or **Roman Catholic.** [48]

President Rutherford B. Hayes, after speaking to the Catholic Knights of America, noted in his diary:

I am a Protestant, born a Protestant, expect to live a Protestant, and shall probably die a Protestant.

I can see in the past, and today, faults in the **Catholic** Church, but I am grateful for:

(1) its work in behalf of temperance;

(2) its example in keeping together poor and rich; care for the poor; influence with the poor;

(3) for its treatment of the blacks; of all the unfortunate races. A negro sat with us at our banquet table;

(4) for its fidelity in spite of party... Archbishop Purcell strung the American flag, in the crisis of our fate, from the top of the Cathedral in Cincinnati, April 16, 1861! The spire was beautiful before, but the **Catholic** prelate made it radiant with hope and glory for our country![49]

After the large waves of Irish and German Catholic immigrants in the middle 1800's, there was a rise of intolerance toward Catholics, but after several decades it subsided.

On November 14, 1896, President Grover Cleveland issued the *Proclamation* respecting the Catholic Church property in the newly acquired Territory of Alaska:

Whereas a treaty of cession was exchanged and proclaimed on June 20, 1867, whereby the Russian Empire ceded to the US the Territory of Alaska; and Whereas said treaty, by Article II, provided...

"It is, however, understood and agreed that the churches which have been built in the ceded territory by the Russian Government shall remain the property of such members of the Greek Oriental Church resident in the territory as may choose to worship therein."

And whereas there were included among the lands...which are claimed by the Holy Orthodox **Catholic** Apostolic Oriental Church, commonly styled the Greco-Russian Church...

Now, therefore, I, Grover Cleveland, President of the United States...proclaim said reservation of lands in the Territory of Alaska...be excluded: The Cathedral Church of St. Michael, built of timber, situated in the center of the city. The Church of the Resurrection, of timber, commonly called the Kalochian Church, situated near the battery number at the palisade separating the city from the Indian village. A double-storied timber building for bishop house.... A timber house for church warden. A timber house for the deacon. Three timber houses...for lodging of priests. Four lots of ground belonging to the parsonages. The place commemorative of the old church. A tomb. Three cemeteries, two outside palisades and one by the Church of the Resurrection.[50]

President Theodore Roosevelt, in his *Fifth Annual Message to Congress*, December 5, 1905, stated:

The income of the Philippine Government has necessarily been reduced by reason of the business and agricultural depression in the islands....
Negotiations and hearings for the settlement of the amount due to the **Roman Catholic Church** for rent and occupation of churches and rectories by the army of the United States are in progress.[51]

Alfred Emanuel Smith (1873-1944), was the four-term Governor of New York, 1919-29, and Democratic Presidential candidate in 1928. Coming under attack during his Presidential Campaign for being a Catholic, he responded in May of 1927:

I am unable to understand how anything I was taught to believe as a **Catholic** could possibly be in conflict with what is good citizenship.

The essence of my faith is built upon the Commandments of God. The law of the land is built on the Commandments of God. There can be no conflict between them....

What is this conflict about which you talk? It may exist in some lands which do not guarantee religious freedom. But in the wildest dreams of your imagination you cannot conjure up a possible conflict between religious principle and political duty in the United States, except on the unthinkable hypothesis that some laws were to be passed which violated the common morality of all God-fearing men.

And if you can conjure up such a conflict, how would a Protestant solve it? Obviously by the dictates of his conscience. That is exactly what a **Catholic** would do. There is no ecclesiastical tribunal which would have the slightest claim upon the obedience of **Catholic** communicants in the resolution of such a conflict. [52]

To gain insight into the struggles Catholics experienced in gaining tolerance, one need only read Pennsylvania State Court's decision *Hysong v. School District of Gallitzin Borough*, 1894, allowing Catholic teachers in the Public Schools:

We cannot infer, from the mere fact that a school board composed of **Catholics** has selected a majority of **Catholic** teachers, that therefore it has unlawfully discriminated in favor of **Catholics**, because the selection of **Catholic** teachers is not a violation of law or, which is the same thing, is not an abuse of discretion. Nor does the fact that these teachers contribute all their earnings beyond their support to the treasury of their order, to be used for religious purposes, have any bearing on the question.

It is none of our business, nor that of these appellants, to inquire into this matter. American men and women, of sound mind and twenty-one years of age, can make such disposition of their surplus earnings as suits their own notions.

We might as well, so far as any law warranted it, inquire of a lawyer before admitting him to the bar, what he intended to do with his surplus fees, and make his answer a test of admission. What he did with his money could no way affect his right to be sworn as an officer of this court... But it is further argued that...they enjoin from appearing in the school room in the habit of their order.

It may be conceded that the dress and crucifix impart at once knowledge to the pupils of the religious belief...of the wearer. But is this, in any reasonable sense of the word, "sectarian" teaching, which the law prohibits?...

The dress is but the announcement of a fact, that the wearer holds a particular religious belief. The religious belief of teachers and all others is generally well known to the neighborhood and to pupils, even if not made noticeable in the dress, for that belief is not secret, but is publicly professed.

Are the courts to decide that the cut of a man's coat or the color of a woman's gown is sectarian teaching, because they indicate sectarian religious belief? If so, then they can be called upon to go further.

The religion of a teacher being known, a pure, unselfish life, exhibiting itself in tenderness to the young, and helpfulness for the suffering, necessarily tends to promote the religion of the man or woman who lives it.

In sensibly, in both young and old, there is a disposition to reverence such a one, and at least, to some extent, consider the life as the fruit of the particular religion. Therefore, irreproachable conduct to that degree is sectarian teaching. But shall the education of the children of the Commonwealth be entrusted only to those men and women who are destitute of any religious belief? [53]

President Theodore Roosevelt stated in his *Fifth Annual Message to Congress*, December 5, 1905:

If the man who seeks to come here is from the moral and social standpoint of such a character as to bid fair to add value to the community he should be heartily welcomed.

We cannot afford to pay heed to whether he is of one creed or another, of one nation, or another. We cannot afford to consider whether he is **Catholic** or Protestant, Jew or Gentile; whether he is Englishman or Irishman, Frenchman or German. [54]

Of note is a few hours after John F. Kennedy was shot, November 22, 1963, Judge Sarah Hughes administered the oath of office to Lyndon Baines Johnson aboard Air Force One at Love Field Airport in Dallas, Texas, with his hand upon a **Catholic** Missal, as a Bible could not be located. [55]

TOLERANCE FOR NEW "LIBERAL" CHRISTIAN SECTS

As French Enlightenment thought experienced a period of popularity in the early 1800's in the eastern United States, tolerance was extended to Unitarians, Universalists, Swedenborgian and other new "liberal" Christian sects or denominations.

As a pebble is dropped in a pond and the ripples go out, tolerance began first for Puritans, then Protestants, then Catholics, then to more unorthodox Christian denominations.

On tolerating new sects, James Madison wrote to Edward Everett, 1823:

> Rival sects, with equal rights, exercise mutual censorship in favor of good morals...**If new sects arise with absurd opinions or overheated maginiations, the proper remedies lie in time, forbearance and example.**[68]

Francis J. Grund, a contemporary of de Tocqueville, wrote in *The Americans in Their Moral, Social and Political Relations,* 1837:

> Yet there are **religious denominations in the United States whose creeds are very nearly verging on Deism; but taking their arguments from the Bible, and calling themselves followers of Christ, they and their doctrines are tolerated,** together with their form of worship. [56]

French historian Alexis de Tocqueville wrote in *Democracy in America,* 1835-40:

> The sects that exist in the United States are innumerable. They all differ in respect to the worship which is due to the Creator; but they all agree in respect to the duties which are due from man to man.
>
> Each sect adores the Deity in its own peculiar manner, but all sects preach the same moral law in the name of God.... **All the sects of the United States are comprised within the great unity of Christianity, and Christian morality is everywhere the same.**[57]

A list denominations in the United States was compiled by Gustave de Beaumont, a French historian who traveled with de Tocqueville, in his work: *Marie ou l'Esclavage aux E'tasUnis,* 1835:

> The principal established religious sects in North America are the Methodists, Anabaptists, Catholics, Presbyterians, Episcopalians, Quakers or Friends, **Universalists,** Congregationalists, **Unitarians,** Dutch Reformed, German Reformed, Moravians, Evangelical Lutherans, etc.
>
> The Anabaptists are divided into Calvinists, Dunkers, etc. The most populous Protestant group is that of the Methodists; it numbered 550,000 members at the beginning of the year 1834. There are no exact figures for the other communions.[58]

Jefferson stated in his *Inaugural Address,* March 4, 1801:

> Enlightened by **a benign religion, professed, indeed, and practiced in various forms,** yet all of them inculcating honesty, truth, temperance, gratitude, and the love of man; acknowledging and adoring an overruling Providence, which by all its dispensations proves that it delights in the happiness of man here and his greater happiness hereafter.[59]

The Library of Congress Exhibition "Religion and the Founding of the Ameircan Republic" (www.loc.gov) stated:

The first services in the Capitol, held when the government moved to Washington in the fall of 1800, were conducted in the "hall" of the House in the north wing of the building. In 1801 the House moved to temporary quarters in the south wing, called the "Oven," which it vacated in 1804, returning to the north wing for three years. Church services were held in what is now called Statuary Hall from 1807 to 1857. Services were conducted in the House until after the Civil War. The Speaker's podium was used as the preacher's pulpit...

A sermon on the millennium was preached by the Baltimore **Swedenborgian minister**, John Hargrove (1750-1839) in the House of Representatives. One of the earliest **millennialist sermons** preached before Congress was offered on July 4, 1801, by the Reverend David Austin (1759-1831), who at the time considered himself "struck in prophesy under the style of the Joshua of the American Temple."

Having proclaimed to his Congressional audience the imminence of the Second Coming of Christ, Austin took up a collection on the floor of the House to support services at "Lady Washington's Chapel" in a nearby hotel where he was teaching that "the seed of the Millennial estate is found in the backbone of the American Revolution."

De Tocqueville wrote in *Democracy in America,* 1835:

In the United States, if a political character attacks a sect, this may not prevent even the partisans of that very sect, from supporting him; b**ut if he attacks all the sects together [Christianity], every one abandons him and he remains alone.** [60]

Lincoln stated in his *Second Inaugural Address*, March 5, 1865:

Neither party expected for the war the magnitude or the duration which it has already attained...Each looked for an easier triumph...
Both read the same Bible and pray to the same God....The prayers of both could not be answered. That of neither has been answered fully. The Almighty has His own purposes. [61]

Unitarians were included in the list of denominations from which chaplains were appointed, as reported to the House Committee on the Judiciary by Mr. Meacham, March 27, 1854:

The 1st day of May, Washington's first speech was read to the House, and the first business after that speech was the appointment of Dr. Linn as chaplain...
The law of 1789 was passed in compliance with their plan, giving chaplains a salary of $500.
It was reenacted in 1816, and continues to the present time. Chaplains have been appointed from all the leading denominations, Methodist, Baptist, Episcopalian, Presbyterian, Congregationalist, Catholic, **Unitarian,** and others. [62]

Giving insight into the heated New England debates between Unitarians and Trinitarians are John Quincy Adams' letters from London after negotiating the *Treaty of Ghent,* 1814, in which he ends with a reaffirmation "doctrine of toleration":

I perceive that the Trinitarians and the **Unitarians** in Boston are sparring together....
Most of the Boston **Unitarians** are my particular friends, but I never thought much of the eloquence or the theology of Priestly. His Socrates and Jesus Compared is a wretched performance. Socrates and Jesus!

A farthing candle and the sun! I pray you to read Massilon's sermon on the divinity of Christ, and then the whole New Testament, after which be a Socinian if you can. [63]

I find in the New Testament, Jesus Christ accosted in His own presence by one of His disciples as God, without disclaiming the appellation.

I see Him explicitly declared by at least two other of the Apostles to be God, expressly and repeatedly announced, not only as having existed before the worlds, but as the Creator of the worlds without beginning of days or end of years. I see Him named in the great prophecy of Isaiah concerning him to be the mighty God!...

The texts are too numerous, they are from parts of the Scriptures too diversified, they are sometimes connected by too strong a chain of argument, and the inferences from them are, to my mind, too direct and irresistible, to admit of the explanations which the Unitarians sometimes attempt to give them, or the evasions by which, at others, they endeavor to escape from them. [64]

You ask me what Bible I take as the standard of my faith the Hebrew, the Samaritan, the old English translation, or what? I answer, the Bible containing the Sermon on the Mount. Any Bible that I can...understand.

The New Testament I have repeatedly read in the original Greek, in the Latin, in the Geneva Protestant, in Sacy's Catholic French translations, in Luther's German translation, in the common English Protestant, and in the Douay Catholic translations. I take any one of them for my standard of faith....

But the Sermon on the Mount commands me to lay up for myself treasures, not upon earth, but in Heaven.

My hopes of a future life are all founded upon the Gospel of Christ....

You think it blasphemous that the omnipotent Creator could be crucified.

God is a spirit. The spirit was not crucified. The body of Jesus of Nazareth was crucified. The Spirit, whether external or created, was beyond the reach of the cross. sYou see, my orthodoxy grows on me, and I still unite with you in the doctrine of toleration. [65]

Regarding transcendentalist Ralph Waldo Emerson, John Quincy Adams wrote:

For many years since the establishment of the theological school at Andover, the Calvinists and **Unitarian**s have been battling with each other upon the atonement, the divinity of Jesus Christ and the Trinity.

This has now very much subsided; but other wanderings of mind takes the place of that, and equally lets the wolf into the fold.

A young man, named Ralph Waldo Emerson, and a classmate of my lamented son George, after failing in the everyday avocation of a **Unitarian** preacher and schoolmaster, starts a new doctrine of transcendentalism, declared all the old revelations superannuated and worn out, and announces the approach of new revelations and prophecies. [66]

Jean Jacques Rousseau (1712-1778), a French philosopher who influenced American thought, wrote in *Emilius and Sophia*, 1762:

Where is the philosopher who could so live, suffer, and die, without weakness... The Jewish authors were incapable of the diction, and strangers to the morality contained in the Gospel...Yes, if the life and death of Socrates are those of a philosopher, the life and death of **Jesus Christ** are those of a God. [67]

TOLERANCE
FOR
ALL CHRISTIANS

"It affords edifying prospects, indeed, to see **Christians of different denominations** dwell together in more charity, and **conduct themselves in respect to each other with a more Christian-like spirit than ever they have done in any former age, or in any other nation.**"
- President Washington, August 1789, to the General Convention of Episcopal Bishops [69]

In early United States, tolerance embraced all Christian denominations, as noted by historians, State Documents, Presidents, Courts, Congressional Reports and Treaties.

HISTORIANS

French historian Alexis de Tocqueville wrote in *The Republic of the United States and Its Political Institutions,* 1835-40:

In the United States the sovereign authority is religious....There is no country in the whole world where the **Christian** religion retains a greater influence over the souls of men than in America, and there can be no greater proof of its utility and of its conformity to human nature than that its influence is powerfully felt over the most enlightened and free nation of the earth. [70]

America is still the place where the **Christian** religion has kept the greatest real power over men's souls; and nothing better demonstrates how useful and natural it is to man, since the country where it now has the widest sway is both the most enlightened and the freest. [71]

In the United States the influence of religion is not confined to the manners, but it extends to the intelligence of the people....

Christianity, therefore reigns without obstacle, by universal consent; the consequence is, as I have before observed, that every principle of the moral world is fixed and determinate. [72]

In his work, *The United States-A Christian Nation,* published in Philadelphia by the John C. Winston Company, 1905, U.S. Supreme Court Justice David Josiah Brewer wrote:

In no charter or constitution is there anything to even suggest that any other than the **Christian** religion is the religion of this country. In none of them is Mohammed or Confucius or Buddha in any manner noticed.

In none of them is Judaism recognized other than by way of toleration of its special creed. While the separation of church and state is often affirmed, there is nowhere a repudiation of **Christianity** as one of the institutions as well as benedictions of society.

In short, there is no charter or constitution that is either infidel, agnostic, or anti-Christian. Wherever there is a declaration in favor of any religion it is of the **Christian** religion. [73]

We classify nations in various ways. As, for instance, by their form of government.

One is a kingdom, another an empire, and still another a republic. Also by race. Great Britain is an Anglo-Saxon nation, France a Gallic, Germany a Teutonic, Russia a Slav.

And still again by religion. One is a Mohammedan nation, others are heathen, and still others are Christian nations. This republic is classified among the Christian nations of the World. It was so formally declared by the Supreme Court of the United States...

We constantly speak of this republic as a Christian nation - in fact, as the leading Christian nation of the world.[74]

STATE DOCUMENTS

Early State documents indicate tolerance was initially for Christian denominations. Though narrow-minded by today's standards, this was liberal compared to European monarchs who only tolerated subjects adhering to their chosen church.

CAMBRIDGE PLATFORM
MASSACHUSETTS BAY COLONY 1648,

Plymouth Colony Records IX, 1663, William Vassall: 1. CHAP: XVII: In Matters Ecclesiastical....It is lawfull, profitable, & necessary for christians to gather themselves into Church estate, and therein to exercise all the ordinances of Christ according unto the word,..because the Apostles & **Christians** in their time did frequently thus practise, when the Magistrates being all of them Jewish or pagan, & mostly persecuting enemies, would give no countenance [favor] or consent to such matters. [75]

MASSACHUSETTS CONSTITUTION 1780:

The Governor shall be chosen annually; and no person shall be eligible to this office, unless, at the time of his election...he shall declare himself to be of the **Christian** religion. [76]

Chapter VI, Article I. Any person chosen governor, or lieutenant-governor, counsellor, senator, or representative, and accepting the trust, shall before he proceed to execute the duties of his place or office, take, make and subscribe the following declaration:

"I,____ do declare, that I believe the **Christian** religion, and have firm persuasion of its truth."[77]

Part I, Article III. Any person chosen governor, lieutenant governor, counsellor, senator, or representative, and accepting the trust, shall subscribe a solemn profession that he believes in the **Christian** religion, and has a firm persuasion of its truth....

And every denomination of **Christians,** demeaning themselves peaceably and as good subjects of the commonwealth, shall be equally under the protection of the law; and no subordination of, any one sect or denomination shall ever be established by law. (until 1863) [78]

The State of Massachusetts paid the salaries of the **Christian** Congregational ministers in that state until 1833. [79]

MARYLAND CONSTITUTION 1776:

Article XXXV. That no other test or qualification ought to be required, on admission to any office of trust or profit, than such oath of support and fidelity to this State and such oath of office, as shall be directed by this Convention, or the Legislature of this State, and a declaration of a belief in the **Christian** religion. [80]

Article XIX; XXXIII. That, as it is the duty of every man to worship God in such a manner as he thinks most acceptable to him; all persons, professing the **Christian** religion, are equally entitled to protection in their religious liberty; wherefore no person ought by any law to be molested in his person or estate on account of his religious persuasion of profession, or for his religious practice; unless under colour of religion, any man shall disturb the good order, peace or safety of the State or shall infringe the laws of morality...

yet the Legislature may, in their discretion, lay a general and equal tax, for the support of the **Christian** religion; leaving to each individual the power of appointing the payment over the money, collected from him, to the support of any particular place of worship or minister, or for the benefit of the poor or his own denomination, of the poor in general if any particular bounty; but the churches, chapels, glebes, and all other property now belonging to the Church of England, ought to remain the Church of England forever. (until 1851).[81]

SOUTH CAROLINA CONSTITUTION 1790:

Article XXXVIII. That all denominations of **Christians**...in this State, demeaning themselves peaceably and faithfully, shall enjoy equal religious and civil privileges. [82]

VIRGINIA CONSTITUTION 1776:

Bill of Rights, Article XVI. It is the mutual Duty of all to practice **Christian** Forbearance, Love, and Charity towards each other. [83]

NORTH CAROLINA CONSTITUTION 1835:

Article XXXII. That no person who shall deny the being of God, or the truth of the **Christian** religion, or the divine authority of the Old or New Testaments, or who shall hold religious principles incompatible with the freedom and safety of the State, shall be capable of holding any office or place of trust or profit in the civil department within this State. (Until 1876) [84]

RHODE ISLAND & PROVIDENCE PLANTATION CHARTER 1663, IN THE CONSTITUTION OF THE COMMONWEALTH UNTIL 1842:

The object of the Colonists is to pursue, with peace and loyal minds, their sober, serious, and religious intentions of godly edifying themselves and one another in the holy **Christian** faith and worship, together with the gaining over and conversion of the poor ignorant Indian natives to the sincere profession and obedience of the same faith and worship. [85]

DELAWARE CONSTITUTION 1776:

Article XXII. Every person who shall be chosen a member of either house, or appointed to any office or place of trust...shall...make and subscribe the following declaration, to wit:

"I, _____, do profess faith in God the Father, and in **Jesus Christ** His only Son, and in the Holy Ghost, one God, blessed for evermore; I do acknowledge the **holy scriptures of the Old and New Testaments to be given by divine inspiration.**" (Until 1792) [86]

PENNSYLVANIA CONSTITUTION 1776:

Frame of Government, Chapter 2, Section 10. And each member [of the legislature], before he takes his seat, shall make and subscribe the following declaration, viz:

"I do believe in one God, the Creator and Governour of the Universe, the Rewarder of the good and Punisher of the wicked, and I do acknowledge the **Scriptures of the Old and New Testament to be given by Divine Inspiration.**"[87]

PRESIDENTS

Many Presidents commented on Christianity in their addresses, quoted Scriptures, said prayers or made Biblical references. JOHN ADAMS stated in his *Inaugural*, March 4, 1797:

With humble reverence, I feel it to be my duty to add, if a veneration for the religion of a people who profess and call themselves **Christians**, and a fixed resolution to consider a decent respect for **Christianity** among the best recommendations for the public service, can enable me in any degree to comply with your wishes, it shall be my strenuous endeavor that this sagacious injunction of the two Houses shall not be without effect.[88]

President THOMAS JEFFERSON wrote of Jesus in a letter to Dr. Benjamin Rush, April 21, 1803:

His system of morals...if filled up in the style and spirit of the rich fragments He left us, would be the most perfect and sublime that has ever been taught by man....

He corrected the deism of the Jews, confirming them in their belief of one only God, and giving them juster notions of His attributes and government....

The precepts of philosophy, and of the Hebrew code, laid hold of actions only. He pushed his scrutinies into the hearts of man, erected his tribunal in the region of thoughts, and purified the waters at the fountainhead....

Of all the systems of morality, ancient and modern, which have come under my observation, none appear to me so pure as that of **Jesus**. [89]

President JOHN QUINCY ADAMS addressed the Inhabitants of Newburyport on the 61st anniversary of the *Declaration of Independence*, July 4, 1837:

Why is it that, next to the birthday of the Saviour of the World, your most joyous and most venerated festival returns on this day. Is it not that, in the chain of human events, the birthday of the nation is indissolubly linked with the birthday of the Savior?

That it forms a leading event in the Progress of the Gospel dispensation? Is it not that the *Declaration of Independence* first organized the social compact on the foundation of the Redeemer's mission upon earth?

That it laid the cornerstone of human government upon the first precepts of **Christianity** and gave to the world the first irrevocable pledge of the fulfillment of the prophecies announced directly from Heaven at the birth of the Saviour and predicted by the greatest of the Hebrew prophets 600 years before. [90]

President WILLIAM HENRY HARRISON stated in his *Inaugural Address*, March 4, 1841:

> I deem the present occasion sufficiently important and solemn to justify me in expressing to my fellow citizens a profound reverence for the **Christian** religion, and a thorough conviction that sound morals, religious liberty, and a just sense of religious responsibility are essentially connected with all true and lasting happiness.[91]

President JOHN TYLER wrote in his *Proclamation*, April 13, 1841:

> When a **Christian** people feel themselves to be overtaken by a great public calamity, it becomes them to humble themselves under the dispensation of Divine Providence. [92]

President JAMES BUCHANAN stated in his *Inaugural Address,* March 4, 1857:

> We ought to cultivate peace, commerce, and friendship with all nations, and this not merely as the best means of promoting our own material interests, but in a spirit of **Christian** benevolence toward our fellow-men, wherever their lot may be cast. [93]

President ABRAHAM LINCOLN stated in his *Inaugural Address,* March 4, 1861:

> Intelligence, patriotism, **Christianity**, and a firm reliance on Him who has never yet forsaken this favored land, are still competent to adjust in the best way all our present difficulty. [94]

President ANDREW JOHNSON, regarding his first *Proclamation,* stated on April 29, 1865:

> My proclamation of the 25th day of next month, was recommended as a day for special humiliation and prayer in consequence of the assassination of Abraham Lincoln...but whereas my attention has since been called to the fact that the day aforesaid is sacred to large numbers of **Christians** as one of rejoicing for the ascension of the Savior:...
>
> I, Andrew Johnson, President of the United States, do hereby suggest that the religious services...be postponed until...the 1st day of June. [95]

President THEODORE ROOSEVELT stated in his first *Proclamation,* September 14, 1901:

> A terrible bereavement has befallen our people. The President of the United States has been struck down; a crime not only against the Chief Magistrate, but against every law-abiding and liberty-loving citizen.
>
> President McKinley crowned a life of largest love for his fellow men, of earnest endeavor for their welfare, by a death of **Christian** fortitude; and both the way in which he lived his life and the way in which, in the supreme hour of trial, he met death will remain forever a precious heritage of our people. [96]

In his *Memorial Day Address,* May 31, 1923, CALVIN COOLIDGE, then Vice-President under President Harding, wrote:

> Throughout all the centuries this land remained unknown to civilization.

Just at a time when **Christianity** was at last firmly established, when there was a general advance in learning, when there was a great spiritual awakening, America began to be revealed to the European world.....

Settlers came here from mixed motives, some for pillage and adventure, some for trade and refuge, but those who have set their imperishable mark upon our institutions came from far higher motives.

Generally defined, they were seeking a broader freedom. They were intent upon establishing a **Christian** commonwealth in accordance to the principle of self-government.

They were an inspired body of men. It has been said that God sifted the nations that He might send choice grain into the wilderness. They had a genius for organized society on the foundations of piety, righteousness, liberty, and obedience of the law.

They brought with them the accumulated wisdom and experience of the ages...Who can fail to see in it the hand of destiny? Who can doubt that it has been guided by a Divine Providence? [97]

President CALVIN COOLIDGE stated in his *Inaugural Address*, March 4, 1925:

America seeks no earthly empires built on blood and force. No ambition, no temptation, lures her to thought of foreign dominions. The legions which she sends forth are armed, not with the sword, but with the **Cross.**

The higher state to which she seeks the allegiance of all mankind is not of human, but Divine origin. She cherishes no purpose save to merit the favor of Almighty God. [98]

COURTS
1799
Maryland Supreme Court, *Runkel v. Winemiller*, 1799:

By our form of government, the **Christian** religion is the established religion; and all sects and denominations of **Christians** are placed upon the same equal footing, and are equally entitled to protection in their religious liberty. [99]

1802
Massachusetts Grand Jury, 1802, appointed by Judge Nathaniel Freeman, defined:

The laws of the **Christian** system, as embraced by The Bible, must be respected as of high authority in all our courts and it cannot be thought improper for the officers of such government to acknowledge their obligation to be governed by its rule....

Our government originating in the voluntary compact of a people who in that very instrument profess the **Christian** religion, it may be considered, not as republic Rome was, a Pagan, but a **Christian** republic.[100]

1811
New York Supreme Court in *People v. Ruggles*, 1811, referred to "Mahomet and the Grand Lama" as "impostors":

The defendant was indicted...in December, 1810, for that he did, on the 2nd day of September, 1810...wickedly, maliciously, and blasphemously, utter, and with a loud voice publish, in the presence and hearing of divers good and **Christian** people, of and concerning the **Christian** religion, and of and concerning Jesus Christ, the false, scandalous, malicious, wicked and blasphemous words following: "Jesus Christ was a bastard, and his mother must be a whore," in contempt of the **Christian** religion...the defendant was tried and found guilty, and was sentenced by the court to be imprisoned for three months, and to pay a fine of $500.[101]

Such words uttered with such a disposition were an offense at common law.

In *Taylor's* case the defendant was convicted upon information of speaking similar words, and the Court...said that **Christianity** was parcel of the law, and to cast contumelious [insulting] reproaches upon it, tended to weaken the foundation of moral obligation, and the efficacy of oaths.

And in the case of *Rex v. Woolston*, on a like conviction, the Court said...that whatever strikes at the root of **Christianity** tends manifestly to the dissolution of civil government....

The authorities show that blasphemy against God and...profane ridicule of Christ or the Holy Scriptures (which are equally treated as blasphemy), are offenses punishable at common law, whether uttered by words or writings...because it tends to corrupt the morals of the people, and to destroy good order.

Such offenses have always been considered independent of any religious establishment or the rights of the Church. They are treated as affecting the essential interests of civil society....

We stand equally in need, now as formerly, of all the moral discipline, and of those principles of virtue, which help to bind society together.

The people of this State, in common with the people of this country, profess the general doctrines of **Christianity**, as the rule of their faith and practice; and to scandalize the author of these doctrines is not only...impious, but...is a gross violation of decency and good order.

Nothing could be more injurious to the tender morals of the young, than to declare such profanity lawful....

The free, equal, and undisturbed enjoyment of religious opinion, whatever it may be, and free and decent discussions on any religious subject, is granted and secured; but to revile...the religion professed by almost the whole community, is an abuse of that right....

We are people whose manners are refined and whose morals have been elevated and inspired with a more enlarged benevolence, by means of the **Christian** religion.

Though the *Constitution* has discarded religious establishments, it does not forbid judicial cognizance of those offenses against religion and morality which have no reference to any such establishment....

This [constitutional] declaration (noble and magnanimous as it is, when duly understood) never meant to withdraw religion in general, and with it the best sanctions of moral and social obligation from all consideration and notice of the law....

To construe it as breaking down the common law barriers against licentious, wanton, and impious attacks upon **Christianity** itself, would be an enormous perversion of its meaning....

Christianity in its enlarged sense, as a religion revealed and taught in the Bible, is part and parcel of the law of the land....

Nor are we bound by any expression of the *Constitution*, as some have strangely supposed, either not to punish at all, or to punish indiscriminately like attacks upon the religion of Mahomet and the Grand Lama;

and for this plain reason, that we are a **Christian** people, and the morality of the country is deeply engrafted upon **Christianity,** and not upon the doctrines or worship of these impostors. [102]

1824

Pennsylvania Supreme Court, in *Updegraph v. The Commonwealth*, 1824, stated::

Abner Updegraph...on the 12th day of December [1821]...not having the fear of God before his eyes...contriving and intending to scandalize, and bring into disrepute, and vilify the **Christian** religion and the scriptures of truth, in the presence and hearing of several persons...did unlawfully, wickedly and premeditatively, despitefully and blasphemously say...

"The Holy Scriptures were a mere fable: that they were a contradiction, and that although they contained a number of good things, yet they contained a great many lies." To the great dishonor of Almighty God, to the great scandal of the profession of the **Christian** religion....

The jury...finds a malicious intention in the speaker to vilify the **Christian** religion and the scriptures, and this court cannot look beyond the record, nor take any notice of the allegation, that the words were uttered by the defendant, a member of a debating association, which convened weekly for discussion and mutual information....

That there is an association in which so serious a subject is treated with so much levity, indecency and scurrility [vulgarity] ...I am sorry to hear, for it would prove a nursery of vice, a school of preparation to qualify young men for the gallows, and young women for the brothel, and there is not a skeptic of decent manners and good morals, who would not consider such debating clubs as a common nuisance and disgrace to the city....

It was the out-pouring of an invective, so vulgarly shocking and insulting, that the lowest grade of civil authority ought not to be subject to it, but when spoken in a **Christian** land, and to a **Christian** audience, the highest offence contra bonos mores; and even if **Christianity** was not part of the law of the land, it is the popular religion of the country, an insult on which would be indictable....

Assertion is once more made, that **Christianity** never was received as part of the common law of this **Christian** land; and...added, that if it was, it was virtually repealed by the *Constitution of the United States*, and of this state....

If the argument be worth anything, all the laws which have **Christianity** for their object - all would be carried away at one fell swoop - the act against cursing and swearing, and breach of the Lord's day; the act forbidding incestuous marriages, perjury by taking a false oath upon the book, fornication and adultery...for all these are founded on **Christianity** - for all these are restraints upon civil liberty....

We will first dispose of what is considered the grand objection - the constitutionality of **Christianity** - for, in effect, that is the question. **Christianity**, general **Christianity,** is and always has been a part of the common law...not **Christianity** founded on any particular religious tenets; not **Christianity** with an established church...but **Christianity** with liberty of conscience to all men....

I would have it taken notice of, that we do not meddle with the difference of opinion, and that we interfere only where the root of **Christianity** is struck as....

The true principles of natural religion are part of the common law; the essential principles of revealed religion are part of the common law; so that a person vilifying, subverting or ridiculing them may be prosecuted at common law; but temporal punishments ought not to be inflicted for mere opinions;

Thus this wise legislature framed this great body of laws, for a **Christian** country and **Christian** people. This is the **Christianity** of the common law...and thus, it is irrefragably proved, that the laws and institutions of this state are built on the foundation of reverence for **Christianity**....

In this the *Constitution of the United States* has made no alteration, nor in the great body of the laws which was an incorporation of the common-law doctrine of **Christianity**...without which no free government can long exist.

To prohibit the open, public and explicit denial of the popular religion of a country is a necessary measure to preserve the tranquillity of a government.

Of this, no person in a **Christian** country can complain....In the Supreme Court of New York it was solemnly determined, that **Christianity** was part of the law of the land, and that to revile the Holy Scriptures was an indictable offence.

The case assumes, says Chief Justice Kent, that we are a **Christian** people, and the morality of the country is deeply engrafted on **Christianity**. *The People v. Ruggles.*

No society can tolerate a wilful and despiteful attempt to subvert its religion, no more than it would to break down its laws - a general, malicious and deliberate intent to overthrow **Christianity**, general **Christianity**.

Religion and morality...are the foundations of all governments. Without these restraints no free government could long exist.

It is liberty run mad to declaim against the punishment of these offenses, or to assert that the punishment is hostile to the spirit and genius of our government.

They are far from being true friends to liberty who support this doctrine, and the promulgation of such opinions, and general receipt of them among the people, would be the sure forerunners of anarchy, and finally, of despotism.

No free government now exists in the world unless where **Christianity** is acknowledged, and is the religion of the country....Its foundations are broad and strong, and deep....it is the purest system of morality, the firmest auxiliary, and only stable support of all human laws....

Christianity is part of the common law; the act against blasphemy is neither obsolete nor virtually repealed; nor is **Christianity** inconsistent with our free governments of the genius of the people.

While our own free *Constitution* secures liberty of conscience and freedom of religious worship to all, it is not necessary to maintain that any man should have the right publicly to vilify the religion of his neighbors and of the country; these two privileges are directly opposed.[103]

1838

Massachusetts Supreme Court, in *Commonwealth v. Abner Kneeland*, 1838, rejected a Universalist's claim of "freedom of the press" as a defense for publishing defamatory remarks about Christianity. The Court stated "freedom of press" was not a license to print without restraint, otherwise:

> According to the argument...every act, however injurious or criminal, which can be committed by the use of language may be committed...if such language is printed.
>
> Not only therefore would the article in question become a general license for scandal, calumny [slander] and falsehood against individuals, institutions and governments, in the form of publication...but all incitation to treason, assassination, and all other crimes however atrocious, if conveyed in printed language, would be dispunishable. [104]
>
> The statute... follows: "That if any person shall willfully blaspheme the holy name of God, by denying, cursing, or contumeliously [insultingly] reproaching God, his creation, government, or final judging of the world..."
>
> In general, blasphemy may be described, as consisting in speaking evil of the Deity...to alienate the minds of others from the love and reverence of God. It is purposely using words concerning God...to impair and destroy the reverence, respect, and confidence due him...

It is a wilful and malicious attempt to lessen men's reverence of God by denying his existence, of his attributes as an intelligent creator, governor and judge of men, and to prevent their having confidence in him....

But another ground for arresting the judgement, and one apparently most relied on and urged by the defendant, is, that this statute itself is repugnant to the *Constitution*...and therefore wholly void....

[This law] was passed very soon after the adoption of the *Constitution*, and no doubt, many members of the convention which framed the *Constitution*, were members of the legislature which passed this law....

In New Hampshire, the *Constitution* of which State has a similar declaration of [religious] rights, the open denial of the being and existence of God or of the Supreme Being is prohibited by statute, and declared to be blasphemy.

In Vermont, with a similar declaration of rights, a statute was passed in 1797, by which it was enacted, that if any person shall publicly deny the being and existence of God or the Supreme Being, or shall contumeliously [insultingly] reproach his providence and government, he shall be deemed a disturber of the peace and tranquility of the State, and an offender against the good morals and manners of society, and shall be punishable by fine....

The State of Maine also, having adopted the same constitutional provision with that of Massachusetts, in her *Declaration of Rights*, in respect to religious freedom, immediately after the adoption of the *Constitution* reenacted, the Massachusetts statue against blasphemy....

In New York the universal toleration of all religious professions and sentiments, is secured in the most ample manner. It is declared in the *Constitution*...that the free exercise and enjoyment of religious worship, without discrimination or preference, shall for ever be allowed in this State to all mankind....

Notwithstanding this constitutional declaration carrying the doctrine of unlimited toleration as far as the peace and safety of any community will allow, the courts have decided that blasphemy was a crime at common law and was not abrogated by the constitution [*People v. Ruggles*]. [105]

[The *First Amendment*] embraces all who believe in the existence of God, as well...as **Christians** of every denomination....This provision does not extend to atheists, because they do not believe in God or religion; and therefore...their sentiments and professions, whatever they may be, cannot be called religious sentiments and professions.[106]

1844

U.S. Supreme Court in *Vidal v. Girard's Executors*, 1844, gave its decision in the case of a deist from France, Stephen Girard, who had moved to Philadelphia and died, stating in his *Will* that his estate of over $7 million be used to establish an orphanage and school, with the stipulation that no religious influence be allowed. The city rejected the proposal, declaring:

The plan of education proposed is anti-christian, and therefore repugnant to the law....The purest principles of morality are to be taught. Where are they found? Whoever searches for them must go to the source from which a **Christian** man derives his faith - the Bible....

There is an obligation to teach what the Bible alone can teach, viz. a pure system of morality... Both in the Old and New Testaments importance is recognized. In the Old it is said, "Thou shalt diligently teach them to thy children," and the New, "Suffer the little children to come unto me and forbid them not..."

No fault can be found with Girard for wishing a marble college to bear his name for ever, but it is not valuable unless is has a fragrance of **Christianity** about it. [107]

The U.S. Supreme Court rendered its unanimous opinion in *Vidal v. Girard's Executors*, 1844, stating:

We cannot overlook the blessings, which such men by their conduct, as well as their instructions, may, nay must impart to their youthful pupils.

Why may not the Bible, and especially the New Testament, without note or comment, be read and taught as a divine revelation in the college - its general precepts expounded, its evidences explained and its glorious principles of morality inculcated [taught]?

What is there to prevent a work, not sectarian, upon the general evidences of **Christianity**, from being read and taught in the college by lay teachers? Certainly there is nothing in the will that proscribes such studies.

Above all, the testator positively enjoins, "that all the instructors and teachers in the college shall take pains to instill into the minds of the scholars the purest principles of morality, so that on their entrance into active life they may from inclination and habit evince benevolence towards their fellow-creatures, and a love of truth, sobriety, and industry, adopting at the same time such religious tenets as their matured reason may enable them to prefer."

Now, it may well be asked, what is there in all this, which is positively enjoined, inconsistent with the spirit or truths of **Christianity**?

Are not these truths all taught by **Christianity,** although it teaches much more? Where can the purest principles of morality be learned so clearly or so perfectly as from the New Testament?

Where are benevolence, the love of truth, sobriety, and industry, so powerfully and irresistibly inculcated [taught] as in the sacred volume?...

It is unnecessary for us, however, to consider what would be the legal effect of a devise in Pennsylvania for the establishment of a school or college, for the propagation of Judaism, or Deism, or any other form of infidelity.

Such a case is not to be presumed to exist in a **Christian** country; and therefore it must be made out be clear and indisputable proof.

Remote inferences, or possible results, or speculative tendencies are not to be drawn or adopted for such purposes. There must be plain, positive, and express provision, demonstrating not only that **Christianity** is not to be taught; but that it is to be impugned or repudiated.[108]

1892

U.S. Supreme Court, February 29, 1892, in *Church of the Holy Trinity v. United State,* stated:

No purpose of action against religion can be imputed to any legislation, state or national, because this is a religious people. This is historically true.

From the discovery of this continent to the present hour, there is a single voice making this affirmation.

The commission to Christopher Columbus...[recited] that "it is hoped that by God's assistance some of the continents and islands in the ocean will be discovered...."

The first colonial grant made to Sir Walter Raleigh in 1584...and the grant authorizing him to enact statutes for the government of the proposed colony provided that they "be not against the true **Christian** faith...."

The *First Charter of Virginia*, granted by King James I in 1606...commenced the grant in these words: "...in propagating of **Christian** Religion to such People as yet live in Darkness...."

Language of similar import may be found in the subsequent charters of that colony...in 1609 and 1611; and the same istrue of the various charters granted to the other colonies.

In language more or less emphatic is the establishment of the **Christian** religion declared to be one of the purposes of the grant.

The celebrated compact made by the Pilgrims in the Mayflower, 1620, recites: "Having undertaken for the Glory of God, and advancement of the **Christian** faith...a voyage to plant the first colony in the northern parts of Virginia...."

The fundamental orders of Connecticut, under which a provisional government was instituted in 1638-1639, commence with this declaration:

"...And well knowing where a people are gathered together the word of God requires that to maintain the peace and union...there should be an orderly and decent government established according to God...to maintain and preserve the liberty and purity of the gospel of our **Lord Jesus** which we now profess...of the said gospel is now practiced amongst us."

In the charter of privileges granted by William Penn to the province of Pennsylvania, in 1701, it is recited:

"...no people can be truly happy, though under the greatest enjoyment of civil liberties, if abridged of...their religious profession and worship...."

Coming nearer to the present time, the *Declaration of Independence* recognizes the presence of the Divine in human affairs in these words:

"We hold these truths to be self-evident, that all men are created equal, that they are endowed by their Creator with certain unalienable Rights....appealing to the Supreme Judge of the world for the rectitude of our intentions....And for the support of this *Declaration*, with firm reliance on the Protection of Divine Providence, we mutually pledge to each other our Lives, our Fortunes, and our sacred Honor."...

We find everywhere a clear recognition of the same truth...because of a general recognition of this truth [that we are a **Christian** nation], the question has seldom been presented to the courts....

There is no dissonance in these declarations. There is a universal language pervading them all, having one meaning; they affirm and reaffirm that this is a religious nation.

These are not individual sayings, declarations of private persons: they are organic utterances; they speak the voice of the entire people.

While because of a general recognition of this truth the question has seldom been presented to the courts, yet we find that in *Updegraph v. The*

Commonwealth, it was decided that, **Christianity**, general **Christianity**, is, and always has been, a part of the common law....not **Christianity** with an established church...but **Christianity** with liberty of conscience to all men.

And in *The People v. Ruggles*, Chancellor Kent, the great commentator on American law, speaking as Chief Justice of the Supreme Court of New York, said: "The people of this State, in common with the people of this country, profess the general doctrines of **Christianity**, as the rule of their faith and practice....We are a **Christian** people, and the morality of the country is deeply engrafted upon **Christianity**, and not upon the doctrines or worship of those impostors."

And in the famous case of *Vidal v. Girard's Executors*, this Court...observed: "It is also said, and truly, that the **Christian** religion is a part of the common law...."

If we pass beyond these matters to a view of American life as expressed by its laws, its business, its customs and its society, we find everywhere a clear recognition of the same truth. Among other matters note the following:

The form of oath universally prevailing, concluding with an appeal to the Almighty; the custom of opening sessions of all deliberative bodies and most conventions with prayer; the prefatory words of all wills, "In the name of God, amen"; the laws respecting the observance of the Sabbath, with the general cessation of all secular business, and the closing of courts, legislatures, and other similar public assemblies on that day; the churches and church organizations which abound in every city, town and hamlet; the multitude of charitable organizations existing everywhere under **Christian** auspices; the gigantic missionary associations, with general support, and aiming to establish **Christian** missions in every quarter of the globe.

These, and many other matters which might be noticed, add a volume of unofficial declarations to the mass of organic utterances that this is a **Christian** nation....we find everywhere a clear recognition of the same truth. [109]

1927

Minnesota Court, in *Kaplan v. Independent School District of Virginia*, 1927, stated:

This government was founded on the principles of **Christianity** by men either dominated by or reared amidst its influence.[110]

1948

U.S. Supreme Court, *McCollum v. Board of Education of School District Number*, 1948, Justice Felix Frankfurter stated:

Traditionally, organized education in the Western world was **Church** education. It could hardly be otherwise when the education of children was primarily study of the Word and the ways of God.

Even in the Protestant countries, where there was a less close identification of Church and State, the basis of education was largely the Bible, and its chief purpose inculcation [teaching] of piety. [111]

CONGRESSIONAL REPORTS

Tolerance was still primarily for Christian denominations, as seen in the March 27, 1854, HOUSE COMMITTEE ON THE JUDICIARY report by Mr. Meachan:

> At the adoption of the *Constitution*, we believe every State - certainly ten of the thirteen - provided as regularly for the support of the Church as for the support of the Government: one, Virginia, had the system of tithes.
>
> Down to the Revolution, every colony did sustain religion in some form. It was deemed peculiarly proper that the religion of liberty should be upheld by a free people. Had the people, during the Revolution, had a suspicion of any attempt to war against **Christianity**, that Revolution would have been strangled in its cradle.
>
> At the time of the adoption of the *Constitution* and the *Amendments*, the universal sentiment was that **Christianity** should be encouraged, not any one sect. Any attempt to level and discard all religion would have been viewed with universal indignation.
>
> The object was not to substitute Judaism or Mohammedanism, or infidelity, but to prevent rivalry among sects to the exclusion of others....In this age there can be no substitute for **Christianity**: that, in its general principles, is the great conservative element on which we must rely for the purity and permanence of free institutions. That was the religion of the founders of the republic, and they expected it to remain the religion of their descendants.[112]

U.S. Congress, January 19, 1853, recorded the report of Mr. Badger of the SENATE JUDICIARY COMMITTEE:

How comes it that Sunday, the **Christian** Sabbath, is recognized and respected by all the departments of Government?

In the law, Sunday is a "dies non;" it cannot be used for the service of legal process, returns of writs, or other judicial purposes. The executive departments, public establishments, are all closed on Sundays; on that day neither House of Congress sits....

Here is a recognition by law, and by universal usage, not only of a Sabbath, but of the **Christian** Sabbath, in exclusion of the Jewish or Mohammedan Sabbath.

Why, then, do the petitioners exclaim against this invasion of their religious rights? Why do they not assert that a national Sabbath, no less than a national Church, is an establishment of religion?...

The recognition of the **Christian** Sabbath is complete and perfect. The officers who receive salaries, or per-diem compensation, are discharged from duty on this day, because it is the **Christian** Sabbath, and yet suffer no loss or diminution of pay on that account. [113]

TREATIES

Some argue that a line from the failed Treaty of Tripoli, 1798, "the [federal] government of the United States is not in any sense founded on the Christian Religion" discounts America's Judeo-Christian heritage, but this is clearly not the case when one examines the context.

Barbary Pirates of Tripoli were terrorizing the high seas, capturing American ships and enslaving sailors. As Tripoli was a Muslim country, its Islamic Shari'a Law instructed them not to make treaties with "infidel" Christians:

"Infidels are those who declare: 'God is the Christ, the son of Mary'" Sura 5:17, "Infidels are those that say 'God is one of three in a Trinity'" Sura 5:73, "Believers, take neither the Jews nor the Christians for your friends" Sura 5:51, "Believers, do not make friends with those who have incurred the wrath of Allah" Sura 60:13

As Muslims fought infidel "Christian" nations of Europe for over a thousand years, U.S. Ambassador Joel Barlow had the challenge of convincing Tripoli that this time they were not negotiating with the Christian religion, but with a nation-state. This was a novel concept to the 18th century Muslim.

If Tripoli did not understand this new concept, then Barbary Pirates would continue capturing "infidel" American sailors and selling them into slavery, as the Koran instructed:

"The infidels are your sworn enemies" Sura 4:101, "Make war on the infidels who dwell around you" Sura 9:123, "When you meet the infidel in the battlefield strike off their heads" Sura 47:4, "Muhammad is Allah's apostle. Those who follow him are ruthless to the infidels" Sura 48:29, "Prophet, make war on the infidels" Sura 66:9

When one understands this background, the sentence of the Treaty, read in its entirety, reveals the intent was not to diminish Christianity's influence on America's founding, but to simply negotiate a treaty that the Muslims would keep:

As the [federal] government of the United States of America is not in any sense founded on the Christian religion, - **as it has in itself no character of enmity against the law, religion or tranquility of the Musselmen**,- and as the **said States never**

have entered into any war or act of hostility against any Mehomitan nation, it is declared by the parties that **no pretext arising from religious opinion shall ever produce an interruption of the harmony existing between the two countries.**[114]

The Muslims did not honor the Treaty, so U.S. Marines captured the city, thus the anthem "From the Halls of Montezuma to the shores of Tripoli." The new treaty drafted under Jefferson's administration, 1806, did not include the misunderstood phrase.

If treaties are a way of uncovering the beliefs of America founders, then other treaties besides Tripoli's must be examined, such as The Treaty of Paris, 1783, which ended the Revolutionary War, signed by Ben Franklin, John Adams, and John Jay - first Chief Justice of the Supreme Court:

In the name of the Most Holy and Undivided Trinity. It having pleased the Divine Providence to dispose the hearts of…Prince George the Third…and of the United States of America, to forget all past misunderstandings….Done at Paris **in the year of our Lord** one thousand seven hundred and eighty-three.[115]

President Thomas Jefferson extended three times a 1787 Act of Congress in which lands were designated by treaty:

For the sole use of Christian Indians and the Moravian Brethren missionaries for civilizing the Indians and **promoting Christianity**.[116]

The Treaty with the Kaskaskia Indians, December 3, 1803, similar to the Wyandot Treaty, 1805, and Cherokees Treaty, 1806, was passed in Jefferson's administration:

Whereas **the greater part of the said tribe have been baptized and received into the Catholic Church,** to which they are much attached, **the United States will give annually, for seven years, one hundred dollars toward the support of a priest of that religion**, who will engage to perform for said tribe the duties of his office, and also to instruct as many of their children as possible, in the rudiments of literature, and **the United States will further give the sum of three hundred dollars, to assist the said tribe in the erection of a church.**[117]

In 1822, Congress ratified the Convention for Indemnity Under Award Of Emperor Of Russia as to the True Construction of the First Article of the Treaty of December 24, 1814, which begins:

In the name of the Most Holy and Indivisible Trinity.[118]

On January 20, 1830, in a Message to Congress, President Andrew Jackson stated:

According to the terms of an **agreement between the United States and the United Society of Christian Indians** the latter have a claim to an annuity of $400, commencing from the 1st of October, 1826, for which an appropriation by law for this amount, as long as they are entitled to receive it, will be proper.[119]

On December 6, 1830, in his Second Annual Message, President Andrew Jackson commented on Indian treaties:

The Indians...gradually, under the protection of the Government and through the influence of good counsels, to cast off their savage habits and **become an interesting, civilized, and Christian community.**[120]

On December 6, 1831, in his Third Annual Message, President Andrew Jackson stated:

The removal of the **Indians** beyond the limits and jurisdiction of the States does not place them beyond the reach of philanthropic aid **and Christian instruction.**[121]

In 1848, Congress ratified the Treaty ending the Mexican War, which brought into the Union California, Nevada, Utah, Arizona, New Mexico, Colorado and Wyoming:

In the Name of Almighty God: The United States and the United Mexican States...have, **under the protection of Almighty God, the Author of Peace,** arranged, agreed upon, and signed the following: Treaty of Peace...

If (**which God forbid**) war should unhappily break out between the two republics, they do now solemnly pledge....**all churches**, hospitals, schools, colleges, libraries, and other establishments for charitable and beneficent purposes, shall be respected, and all persons connected with the same protected in the discharge of their duties, and the pursuit of their vocations....Done at city of Guadalupe Hidalgo, on the second day of February, **in the year of the Lord** one thousand eight hundred and forty-eight.[122]

Referring to Indian treaties, President Abraham Lincoln stated in his Third Annual Message, December 3, 1863:

It is hoped that the **treaties** will result in the establishment of permanent friendly relations **with such of these tribes** as have been brought into frequent and bloody collision with our outlying settlements and emigrants. Sound policy and our imperative duty to these wards of the Government demand our anxious and constant attention to their material well-being, to their progress in the arts of civilization, and, above all, **to that moral training which under the blessing of Divine Providence will confer upon them the elevated and sanctifying influences, hopes and consolations, of the Christian faith.**[123]

Of the treaty to end Turkish Genocide of Armenian Christians, President Cleveland wrote December 2, 1895:

By treaty several of the most powerful European powers have secured a right and have assumed a duty not only in behalf of their own citizens and in furtherance of their own interests, **but as agents of the Christian world**. Their right to enforce such conduct of **Turkish government as will refrain fanatical brutality**, and if this fails their duty is to so interfere as to insure against such dreadful occurrences in Turkey as have shocked civilization.[124]

President Wilson wrote to the Senate, July 10, 1919, on the Treaty of Peace with Germany signed at Versailles:

A new responsibility has come to this great nation…

The stage is set, the destiny disclosed. It has come about by no plan of our conceiving, but by **the hand of God** who led us into this way.[125]

Of the U.S. delegation drawing up the Four-Power Treaty, President Warren Harding wrote December 23, 1921:

He has full confidence now and is more than gratified over their efforts, because they are working out the greatest contribution to **peace and good-will which has ever marked the Christmas time in all the Christian era**.[126]

GREED AND THE GOSPEL

To clear up a misunderstanding of the term "Christian," it is important to understand there are two threads traceable throughout history, GREED and the GOSPEL.

Those motivated by GREED, though they may have called themselves Christian, were so in name only, and often fought against genuine Christian work, giving the faith a bad name. The Apostle Paul referred to these people in his letter to Titus, chapter 1, verse 16: "They profess that they know God; but in works they deny him, being abominable, and disobedient, and unto every good work reprobate."

These includes merchants of the East India Tea Company that hindered the work of Christian missionaries in India, or those who traded slaves, or took land from Indians, or discriminated against women, or held racial prejudice, or voted their pocketbook even though they knew it meant the spread of immorality and disregard for innocent human life.

The sole concern of people motivated by greed is their job, financial security, the bottom line, in other words, "whoever has the gold rules," yet true Christians are motivated by Jesus' Golden Rule "do unto others as you would have them do unto you." (Mark 7:12)

These true Christians fought to abolish slavery, built orphanages, medical clinics, hospitals, donated money, gave free food and clothes, took in homeless, dug wells, dispensed emergency aid, inoculated, taught farming techniques, visited those in prison, provided literacy programs and disaster relief.

These included missionaries like Lottie Moon, who helped famine victims in China; Mary Slessor who helped end twin killing in Africa; Gladys Aylward, who helped end the binding of girls' feet in China; William Carey, who helped end the Hindu Sati practice of burning a widow to death on her husband's ashes; or Detrich Bonhoffer, who stood up to Hitler.

Even concepts like "women and children first," philanthropy, volunteerism, civil rights, and tolerance have roots traceable to Judeo-Christian thought.

It is unfortunate that Conquistadors lusted for gold, but thankfully they were followed by sincere missionaries, like Bartolome' de Las Casas, who ministered to the natives and helped end cannibalism and human sacrifice.

True Christians tried to follow Jesus' teaching "whatever you have done unto the least of these my brethren, you have done unto me"(Mat. 25:40), as Mother Teresa of Calcutta said:

> "I see Jesus in every human being. I say to myself, this is hungry Jesus, I must feed him. This is sick Jesus. This one has leprosy or gangrene; I must wash him and tend to him. I serve because I love Jesus."[127]

CHRISTIANS PROMOTE TOLERANCE OF NON-CHRISTIANS

"What gave to us this noble safeguard of religious toleration? It was Christianity."
- South Carolina Supreme Court, *City of Charleston v. S.A. Benjamin*, 1846.[128]

The **U.S. Government's www.CIA.gov World Factbook link** lists Americans in 2002 as 78% Christian (52% Protestant, 24% Catholic, 2% Mormon), 1% Jewish, 1% Muslim, 10% other, 10% none. Ten years ago, that site listed Americans as 84% Christian. The further one goes back in time, the greater the percentage of Christians in America. Patricia U. Bonomi, Professor Emeritus of New York University, in her article *The Middle Colonies as the Birthplace of American Religious Pluralism,* wrote: "The colonists were about 98 percent Protestant."

Given that America's population was predominately Christian at the time the nation's founding gives rise to the question: What would motivate a predominently Christian populace to promote tolerance of non-Christians?

1) SHARING THE GOSPEL

The idea of going to another culture to evangelize non-christians was not common until 1812, when America's first foreign missionary, Adonirum Judson, left for Rangoon, Burma.

Prior to 1812, the concept of communicating the Gospel to those of other religions was to invite them to live in one's community. James Madison used this reasoning in his *Memorial & Remonstrance* to the Virginia Assembly, 1785.

Though other States, such as Massachusetts, Maryland and New Hampshire, supported Christian teachers of piety and religion, Madison opposed the measure in Virginia, as those responsible for hiring the teachers would be tempted to hire from their own denomination, thus having the same effect as setting up a State church..

Madison explained that establishing a State religion would discourage those "still remaining under the dominions of false religions" from immigrating and being reached with "the light of Christianity....the light of Truth."

In his *Memorial & Remonstrance*, 1785,Madison wrote:

The policy of the bill is adverse to the diffusion of the light of Christianity. The first wish of those who ought to enjoy this precious gift, ought to be, that it may be **imparted to the whole race of mankind.**

Compare the number of those who have as yet received it, with the number still remaining under the dominions of **false religions,** and how small is the former!

Does the policy of the bill tend to lessen the disproportion? No; it at once discourages those who are **strangers to the light of Truth**, from coming into the regions of it. [129]

Madison continued:

Whilst we assert for ourselves a freedom to embrace, to profess, and to observe the Religion which we believe to be of divine origin, **we cannot**

deny an equal freedom to those whose minds have not yet yielded to the evidence which has convinced us.

If this freedom be abused, it is an offence against God, not against man: To God, therefore, not to man, must an account of it be rendered. [130]

Colonial leader Roger Williams had written earlier in his *Plea for Religious Tolerance,* 1644:

In holding an enforced uniformity of religion in a civil state, we must necessarily disclaim our desires and hopes of the Jew's conversion to Christ....

It is the will and command of God that (since the coming of his Son the Lord Jesus) a permission of the most paganish, Jewish, Turkish, or antichristian consciences and worships, be granted to all men in all nations and countries; and they are only to be fought against with that sword which is only (in soul matters) able to conquer, to wit, the sword of God's Spirit, the Word of God....

I acknowledge that to molest any person, Jew or Gentile, for either professing doctrine, or practicing worship merely religious or spiritual, it is to persecute him, and such a person (whatever his doctrine or practice be, true or false) suffereth persecution for conscience...

The sufferings of false and antichristian teachers harden their followers, who being blind, by this means are occasioned to tumble into the ditch of hell after their blind leaders, with more inflamed zeal of lying confidence...

To batter down idolatry, false worship, heresy, schism, blindness, hardness, out of the soul and spirit, it is vain, improper, and unsuitable to bring those weapons which are used by persecutors, stocks, whips, prisons, swords,....but against these spiritual strongholds in the souls of men, spiritual artillery and weapons are proper, which are mighty through God to subdue and bring under the very thought to obedience.[131]

William Penn wrote: "Force makes hypocrites, 'tis persuasion only that makes converts."

2) CHRISTIAN TEACHING ON TOLERANCE

Christian leaders in America advocated Jesus' teaching from the Sermon on the Mount know as the Golden Rule - "do unto others as you would have them do unto you."

President Madison said in a *Proclamation,* July 9, 1812:

With a reverence for the unerring precept of our holy religion, to **do to others as they would require that others should do to them**.[132]

In An Address on the Bank of North America, 1785, Gouverneur Morris stated:

How can we hope for public peace and national prosperity, if the faith of governments so solemnly pledged can be so lightly infringed?...It is He who tells you, **"do unto others as ye would that they would do unto you."**[133]

President Andrew Jackson, in his Third Annual Message, December 6, 1831, stated:

A small sum is stipulated on our part to go to the extinction of claims by French citizens on our Government....Payment, though unsupported by legal proof, affords a practical illustration of our submission to **the divine rule of doing to others what we desire they should do unto us.**[134]

"Christian" was synonymous with "tolerance," as Samuel Adams wrote in *The Rights of the Colonists*, 1772, "the spirit of toleration" is the "chief characteristic of the church":

> In regards to religion, mutual toleration in the different professions thereof is what all good and candid minds in all ages have ever practiced...
> and it is now **generally agreed among Christians that this spirit of toleration**, in the fullest extent consistent with the being of civil society, **is the chief characteristical mark of the church.** [135]

The concept of "doing unto others as you would have them do unto you," called "Christian Forbearance," was cited in "The *Virginia Bill of Rights*, 1776, written with the help of James Madison, George Mason and Patrick Henry:

> That Religion, or the Duty which we owe our Creator, and the Manner of discharging it, can be directed only by Reason and Convictions, not by Force or Violence; and therefore all Men are equally entitled to the free exercise of Religion, according to the Dictates of Conscience; and that it is the mutual Duty of all to practice **Christian Forbearance**, Love, and Charity towards each other. [136]

Patrick Henry said Christianity promoted forbearance:

> I know, sir, how well it becomes a liberal man and a **Christian** to forget and forgive. **Our mild and holy system of religion inculcates an admirable maxim of forbearance.**[137]

Patrick Henry is attributed with a comment expressing the idea that a Christian umbrella gives tolerance to all faiths:

> It cannot be emphasized too strongly or too often that this great nation was founded, not by religionists, but by Christians; not on religions, but on the Gospel of Jesus Christ. For this very reason **peoples of other faiths** have been afforded asylum, prosperity, and freedom of worship here. [138]

3) JESUS' EXAMPLE

America's leaders put into law Jesus' example of never forcing anyone to believe in him, realizing that the only worship pleasing to God was a voluntary free-will offering from "the impulse of their hearts and the dictates of their consciences."

As explored later in this book, they saw true religion as being from the inside-out, not forced from the outside-in, a policy foreign to Medieval Europe or Islamic Caliphs.

James Madison alluded to this in his *Proclamation of a National Day of Public Humiliation & Prayer*, July 23, 1813:

> If the public homage of a people can ever be worthy of the favorable regard of the Holy and Omniscient Being to whom it is addressed, it must be...**guided only by their free choice, by the impulse of their hearts and the dictates of their consciences;**
>
> and such a spectacle must be interesting to all Christian nations as proving that **religion, that gift of Heaven for the good of man is freed from all coercive edicts.** [139]

Jefferson composed his own epitaph and, interestingly, did not mention being President. Instead he wrote:

Here lies buried Thomas Jefferson, author of the *Declaration of Independence*, author of the Statutes for Religious Freedom in Virginia, and father of the University of Virginia. [140]

What was in this *Statute for Religious Freedom in Virginia, 1786?* In it, Jefferson appealed to "the plan of the Holy Author of religion...not to propagate it by coercion":

Well aware that Almighty God hath created the mind free, and manifested His Supreme Will that free it shall remain by making it altogether insusceptible of restraints; that all attempts to influence it by temporal punishments, or burdens, or by civil incapacitations, tend only to begat habits of hypocrisy and meanness, and are a departure from the plan of **the Holy Author of religion, who being Lord both of body and mind, yet chose not to propagate it by coercions** on either, **as was in his Almighty power to do, but to extend it by its influence on reason alone.**[141]

Who did the country think Jefferson was referring to when he said "***...the Holy Author of religion...chose not to propagate it by coercions.***"

He could not have been referring to polytheistic Hinduism or Buddhism or Greek Mythology, as he used the singular term "Author" not the plural "Authors." Besides, there were no Buddhists or Hindus in America at that time.

He could not have been referring to Islam, as there were virtually no Muslims living in the United States at the time, additionally, they had a reputation of propagating through "coercion," as Mohammed himself led an army which killed many who would not submit.

Jefferson was probably was not referring to Judaism, though several congregations existed in America, as Hebrews were not known for "propagating" religion.

Jefferson's "Holy Author of religion" is similar to George Washington's "Divine Author of our blessed Religion" used in his *Prayer for the United States,* engraved in St. Paul's Chapel,, the oldest continuously used structure in New York City. Though across from the World Trade Center, it was not damaged during the September 11, 2001, terrorist attack:

> Almighty God; We make our earnest prayer that Thou wilt keep the United States in Thy Holy protection...that Thou wilt most graciously be pleased to dispose us all to do justice, to love mercy, and to **demean ourselves with that Charity, humility, and pacific temper of mind which were the Characteristics of the *Divine Author of our blessed Religion,*** and without a humble imitation of whose example in these things we can never hope to be a happy nation. Grant our supplication, we beseech Thee, through Jesus Christ our Lord. Amen.[142]

Cotton Mather used the term "Holy Author of that Religion" in his *Magnalia Christi Americana*, 1702:

> I write the wonders of the Christian religion, flying from the depravations of Europe, to the American strand: and, assisted by the **Holy Author of that Religion.** [143]

Pennsylvania Frame of Government, April 25, 1682, had a similar reference to "Author...of Pure Religion":

> The same Divine Power, that is both the **Author and Object of Pure Religion.**[144]

Jefferson concluded his *Statute for Religious Freedom in Virginia,* 1786, with the well-known words:

> Be it, therefore, enacted...That no man shall be compelled to frequent or support any religious worship, place, or ministry, whatsoever, nor shall be enforced, restrained, molested, or burdened in his body or goods, nor shall otherwise suffer, on account of his religious opinions or belief;
>
> but that all men shall be free to profess and by argument to maintain their opinions in matters of religion, and that the same shall in no wise diminish, enlarge, or affect their civil capacities. [145]

This is what Rhode Island founder Roger Williams had written over a century earlier in his *Plea for Religious Liberty,* 1644, stating that even if one believes in "false worship" the magistrate must guarantee "no injury" to his person or goods:

> The civil magistrate either respecteth that religion which...is true, or...that which is false. If that which the magistrate believeth to be true, be true, I say he owes a threefold duty...
>
> First...according to Isa. 49, Revel. 21, a tender respect of truth and the professors of it. Secondly, personal submission of his own soul to the power of the Lord Jesus in that spiritual government and kingdom...Matt. 18, 1 Cor. 5. Thirdly, protection of such true professors of Christ, whether apart, or met together, as also of their estates from violence and injury...Rom. 13.
>
> Now, secondly, if it be a false religion (unto which the civil magistrate dare not adjoin, yet) he owes:

First, permission (for approbation he owes not what is evil) and this according to Matthew 13:30, for public peace and quiet's sake. **Secondly, he owes protection to the persons of his subjects (though of a false worship), that no injury be offered either to the persons or goods of any.** [146]

The U.S. Supreme Court, in *Church of the Holy Trinity v. United States,* 1892, described two different definitions of the term "Christianity." The first being "an established church" with "particular religious tenets," and the second being "general Christianity" with a "liberty of conscience for all men":

In *Updegraph v. The Commonwealth,* it was decided that, "Christianity, **general Christianity**, is, and always had been, a part of the common law...not Christianity founded on any particular religious tenets; not Christianity with an established church, and tithes, and spiritual courts, **but Christianity with liberty of conscience to all men.**"[147]

Historian Alexis de Tocqueville wrote in *The Republic of the United States of America & Its Political Institutions,* 1851:

From the earliest settlement of the emigrants, politics and religion contracted an alliance which has never been dissolved...**The Americans combine the notions of Christianity and of liberty** so intimately in their minds, that **it is impossible to make them conceive the one without the other**. [148]

Tolerance of non-Christians was promoted by early America's predominately Christian populace to 1) share the Gospel, 2) practice Christian teaching on tolerance, and 3) follow Jesus' example.

TOLERANCE
FOR
JEWS

Early Americans studied Hebrew language, laws and scriptures, and small communities of Jews experienced degrees of tolerance, but complete acceptance was gradual.

Their journey began when King Ferdinand and Queen Isabella, who sent Columbus on his voyage, not only drove Muslims out of Spain, but also over 150,000 Jews, many to Portugal and Amsterdam. Hundreds sailed with Dutch merchants to South America, but were forced to flee after Spanish and Portuguese attacks. In 1654, twenty-three refugees arrived on the French ship *Sainte Catherine* in New Amsterdam.

Governor Peter Stuyvesant tried to evict them, but pleas from Jewish investors in the Dutch West India Company in Amsterdam prevailed. Though Jews were not allowed to worship outside their homes, they were allowed to purchase land for a cemetery in 1656. In 1664, New Amsterdam became New York and there the first synagogue in North America was built in 1730. The Jewish population grew to 1,500 during the colonial period, in seven synagogues: New York, Newport, Philadelphia, Lancaster. Richmond, Charleston and Savannah.

The 6,000 Jews in America in 1800 grew to 17,000 by 1830, when New York's Ellis Island saw over a hundred thousand German Jews immigrate to escape persecution in Bavaria. Beginning in 1881, over a million Jews immigrated to escape the Czar's pogroms in Russia.

Early Americans referenced Israel. Puritan leader John Winthrop wrote in his *Model of Christian Charity,* June 11, 1630:

We shall find the God of **Israel** is among us.[149]

The alphabet in the *New England Primer*, 1737, included:

"M" MOSES was he Who **Israel's** Host Led thro' the Sea. [150]

In 1773, after the Boston Massacre, the men of Marlborough, Massachusetts, declared:

We implore the Ruler above the skies, that He would make bare His arm in defense of His Church and people, and let **Israel** go. [151]

Abigail Adams wrote to her husband, June 18, 1775:

The God of **Israel** is He that giveth strength and power unto His people. [152]

Connecticut Governor Jonathan Trumbull wrote General George Washington, July 13, 1775:

May the God of the armies of **Israel** shower down the blessings of his Divine Providence on you.[153]

Thomas Jefferson, July 3, 1776, proposed the seal of the United States be:

The children of **Israel** in the wilderness, led by a cloud by day, and a pillar of fire by night. [154]

Abigail Adams wrote to her husband, John, in Philadelphia, June 20, 1776:

> He who fed the **Israelites** in the wilderness, who clothes the lilies of the field and who feeds the young ravens when they cry, will not forsake a people engaged in so right a cause.[155]

President Thomas Jefferson remarked in his *Second Inaugural Address*, March 4, 1805:

> I shall need, too, the favor of that Being in whose hands we are, who led our forefathers, as **Israel** of old.[156]

John Adams wrote to Judge F.A Van der Kemp, February 16, 1809:

> The **Hebrews** have done more to civilize men than any other nation....God ordered the **Jews** to preserve and propagate to all mankind the doctrine of a Supreme, Intelligent, Wise, Almighty Sovereign of the Universe....which is to be the great essential principle of morality, and consequently all civilization.[157]

Francis J. Grund, a contemporary of de Tocqueville, commented on the tolerance enjoyed by Jews in his work *The Americans in Their Moral, Social and Political Relations,* 1837:

> Although the most perfect tolerance exists with regard to particular creeds, yet it is absolutely necessary that a man should belong to some persuasion or other, lest his fellow citizens should consider him an outcast from society.

The **Jews** are tolerated in America with the same liberality as any denomination of Christians; but if a person were to call himself a Deist or an Atheist, it would excite universal execration.[158]

It was not until the middle 1800's that Jews were allowed to hold office. For example, Maryland's 1776 "Oath of Office" required a: "declaration of belief in the Christian religion,"[159] but in 1851, it added:

And if the party shall profess to be a **Jew** the declaration shall be of his belief in a future state of rewards and punishments. [160]

PRESIDENTS & LEADERS WRITING OF JEWS

Dr. Benjamin Rush, a signer of the *Declaration of Independence*, wrote to Elias Boudinot, July 9, 1788, regarding a parade in Philadelphia:

The Rabbi of the **Jews** locked arms of two ministers of the Gospel was a most delightful sight. There could not have been a more happy emblem.[161]

President Washington wrote to the **Hebrew** Congregations of Philadelphia, Newport, Charlestown and Richmond, January 1790:

The liberal sentiment towards each other which marks every political and religious denomination of men in this country stands unrivalled in the history of nations....

The power and goodness of the Almighty were strongly manifested in the events of our late glorious revolution and His kind interpositions in our behalf has been no less visible in the establishment on our present equal government.

In war He directed the sword and in peace He has ruled in our councils. My agency in both has been guided by the best intentions, and a sense of the duty which I owe my country....May the same temporal and eternal blessings which you implore for me, rest upon your **congregations.**[162]

President Washington addressed the **Hebrew** Congregation in Newport, Rhode Island, August 17, 1790:

It is now no more that toleration is spoken of as if it were the indulgence of one class of people that another enjoyed the exercise of their inherent natural rights, for, happily, the Government of the United States, which gives to bigotry no sanction, to persecution no assistance, requires only that they who live under its protection should demean themselves as good citizens in giving it on all occasions their effectual support....

May the **children of the stock of Abraham** who dwell in this land continue to merit and enjoy the good will of the other inhabitants - while every one shall sit in safety under his own vine and fig tree and there shall be none to make him afraid.

May the Father of all mercies scatter light, and not darkness, upon our paths, and make us all in our several vocations useful here, and in His own due time and way everlastingly happy. [163]

President George Washington wrote to the Hebrew Congregations of the city of Savannah, Georgia:

May the same wonder-working Deity, who long since delivering the **Hebrews** from their Egyptian Oppressors planted them in the promised land-whose Providential Agency has lately been conspicuous in establishing these United States as an independent Nation-still continue to water them with the dews of Heaven and to make the inhabitants of every denomination participate in the temporal and spiritual blessings of that people whose God is Jehovah.[164]

President James Buchanan wrote to the House of Representatives, April 24, 1860:

In compliance with the resolution of the House of Representatives of the 2d March, 1859, and of the 26th ultimo, requesting information relative to discriminations in Switzerland against citizens of the United States of the **Hebrew** persuasion, I transmit a report of the Secretary of State. [165]

In 1860, Dr. Rabbi Morris Jacob Raphall (1798-1868), who corresponded with President Lincoln, was the first **Jewish** rabbi invited to open a U.S. House session with prayer.[166]

During the Civil War, July 12, 1862, new wording was written to include chaplains of the **Hebrew** faith, following a complaint of the lack of chaplains to serve **Jewish** soldiers. The law previously read: "The chaplain so appointed must be a regular ordained minister of a Christian denomination."[167]

Jefferson Davis, President of the Confederacy, included in his cabinet Judah P. Benjamin, the first Jewish Cabinet member in North America.

President Grant wrote to the Senate, May 14, 1872:

I transmit herewith copies of the correspondence between the Department of State and the consul of the United States at Bucharest relative to the persecution and oppression of the **Israelites** in the Principality of Romania.[168]

President Ulysses S. Grant wrote to the House of Representatives, May 22, 1872:

In answer to a resolution of the House of Representatives of the 20th instant, requesting me to join the Italian Government in a protest against the intolerant and cruel treatment of the **Jews** in Romania, I transmit a report from the Secretary of State relative to the subject.[169]

President Chester A. Arthur stated in his *First Annual Message to Congress*, December 6, 1881:

It is desirable that our cordial relations with Russia should be strengthened by proper engagements assuring to peaceable Americans who visit the Empire the consideration which is due to them as citizens of a friendly state.

This is especially needful with respect to American **Israelites**, whose classification with the native **Hebrew** has evoked energetic remonstrances.[170]

President Chester A. Arthur wrote to the U.S. House of Representatives, May 2, 1882:

In answer to a resolution of the House of Representatives of the 30th of January last, calling for correspondence respecting the condition of **Israelites** in Russia, I transmit herewith a report from the Secretary of State and its accompanying papers.[171]

President Chester A. Arthur stated in his *Second Annual Message to Congress*, December 4, 1882:

Our long-established friendliness with Russia has remained unshaken. It has prompted me to proffer the earnest counsels of this Government that measures by adopted for suppressing the proscription which the **Hebrew** race in that country has lately suffered.

It has not transpired that any American citizen has been subjected to arrest or injury, but our courteous remonstrance has nevertheless been courteously received. There is reason to believe that the time is not far distant when Russia will be able to secure toleration to all faiths within her borders. [172]

President Benjamin Harrison proclaimed a *National Day of Prayer* at the Centennial of George Washington's Inauguration, April 4, 1889:

That the joy of the occasion may be associated with a deep thankfulness in the minds of the people for all our blessings in the past and a devout supplication to God for their gracious continuance in the future, the representatives of the religious creeds, both Christian and **Hebrew,** have memorialized the Government to designate an hour for prayer and thanksgiving on that day. [173]

President Benjamin Harrison stated in his *Third Annual Message*, December 9, 1891:

This Government has found occasion to express in a friendly spirit, but with much earnestness, to the Government of the Czar its serious concern because of the harsh measures now being enforced against the **Hebrews** in Russia.

By the revival of antisemitic laws, long in abeyance, great numbers of those unfortunate people have been constrained to abandon their homes and leave the Empire by reason of the impossibility of finding subsistence within the pale to which it is sought to confine them.

The immigration of these people to the United States - many others countries being closed to them - is largely increasing and is likely to assume proportions which may make it difficult to find home and employment for them here and to seriously affect the labor market. It is estimated that over 1,000,000 will be forced from Russia within a few years.

The **Hebrew** is never a beggar; he has always kept the law - life by toil - often under severe and oppressive civil restrictions. It is also true that no race, sect, or class has more fully cared for its own than the **Hebrew** race....

This consideration, as well as the suggestion of humanity, furnishes ample ground for the remonstrances which we have presented to Russia.[174]

President Grover Cleveland wrote to Congress in his *Seventh Annual Message,* December 2, 1895:

Correspondence is on foot touching the practice of Russian consuls within the jurisdiction of the United States to interrogate citizens as to their race and religious faith, and upon ascertainment thereof to deny to **Jews** authentication of passports of legal documents for use in Russia.

Inasmuch as such a proceeding imposes a disability which in the case of succession to property in Russia may be found to infringe the treaty rights of our citizens, and which is an obnoxious invasion of our territorial jurisdiction, it has elicited fitting remonstrance, the result of which, it is hoped, will remove the cause of the compliant. [175]

President Theodore Roosevelt, who appointed Oscar Strauss as the first Jew to a U.S. Cabinet position, stated in his *Fourth Annual Message to Congress,* December 6, 1904:

It is inevitable that such a nation should desire eagerly to give expression to its horror on an occasion like that of the massacre of the **Jews** in Kishenef....

It has proved very difficult to secure from Russia the right for our **Jewish** fellow-citizens to receive passports and travel through Russian territory. Such conduct is not only unjust and irritating toward us, but it is difficult to see its wisdom from Russia's standpoint.

No conceivable good is accomplished by it. If an American **Jew** or an American Christian misbehaves himself in Russia he can at once be driven out; but the ordinary American **Jew**, like the ordinary American Christian, would behave just about as he behaves here. [176]

President Theodore Roosevelt stated in his *Fifth Annual Message to Congress*, December 5, 1905:

It is unwise to depart from the old American tradition and to discriminate for or against any man who desires to come here and become a citizen, save on the ground of that man's fitness for citizenship. It is our right and duty to consider his moral and social quality....

If the man who seeks to come here is from the moral and social standpoint of such a character as to bid fair to add value to the community he should be heartily welcomed.

We cannot afford to pay heed to whether he is of one creed or another, of one nation, or another. We cannot afford to consider whether he is Catholic or Protestant, **Jew** or Gentile; whether he is Englishman or Irishman, Frenchman or German.[177]

President Theodore Roosevelt stated in his *Sixth Annual Message to Congress*, December 3, 1906:

Not only must we treat all nations fairly, but we must treat with justice and good will all immigrants who come here under the law. Whether they are Catholic or Protestant, **Jew** or Gentile; whether they come from England or Germany.[178]

President Woodrow Wilson proclaimed a *Contribution Day* for the aid of stricken Jewish people, January 11, 1916:

Whereas, I have received from the Senate of the United States a Resolution, passed January 6, 1916, reading as follows:

"Whereas in the various countries now engaged in war there are nine millions of **Jews**, the great majority of whom are destitute of food, shelter, and clothing; and

"Whereas millions of them have been driven from their homes without warning, deprived of an opportunity to make provision for their most elementary wants, causing starvation, disease and untold suffering; and

"Whereas the people of the United States of America have learned with sorrow of this terrible plight of millions of human beings and have most generously responded to the cry for help whenever such an appeal has reached them;

"Therefore be it Resolved, That, in view of the misery, wretchedness, and hardships which these nine millions of **Jews** are suffering, the President of the United States be respectfully asked to designate a day on which the citizens of this country may give expression to their sympathy by contributing to the funds now being raised for the relief of the **Jews** in the war zones." And

Whereas, I feel confident that the people of the United States will be moved to aid the war-stricken people of a race which has given to the United States so many worthy citizens;

Therefore, I, Woodrow Wilson, President of the United States, in compliance with the suggestion of the Senate thereof, do appoint and proclaim January 27, 1916, as a day upon which the people of the United States may make such contributions as they feel disposed for the aid of the stricken **Jewish** people. Contributions may be addressed to the American Red Cross, Washington, D.C., which will care for their proper distribution...Done this eleventh day of January, in the year of Our Lord one thousand nine hundred and sixteen.[179]

President Woodrow Wilson wrote to Rabbi Stephen S. Wise of New York City, September 1, 1918:

My Dear Rabbi Wise: I have watched with deep and sincere interest the reconstructive work which the Weizmann commission has done in

Palestine at the instance of the British Government, and I welcome an opportunity to express the satisfaction I have felt in the progress of the Zionist movement in the United States and in the allied countries since the declaration of Mr. Balfour, on behalf of the British Government, of Great Britain's approval of the establishment in Palestine of a national home for the **Jewish** people, and his promise that the British Government would use its best endeavors to facilitate the achievement of that object, with the understanding that nothing would be done to prejudice the civil and religious rights of non-Jewish people in Palestine or the rights and political status enjoyed by **Jews** in other countries.

I think that all Americans will be deeply moved by the report that even in this time of stress the Weizmann commission has been able to lay the foundation of the **Hebrew** University at Jerusalem, with the promise that that bears of spiritual rebirth. Cordially and sincerely yours, Woodrow Wilson. [180]

President Calvin Coolidge spoke via phone from the White House to the Federation of Jewish Philanthropic Societies of New York City, October 26, 1924:

Your Federation for the Support of **Jewish** Philanthropic Societies in New York is the central financial agency, I am told, for no less than ninety-one various philanthropies, which receive annual support aggregating $7,000,000.

Among them are hospitals, orphanages, a great relief society, a loaning organization, a home for Aged and Infirm.

The Young Men's **Hebrew** Association and the Young Women's **Hebrew** Association do social and educational work of the greatest value.

Especial attention is devoted indeed to educational effort for which technical schools are maintained.

That is, of course, precisely what we should expect from a great **Jewish** organization; for the Jews are always among the first to appreciate and to utilize educational opportunities....

The **Jewish** people have always and everywhere been particularly devoted to the ideal of taking care of their own. This Federation is one of the monuments to their independence and self-reliance.

They have sought to protect and preserve that wonderful inheritance of tradition, culture, literature and religion, which has placed the world under so many obligations to them....

I want you to know that I feel you are making good citizens, that you are strengthening the Government, that you are demonstrating the supremacy of the spiritual life and helping establish the Kingdom of God on earth. [181]

President Calvin Coolidge gave a detailed account of the overlooked story of Jewish contributions to the American Revolution in a ceremony laying the cornerstone of the Jewish Community Center, Washington, D.C., May 3, 1925:

We have gathered this afternoon to lay with appropriate ceremony and solemnity the cornerstone of a temple. The splendid structure which is to rise here will be the home of the **Jewish** Community Center of Washington....

About this institution will be organized, and from it will be radiated, the influences of those civic works in which the genius of the **Jewish** people has always found such eloquent expression....

This year 1925 is a year of national anniversaries, States, cities, and towns throughout all the older parts of the country will be celebrating their varied parts in the historic events which a century and a half ago marked the beginning of the American Revolution....

It will remind us, as a nation, of how a common spiritual inspiration was potent to bring and mold and weld together into a national unity, the many and scattered colonial communities that had been planted along the Atlantic seaboard....There were well-nigh as many divergencies of religious faith as there were of origin, politics and geography....

From its beginning, the new continent had seemed destined to be the home of religious tolerance. Those who claimed the right of individual choice for themselves finally had to grant it to others.

Beyond that - and this was one of the factors which I think weighed heaviest on the side of unity - **the Bible was the one work of literature that was common to all of them**. The Scriptures were read and studied everywhere. There are many testimonies that their teachings became the most important intellectual and spiritual force for unification.

I remember to have read somewhere, I think in the writings of the historian William Lecky, the observation the "**Hebraic** mortar cemented the foundations of American democracy." Lecky had in mind this very influence of the Bible in drawing together the feelings and sympathies of the widely scattered communities.

All the way from New Hampshire to Georgia, they found a common ground of faith and reliance in the Scriptural writings.

In those days books were few, and even those of a secular character were largely the product of a scholarship which used the Scriptures as the model and standard of social interpretation.

It was to this, of course, that Lecky referred. He gauged correctly a force too often underestimated and his observation was profoundly wise. It suggested, in a way which none of us can fail to understand, the debt which the young American nation owed to the sacred writing that the **Hebrew** people gave to the world.

This biblical influence was strikingly impressive in all the New England colonies, and only less so in the others. In the Connecticut Code of 1650, the **Mosaic** model is adopted. The magistrates were authorized to administer justice "according to the laws here established, and, for want of them, according to the word of God."

In the New Haven Code of 1655, there were 79 topical statutes for the Government, half of which contained references to the Old Testament. The founders of the New Haven, John Davenport and Theophilus Eaton, were expert **Hebrew** scholars.

The extent to which they leaned upon the moral and administrative system, laid down by the **Hebrew** lawgivers, was responsible for their conviction that the **Hebrew** language and literature ought to be made as familiar as possible to all the people.

So it was that John Davenport arranged that in the first public school in New Haven the **Hebrew** language should be taught. The preachers of those days, saturated in the religion and literature of the **Hebrew** prophets, were leaders, teachers, moral mentors and even political philosophers for their flocks.

A people raised under such leadership, given to much study and contemplation of the Scriptures, inevitably became more familiar with the great figures of **Hebrew** history, with Joshua, Samuel, Moses, Joseph, David, Solomon, Gideon, Elisha - than they were with the stories of their own ancestors as recorded in the pages of profane history.

The sturdy old divines of those day found the Bible a chief source of illumination for their arguments in support of the patriot cause. They knew the Book. They were profoundly familiar with it, and eminently capable in the exposition of all its justifications for rebellion.

To them, the record of the exodus from Egypt was indeed an inspired precedent. They knew what arguments from holy writ would most powerfully influence their people. It required no great stretch of logical processes to demonstrate that the children of **Israel**, making bricks without straw in Egypt, had their modern counterpart in the people of the colonies, enduring the imposition of taxation without representation!

And the **Jews** themselves, of whom a considerable number were already scattered throughout the colonies, were true to the teachings of their own prophets. The **Jewish** faith is predominantly the faith of liberty.

From the beginning to the conflict between the colonies and the mother country, they were overwhelmingly on the side of the rising revolution. You will recognize them when I read the names of some among the merchants who unhesitatingly signed the non-importation resolution of 1765:

Isaac Moses, Benjamin Levy, Samson Levy, David Franks, Joseph Jacobs, Hayman Levy, Jr., Mathias Bush, Michael Gratz, Bernard Gratz, Isaac Franks, Moses Mordecai, Benjamin Jacobs, Samuel Lyon and Manuel Mordecai Noah. Not only did the colonial **Jews** join early and enthusiastically in the non-intercourse program, but when the time came for raising and sustaining an army, they were ready to serve wherever they could be most useful.

There is a romance in the story of Haym Solomon, Polish **Jew** financier of the Revolution. Born in Poland, he was made prisoner by the British forces in New York, and when he escaped set up in business in Philadelphia.

He negotiated for Robert Morris all the loans raised in France and Holland, pledged his personal faith and fortune for enormous amounts, and personally advanced large sums to such men as James Madison, Thomas Jefferson, Baron Steuben, General St. Clair, and many other patriot leaders who testified that without his aid they could not have carried on in the cause.

A considerable number of **Jews** became officers in the continental forces. The records show at least four **Jews** who served as Lieutenant Colonels, three and Majors and certainly six, probably more, as Captains. Major Benjamin Nones has been referred to as the Jewish Lafayette.

He came from France in 1777, enlisted in the continentals as a volunteer private, served on the staffs of both Washington and Lafayette, and later was attached to the command of Baron De Kalb, in which were a number of **Jews**.

When De Kalb was fatally wounded in the thickest of the fighting at the Battle of Camden, the three officers who were at hand to bear him from the field were Major Nones, Captain De La Motta, and Captain Jacob De Leon, all of the **Jews**.

It is interesting to know that at the time of the Revolution there was a larger **Jewish** element in the southern colonies than would have been found there at most later periods; and these Jews of the Carolinas and Georgia were ardent supporters of the Revolution. One corps of infantry raised in Charleston, South Carolina, was composed preponderantly of **Jews**, and they gave a splendid account of themselves in the fighting in that section.

It is easy to understand why a people with the historic background of the **Jew** should thus overwhelmingly and unhesitatingly have allied themselves with the cause of freedom.

From earliest colonial times, America has been a new land of promise to this long-persecuted race. The **Jewish** community of the United States is not only the second most numerous in the world, but in respect of its old world origins it is probably the most cosmopolitan....

The 14,000 **Jews** who live in this Capital City have passed, under the favoring auspices of American institutions, beyond the need for any other benevolence.

They are planting here a home for community service....Here will be the seat of organized influence for the preservation and dissemination of all that is best and most useful, of all that is leading and enlightening, in the culture and philosophy of this "peculiar people" who have so greatly given to the advancement of humanity.

Our country has done much for the **Jews** who have come here to accept its citizenship and assume their share of its responsibilities in the world....

Every inheritance of the **Jewish** people, every teaching of their secular history and religious experience, draws them powerfully to the side of charity, liberty and progress.....

This capacity for adaptation in detail, without sacrifice of essentials, has been one of the special lessons which the marvelous history of the **Jewish** people has taught....

In advancing years, as those who come and go shall gaze upon this civic and social landmark, may it be a constant reminder of the inspiring service that has been rendered to civilization by men and women of the **Jewish** faith.

May they recall the long array of those who have been eminent in statecraft, in science, in literature, in art, in the professions, in business, in finance, in philanthropy and in the spiritual life of the world. May they pause long enough to contemplate that the patriots who laid the foundation of this Republic drew their faith from the Bible.

May they give due credit to the people among whom the Holy Scriptures came into being.

And as they ponder the assertion that **"Hebraic** mortar cemented the foundations of American democracy," they cannot escape the conclusion that if American democracy is to remain the greatest hope of humanity, it must continue abundantly in the faith of the Bible. [182]

President Harry S. Truman, the day after Franklin D. Roosevelt's funeral, concluded his *First Address before a Joint Session of Congress,* April 12, 1945:

I humbly pray to Almighty God in the words of **King Solomon**: "Give therefore Thy servant an understanding heart to judge Thy people that I may discern between good and bad; for who is able to judge this Thy so great a people?"[183]

President Harry S. Truman wrote in his *Memoirs - Volume Two: Years of Trial and Hope*, published 1956:

When I was in the Senate, I had told my colleagues, Senator Wagner of New York and Senator Taft of Ohio, that I would go along on a resolution putting the Senate on record in favor of the speedy achievement of the **Jewish** homeland. [184]

President Harry S. Truman wrote a memorandum to Winston Churchill, July 24, 1945:

The drastic restrictions imposed on the **Jewish** immigration by the British White Paper of May, 1939, continue to provoke passionate protest from Americans most interested in Palestine and in the Jewish problem.

They fervently urge the lifting of these restrictions which deny to **Jews**, who have been so cruelly uprooted by ruthless Nazi persecutions, entrance into the land which represents for so many of them their only hope of survival. [185]

President Truman stated to the press, 1945:

The American view on Palestine is that we want to let as many of the **Jews** into Palestine as its possible to let into that country. [186]

In his *Memoirs - Volume Two: Years of Trial and Hope,* 1956, Harry S. Truman included a note to his assistant:

I surely wish God Almighty would give the Children of **Israel** an Isaiah, the Christians a St. Paul, and the Sons of Ishmael a peep at the Golden Rule.[187]

In 1946, President Harry S. Truman acknowledged America's Judeo-Christian tradition:

The Protestant church, the Catholic church, and the **Jewish** synagogue bound together in the American unity of brotherhood - must provide the shock forces to accomplish this moral and spiritual awakening. No other agency can do it. Unless it is done, we are headed for the disaster we would deserve.[188]

President Harry S. Truman stated at the dedication of Everglades National Park, On December 6, 1947:

For conservation of the human spirit, we need places such as Everglades National Park where we may be more keenly aware of our Creator's infinitely beautiful, and infinitely bountiful handiwork...

Here we can truly understand what that great **Israelite** Psalmist meant when he sang: "He maketh me to lie down in green pastures, He leadeth me beside still water; He restoreth my soul."[189]

On the frigid night of February 3, 1943, the Allied ship Dorchester plowed through the waters near Greenland. At 1:00am, a Nazi submarine fired a torpedo into its flank, killing many in the explosion and trapping others below deck. It the ensuing chaos, four chaplains: a priest, **a rabbi** and two protestant ministers; distributed life jackets.

When there were none left, the four chaplains ripped off their own jackets and put them on four young men. Standing embraced on the slanting deck, the chaplains bowed their heads in prayer as they sank to their icy deaths. Congress honored them by declaring a "Four Chaplains Day." In February of 1954, President Eisenhower remarked:

> We remember that, only a decade ago, aboard the transport Dorchester, four chaplains of four faiths together willingly sacrificed their lives so that four others might live. In the three centuries that separate the Pilgrims of the Mayflower from the chaplains of the Dorchester, America's freedom, her courage, her strength, and her progress have had their foundation in faith.[191]

In 1947, the United States Corp of Cadets contained in their regulations:

> Attendance at chapel is part of a cadet's training; no cadet will be exempted. Each cadet will receive religious training in one of the three particular faiths: Protestant, Catholic or **Jewish**.[191]

In a display of Judeo-Christian heritage, President Kennedy, at his Inauguration, 1961, had prayers by a **Jewish** rabbi, a Protestant minister, a Catholic cardinal, a Greek Orthodox archbishop, and a poem by Robert Frost.[192]

Martin Luther King, Jr. wrote from his jail cell in Birmingham, Alabama, April 16, 1963:

> I must make two honest confessions to you, my Christian and **Jewish** brothers...I began thinking about the fact that I stand in the middle of two opposing forces in the Negro community.

One is a force of complacency made up of Negroes who, as a result of long years of oppression, are so completely drained of self-respect and a sense of "somebodiness" that they have adjusted to segregation, and of a few middle-class Negroes who, because of a degree of academic and economic security and because in some ways they profit by segregation, have consciously become insensitive to the problem of the masses.

The other force is one of bitterness and hatred, and it comes perilously close to advocating violence. It is expressed in the various black nationalist groups that are springing up across the nation, the largest and best-known being Elijah Muhammad's Muslim movement.

Nourished by the Negro's frustration over the continued existence of racial discrimination, this movement is made up of people who have lost faith in America, who have absolutely repudiated Christianity, and who have concluded that the white man is an incorrigible "devil."

I have tried to stand between these two forces, saying that we need emulate neither the "do-nothingism" of the complacent nor the hatred of the black nationalist...

One day the South will know that when these disinherited children of God sat down at lunch counters they were in reality standing up for what is best in the American dream and for the most sacred values in our **Judeo-Christian** heritage, thereby bringing our nation back to those great wells of democracy which were dug deep by the founding fathers in their formulation of the *Constitution* and the *Declaration of Independence*.[193]

Martin Luther King, Jr. stated at the Civil Rights March on Washington, August 28, 1963:

> When we let freedom ring, when we let it ring from every village and every hamlet, from every state and every city, we will be able to speed up that day when all of God's children, black men and white men, **Jews** and Gentiles, Protestants and Catholics, will be able to join hands and sing in the words of the old Negro spiritual, "Free at last! Free at last! Thank God Almighty, we are free at last!" [194]

President Lyndon B. Johnson stated at the dedication of the new **synagogue** of the Agudas Achim Congregation in Austin, Texas, December 30, 1963:

> Our *Constitution* wisely separates church and state, separates religion and Government. But this does not mean that men of Government should divorce themselves from religion.
>
> On the contrary, a first responsibility of national leadership, as I see it, is spiritual leadership, for I deeply believe that America will prevail not because her pocketbooks are big, but because the principles of her people are strong...
>
> It is my hope, and your prayer, that the tests of the future will find us all working in brotherhood to put down the hate of the present, to prevail over evil, to work with mercy and compassion among the afflicted, to be in all that we do worthy to be called God's children....
>
> If we have leaders like this good man who introduced me, who has spent so many of his hours in the years past trying to build **temples** like this, **temples** where men can worship, **temples** where

justice reigns, **temples** where the free are welcome, **temples** where the dignity of man prevails, then America will truly be worthy of the leadership that we claim, and the rest of the world will follow where we lead. [195]

President Ronald Reagan told the National Conference of Christians and Jews in New York, March 23, 1982:

A strong, credible America is also an indispensable incentive for a peaceful resolution of differences between **Israel** and her neighbors. America has never flinched from its commitment to the State of **Israel** - a commitment which remains unshakable. [196]

President Ronald Reagan addressed the annual National Religious Broadcasters Convention, January 31, 1983:

All of us, as Protestants, Catholics, and **Jews,** have a special responsibility to remember our fellow believers who are being persecuted in other lands. We're all **children of Abraham**. We're children of the same God.[197]

President Ronald Reagan stated in a *Radio Address* to the Nation, April 2, 1983:

This week **Jewish** families and friends have been celebrating Passover, a tradition rich in symbolism and meaning.

Its observance reminds all of us that the struggle for freedom and the battle against oppression waged by the **Jews** since ancient times is one shared by people everywhere. And Christians have been commemorating the last momentous days leading to the crucifixion of Jesus 1,950 years ago.

Tomorrow, as morning spreads around the planet, we'll celebrate the triumph of life over death, the resurrection of Jesus. Both observances tell of sacrifice and pain but also of hope and triumph....

Men and women around the world who love God and freedom - bear a message of world hope and brotherhood like the rites of Passover and Easter that we celebrate this weekend. [198]

President Ronald Reagan stated in a *Hanukkah Message*, December 21, 1984:

This holiday commemorates the Maccabees victory over their oppressors and the valiant spirit of their battle. Two thousand years ago, God blessed their efforts to retain an independent **Jewish** commonwealth and to preserve the **Jewish** Religion.[199]

President George H.W. Bush stated in a *Hanukkah Message*, December 21, 1989:

This menorah, this ancient vessel of light, is an eloquent statement of the **Jewish** people's struggle in history's first recorded battle for religious freedom. It shines with courage and with constancy, with conscience and with strength in the centuries-long struggle for religious tolerance.[200]

On August 17, 1992, at the Republican National Convention, Houston, Texas, Ronald Reagan stated:

Whether we come from poverty or wealth; whether we are Afro-American or Irish-American; Christian or **Jewish,** from big cities or small towns, we are all equal in the eyes of God.[201]

President George W. Bush stated at the first lighting of a menorah in the White House, December 10, 2001:

> For the first time in American history, the Hanukkah menorah will be lit at the White House residence...We can see the heroic spirit of the Maccabees lives on in **Israel** today, and we trust that a better day is coming when this Festival of Freedom will be celebrated in a world free from terror. [202]

Rush H. Limbaugh wrote in his book, *See, I Told You So* (New York, NY: Pocket Books, 1993):

> The Pilgrims were a people completely steeped in the lessons of the Old and New Testaments. They looked to the ancient **Israelites** for their example. And, because of the biblical precedents set forth in Scripture, they never doubted that their experiment would work. [203]

Margaret Hilda Thatcher, the first woman Prime Minister of the United Kingdom, stated on February 5, 1996:

> Schools were places where children learned the great hymns which stayed them the rest of their lives. Hymns, Prayers, Bible readings...even if your parents are not practicing Christians, or **Jews,** or what have you.[204]
>
> We have to remember that the **Jewish** people never, ever lost their faith in the face of all the persecution and as a result have come to have their own promised land and to have Jerusalem as a capital city again. [205]

TOLERANCE
FOR
MONOTHEISTS

"Before any man can be considered as a member of Civil Society, he must be considered as a subject of the **Governor of the Universe**....Much more must every man who becomes a member of any particular Civil Society, do it with a saving of his allegiance to the **Universal Sovereign**."
    -James Madison, *Memorial & Remonstrance,* 1785[206]

The common denominator of tolerance enlarged to include Monotheists - such as Christians, Jews or Muslims, or anyone who had a belief in one God.

The U.S. national currency is inscribed with the *National Motto* "**In God We Trust**," not plural "In gods we trust." The *Pledge of Allegiance* has a monotheistic reference "**One Nation under God**," not a polytheistic "under gods." Adopted by Congress March 3, 1931, the *National Anthem's* fourth verse is:

O! thus be it ever, When free men shall stand,
Between their loved home and the war's desolation;
Blest with vict'ry and peace, may the **Heav'n**-rescued land,
Praise the **Pow'r** that hath made and preserved us a nation!
Then conquer we must, When our cause it is just;
And this be our motto, "In **God** is our trust!"
And the star spangled banner, In triumph shall wave
O'er the land of the free And the home of the brave![207]

The U.S. Supreme Court and U.S. Federal Courts open, not with a polytheistic invocation to "the gods," but instead the monotheistic invocation:

> **God** save the United States and this honorable Court.[208]

President Harry S. Truman addressed the national Conference of Christians and Jews in Washington, D.C., November 11, 1949:

> The only sure bedrock of human brotherhood is the knowledge that **God** is the Father of mankind.[209]

Ben Franklin cited tolerance (forbearance) by believers in God as the reason for America's prosperity in his pamphlet titled *Information to Those Who Would Remove to America,* 1754:

> Serious religion, under its various denominations, is not only tolerated, but respected and practised. Atheism is unknown there....
> The **Divine Being** seems to have manifested his approbation of the mutual forbearance and kindness with which the different sects treat each other; by the remarkable prosperity with which he has been pleased to favor the whole country. [210]

French historian Alexis de Tocqueville, while traveling through New York in 1831, had the opportunity to observe the importance of a belief in God during a court case:

> While I was in America, a witness, who happened to be called at the assizes of the county of Chester (state of New York), declared that he did not believe in the existence of **God** or in the immortality of the soul.

The judge refused to admit his evidence, on the ground that the witness had destroyed beforehand all confidence of the court in what he was about to say. The newspapers related the fact without any further comment. *The New York Spectator* of August 23d, 1831, relates the fact in the following terms:

"The court of common pleas of Chester county (New York), a few days since rejected a witness who declared his disbelief in the existence of **God**. The presiding judge remarked, that he had not before been aware that there was a man living who did not believe in the existence of **God**; that this belief constituted the sanction of all testimony in a court of justice: and that he knew of no case in a Christian country, where a witness had been permitted to testify without such belief." [211]

The progression of tolerance from just "Christian" to "Jewish" to "Monotheist" can be observed in the oaths of office of sequential versions of the *Constitution of the State of Maryland.* In 1776, the oath to hold office required:

A declaration of belief in the Christian religion.[212]

In 1851, the oath of office broadened for Jews:

A declaration of belief in the Christian religion; and if the party shall profess to be a Jew the declaration shall be of his belief in a future state of rewards and punishments. [213]

In 1864, the oath allowed for belief in one God:

A declaration of belief in the Christian religion, or of the **existence of God**, and in a future state of rewards and punishments. [214]

The Oath of Office for U.S. Senators, usually administered by the Vice President, and U.S. Representatives, administered by the Speaker of the House, acknowledges God:

I, _____, do solemnly swear (or affirm) that I will support and defend the *Constitution of the United States* against all enemies, foreign and domestic; that I will bear true faith and allegiance to the same; that I take this obligation freely, without any mental reservation or purpose of evasion; and that I will well and faithfully discharge the duties of the office on which I am about to enter: So help me **God**. [215]

U.S. PRESIDENTS

Presidents have continued the tradition of swearing in with their hand on a Bible, ending their oath "So Help Me God," and acknowledging God in their *Inaugural Addresses*:[216]

1st- GEORGE WASHINGTON, April 30, 1789: "My fervent supplications to that **Almighty Being** who rules over the universe...the **Great Author** of every public and private good"

2nd- JOHN ADAMS, March 4, 1797: "May that **Being** who is supreme over all, the **Patron of Order**, the **Fountain of Justice**, and the **Protector** in all ages of the world of virtuous liberty, continue His blessings upon this nation."

3rd- THOMAS JEFFERSON, March 4, 1801: "Acknowledging and adoring an overruling **Providence**

3rd- THOMAS JEFFERSON, March 4, 1805: "The favor of that **Being** in whose hands we are, who led our forefathers, as Israel of old."

4th- JAMES MADISON, March 4, 1809: "The guardianship and guidance of that **Almighty Being** whose power regulates the destiny of nations."

4th- JAMES MADISON, March 4, 1813: "Justice which invites the **smiles of Heaven**."

5th- JAMES MONROE, March 4, 1817: "**Divine Author** of his being...favor of a gracious **Providence**...my fervent prayers to the **Almighty** that He will be graciously pleased to continue to us that protection which He has already so conspicuously displayed."

5th- JAMES MONROE, March 5, 1821: "My most fervent prayers to the **Supreme Author of All Good**....with a firm reliance on the protection of **Almighty God**."

6th- JOHN QUINCY ADAMS, March 4, 1825: "'Except the **Lord** keep the city, the watchman waketh in vain,' with fervent supplications for His favor, to His overruling providence."

7th- ANDREW JACKSON, March 4, 1829: "A firm reliance on the goodness of that **Power** whose providence mercifully protected our national infancy...my ardent supplications that He will continue to make our beloved country the object of His divine care and gracious benediction."

7th- ANDREW JACKSON, March 4, 1833: "My fervent prayer to that **Almighty Being** before whom I now stand, and who has kept us in His hands from the infancy of our Republic to the present day...that He will so overrule all my intentions and actions."

8th- MARTIN VAN BUREN, March 4, 1837: "To hope for the sustaining of an ever-watchful and beneficent **Providence**...I only look to the gracious protection of that **Divine Being** whose strengthening support I humbly solicit...May it be among the dispensations of His Providence"

9th- WILLIAM HENRY HARRISON, March 4, 1841: "Confidence upon the aid of that **Almighty Power** which has hitherto protected me....the **Beneficent Creator** has made no distinction amongst men.....like the false christs whose coming was foretold by the **Savior**....good **Being** who has blessed us"

10th- JOHN TYLER, April 9, 1841: "My earnest prayer shall be constantly addressed to the all-wise and **all-powerful Being** who made me...Confiding in the protecting care of an everwatchful and overruling **Providence**."

11th- JAMES K. POLK, March 4, 1845: "I fervently invoke the aid of that **Almighty Ruler of the Universe** in whose hands are the destinies of nations and of men to guard this Heaven-favored land....again humbly supplicating that **Divine Being**,"

12th - ZACHARY TAYLOR, March 5, 1849: "The goodness of **Divine Providence** has conducted our common country."

13th- MILLARD FILLMORE, July 10, 1850: "I rely upon **Him** who holds in His hands the destinies of nations."

14th- FRANKLIN PIERCE, March 4, 1853: "The guidance of a manifest and beneficent **Providence**....there is no national security but in the nation's humble, acknowledged dependence upon **God** and His overruling providence."

15th- JAMES BUCHANAN, March 4, 1857: "Invoke the **God** of our fathers for wisdom and firmness to execute its high and responsible duties...humbly invoking the blessing of **Divine Providence** on this great people."

16th- ABRAHAM LINCOLN, March 4, 1861: "Intelligence, patriotism, Christianity, and a firm reliance on **Him** who has never yet forsaken this favored land, are still competent to adjust in the best way all our present difficulty."

16th- ABRAHAM LINCOLN, March 4, 1865: "Both read the same Bible and pray to the same **God**....The **Almighty** has His own purposes....Yet, if **God** will that it continue...'the Judgements of the **Lord** are true and righteous altogether.'"

17th- ANDREW JOHNSON, April 15, 1865: "Duties have been mine; consequences are **God's**."

18th- ULYSSES S. GRANT, March 4, 1869: "I ask the prayers of the nation to **Almighty God**...

18th- ULYSSES S. GRANT, March 4, 1873: "Under **Providence**, I have been called a second time...I do believe that our **Great Maker** is preparing the world, in His own good time."

19th- RUTHERFORD B. HAYES, March 5, 1877: "Looking for the guidance of that **Divine Hand** by which the destinies of nations and individuals are shaped."

20th- JAMES A. GARFIELD, March 4, 1881: "Bless their fathers and their fathers' **God** that the Union was preserved, that slavery was overthrown, and that both races were made equal before the law...'followed the light as **God** gave them to see the light.'...I reverently invoke the support and blessings of **Almighty God**."

21st- CHESTER A. ARTHUR, September 22, 1881: "I assume the trust imposed by the *Constitution*, relying for aid on **Divine Guidance** and the virtue, patriotism, and intelligence of the American people."

22nd- GROVER CLEVELAND, March 4, 1885: "Let us not trust to human effort alone, but humbly acknowledge the power and goodness of **Almighty God** who presides over the destiny of nations, and who has at all times been revealed in our country's history, let us invoke His aid and His blessings."

23rd- BENJAMIN HARRISON, March 4, 1889: "Reverently invoke and confidently extend the favor and help of **Almighty God** - that He will give to me wisdom, strength, and fidelity, and to our people a spirit of fraternity and a love of righteousness and peace....**God** has placed upon our head a diadem."

24th- GROVER CLEVELAND, March 4, 1893: "I now give before **God** and these witnesses...the laws of **God**...Above all, I know there is a **Supreme Being** who rules the affairs of men and whose goodness and mercy have always followed the American people, and I know He will not turn from us now if we humbly and reverently seek His powerful aid."

25th- WILLIAM MCKINLEY, March 4, 1897: "Guidance of **Almighty God**. Our faith teaches that there is no safer reliance than upon the **God** of our fathers...as we obey His commandments and walk humbly in His footsteps....under **Providence**...the obligation I have reverently taken before the **Lord Most High**."

25th- WILLIAM MCKINLEY, March 4, 1901: "Reverently invoking for my guidance the direction and favor of **Almighty God**...and in the fear of **God** will 'take occasion by the hand and make the bounds of freedom wider yet.'"

26th- THEODORE ROOSEVELT, September 14, 1901: "Bow down in submission to the will of **Almighty God**."

26th- THEODORE ROOSEVELT, March 4, 1905: "Gratitude to the **Giver of Good** who has blessed us."

27th- WILLIAM HOWARD TAFT, March 4, 1909: "I invoke the considerate sympathy and support of my fellow-citizens and the aid of the **Almighty God**."

28th- WOODROW WILSON, March 4, 1913: "Sweep across our heartstrings like some air out of **God**'s own presence, where justice and mercy are reconciled and the judge and the brother are one....**God** helping me, I will not fail them."

28th- WOODROW WILSON, March 5, 1917: "In **God**'s Providence, let us hope...I pray **God** I may be given the wisdom and the prudence to do my duty in the true spirit of this great people"

29th- WARREN G. HARDING, March 4, 1921: "Belief in the **Divine Inspiration** of the founding fathers.... **God**'s intent in the making of this new world Republic.... brotherhood of mankind which must be **God**'s highest conception.... **God** given destiny... answerable to **God**... guidance of **God** in His Heaven... 'What doth the **Lord** require of thee but to do justly, and to love mercy, and to walk humbly with thy **God**.' This I plight to **God** and country."

30th- CALVIN COOLIDGE, August 4, 1923: "Wisdom of **Divine Providence**, Warren Gamaliel Harding, twenty-ninth President of the United States, has been taken from us...bow down in submission to the will of **Almighty God**."

30th- CALVIN COOLIDGE, March 4, 1925: "America seeks no earthly empires built on blood and force...The legions which she sends forth are armed, not with the sword, but with the Cross. The higher state to which she seeks the allegiance of all mankind is not of human, but **Divine** origin. She cherishes no purpose save to merit the favor of **Almighty God**."

31st- HERBERT HOOVER, March 4, 1929: "Consecration under **God** to the highest office...the guidance of **Almighty Providence**....I ask the help of **Almighty God**."

32nd- FRANKLIN D. ROOSEVELT, March 4, 1933: "We face our common difficulties. They concern, thank **God**, only material things....we humbly ask the blessing of **God**. May He protect each and every one of us! May He guide me."

32nd- FRANKLIN D. ROOSEVELT, January 20, 1937: "I shall do my utmost to speak their purpose and to do their will, seeking **Divine Guidance** to help each and every one to give light to them that sit in darkness."

32nd- FRANKLIN D. ROOSEVELT, January 20, 1941: "As Americans, we go forward in the service of our country by the will of **God**."

32nd- FRANKLIN D. ROOSEVELT, January 20, 1945: "In the presence of **God**...The **Almighty God** has blessed our land...He has given our people stout hearts...He has given to our country a faith...we pray to Him...to the achievement of His will...In the presence of **God**."

33rd- HARRY S TRUMAN, April 12, 1945: "I humbly pray to **Almighty God** in the words of King Solomon: 'Give therefore Thy servant an understanding heart to judge Thy people...I ask only to be a good and faithful servant of my **Lord**."

33rd- HARRY S TRUMAN, January 20, 1949: "We believe that all men are created equal because they are created in the image of **God**...the right to believe in and worship **God**....With **God**'s help."

34th- DWIGHT D. EISENHOWER, January 20, 1953: "**Almighty God**...beseeching that Thou will make full and complete our dedication...that all may work for the good of our beloved country and Thy glory...in the presence of **God**...we beseech **God**'s guidance....gifts of the **Creator**...all men equal in His sight....watchfulness of a **Divine Providence**...prayer to **Almighty God**."

34th- DWIGHT D. EISENHOWER, January 21, 1957: "Before all else, we seek upon our common labor as a nation, the blessings of **Almighty God**."

35th- JOHN F. KENNEDY, January 20, 1961: "I have sworn before you and **Almighty God**...rights of man come not from the generosity of the state but from the hand of **God**...asking His blessing and His help...on earth **God**'s work must truly be our own."

36th- LYNDON B. JOHNSON, November 22, 1963: "For me, it is a deep personal tragedy. I know that the world shares the sorrow that Mrs. Kennedy and her family bear. I will do my best. That is all I can do. I ask for your help - and **God**'s."

36th- LYNDON B. JOHNSON, January 20, 1965: "We have no promise from **God** that our greatness will endure. We have been allowed by Him to seek greatness...the judgement of **God** is harshest on those who are most favored."

37th- RICHARD M. NIXON, January 20, 1969: "They concern, thank **God**, only material things.'...all are born equal in dignity before **God**....I have taken an oath in the presence of **God**...the world as **God** sees it...invoke **God**'s blessing...the will of **God**."

37th- RICHARD M. NIXON, January 20, 1973: "**God**-given right...We shall answer to **God**...in the years ahead I may have **God**'s help...sustained by our faith in **God** who created us, and striving always to serve His purpose."

38th- GERALD R. FORD, August 9, 1974: "There is a **Higher Power**, by whatever name we honor Him, who ordains not only righteousness but love, not only justice but mercy...May **God** bless and comfort...do what is right as **God** gives me to see the right...**God** helping me."

39th- JIMMY CARTER, January 20, 1977: "Before me is the Bible used in the inauguration of our first President...I have just taken the oath of office on the Bible my mother gave me... 'He hath showed thee, O man, what is good; and what does the **Lord** require of thee, but to do justly, and to love mercy, and to walk humbly with thy **God**."

40th- RONALD REAGAN, January 20, 1981: "So help me **God**....We are a nation under **God**, and I believe **God** intended for us to be free....together, with **God**'s help, we can and will resolve the problems...why shouldn't we believe that? We are Americans. **God** bless you."

40th- RONALD REAGAN, January 21, 1985: "**God** bless you and welcome back....When the first President, George Washington, placed his hand upon the Bible....One people under **God** determined that our future shall be worthy of our past."

41st- GEORGE H.W. BUSH, January 20, 1989: "The Bible on which I place my hand is the Bible on which he placed his....**Heavenly Father**, we bow our heads and thank You for Your love...Make us strong to do Your work, willing to heed...Your will...Help us to remember it, **Lord**. Amen....**God**'s love is truly boundless...**God** bless you and **God** bless the United States."

42nd- BILL CLINTON, January 20, 1993: "When our Founders boldly declared America's Independence...and our purposes to the **Almighty**, they knew that America, to endure, would have to change...Scripture says, 'And let us not be weary in well-doing, for in due season, we shall reap, if we faint not'...With **God**'s help...**God** bless you."

42nd- BILL CLINTON, January 20, 1997: "Our rich texture of racial, religious and political diversity will be a **Godsend** in the 21st Century....May **God** strengthen our hands for the good work ahead - and always, always bless our America."

43rd- GEORGE W. BUSH, January 20, 2001: "A **Power** larger than ourselves, **Who** creates us equal in His image...an Angel rides in the Whirlwind and directs this Storm?...this story's **Author**, Who fills time and eternity with His purpose. His purpose is achieved in our duty...An Angel still rides in the whirlwind and directs this storm. **God** bless you, and **God** bless America."

43rd- GEORGE W. BUSH, January 20, 2005: "The day of our founding, we have proclaimed that every man and woman on this Earth has rights and dignity and matchless value, because they bear the image of the **Maker** of heaven and earth...We still believe as Abraham Lincoln did: "Those who deny freedom to others deserve it not for themselves, and, under the rule of a just **God**, cannot long retain it."...**God** moves and chooses as **He** wills...but history also has a visible direction, set by liberty and the **Author of Liberty**...May **God** bless you, and may **He** watch over the United States.

STATE CONSTITUTIONS
All 50 *States Constitutions* have acknowledged God:[217]

ALABAMA 1901: "We, the people of the State of Alabama...invoking the favor and guidance of **Almighty God**, do ordain and establish the following..."

ALASKA 1956: "We, the people of Alaska, grateful to **God** and to those who founded our nation...

ARIZONA 1911: "We, the people of the State of Arizona, grateful to **Almighty God** for our liberties..."

ARKANSAS 1874: "We, the people of the State of Arkansas, grateful to **Almighty God** for the privilege of choosing our own form of government..."

CALIFORNIA 1879: "We, the people of the State of California, grateful to **Almighty God** for our freedom..."

COLORADO 1876: "We, the people of Colorado, with profound reverence for the **Supreme Ruler of Universe**..."

CONNECTICUT 1818: "The people of Connecticut, acknowledging with gratitude the good **Providence of God** in permitting them to enjoy..."

DELAWARE 1897: "Through **Divine Goodness** all men have, by nature, the rights of worshipping and serving their **Creator** according to the dictates of their consciences..."

FLORIDA 1885: "We, the people of the State of Florida, grateful to **Almighty God** for our constitutional liberty..."

GEORGIA 1777: "We, the people of Georgia, relying upon protection and guidance of **Almighty God**..."

HAWAII 1959: "We, the people of Hawaii, grateful for **Divine Guidance**..."

IDAHO 1889: "We, the people of the State of Idaho, grateful to **Almighty God** for our freedom..."

ILLINOIS 1870: "We, the people of the State of Illinois, grateful to **Almighty God** for the civil, political and religious liberty which He hath so long permitted us to enjoy and looking to Him for a blessing...."

INDIANA 1851: "We, the people of the State of Indiana, grateful to **Almighty God** for the free exercise of the right to choose our form of government..."

IOWA 1857: "We, the people of the State of Iowa, grateful to the **Supreme Being** for the blessings hitherto enjoyed, and feeling our dependence on Him for a continuation of these blessings..."

KANSAS 1859: "We, the people of Kansas, grateful to **Almighty God** for our civil and religious privileges..."

KENTUCKY 1891: "We, the people of the Commonwealth of Kentucky, grateful to **Almighty God** for the civil, political and religious liberties..."

LOUISIANA 1921: "We, the people of the State of Louisiana, grateful to **Almighty God** for the civil, political and religious liberties we enjoy..."

MAINE 1820: "We, the people of Maine, acknowledging with grateful hearts the goodness of the **Sovereign Ruler of the Universe** in affording us an opportunity...and imploring His aid and direction..."

MARYLAND 1776: "We, the people of the State of Maryland, grateful to **Almighty God** for our civil and religious liberty..."

MASSACHUSETTS 1780: "We...the people of Massachusetts, acknowledging with grateful hearts, the goodness of the **Great Legislator of the Universe**...in the course of His Providence, an opportunity...and devoutly imploring His direction..."

MICHIGAN 1908: "We, the people of the State of Michigan, grateful to **Almighty God** for the blessings of freedom..."

MINNESOTA 1857: "We, the people of the State of Minnesota, grateful to **God** for our civil and religious liberty..."

MISSISSIPPI 1890: "We, the people of Mississippi in convention assembled, grateful to **Almighty God**, and invoking His blessing on our work..."

MISSOURI 1945: "We, the people of Missouri, with profound reverence for the **Supreme Ruler of the Universe**, and grateful for His goodness..."

MONTANA 1889: "We, the people of Montana, grateful to **Almighty God** for the blessings of liberty..."

NEBRASKA 1875: "We, the people, grateful to **Almighty God** for our freedom..."

NEVADA 1864: "We, the people of the State of Nevada, grateful to **Almighty God** for our freedom..."

NEW HAMPSHIRE 1792: "Every individual has a natural and unalienable right to worship **God** according to the dictates of his own conscience..."

NEW JERSEY 1844: "We, the people of the State of New Jersey, grateful to **Almighty God** for civil and religious liberty which He hath so long permitted us to enjoy, and looking to Him for a blessing..."

NEW MEXICO 1911: "We, the people of New Mexico, grateful to **Almighty God** for the blessings of liberty..."

NEW YORK 1846: "We, the people of the State of New York, grateful to **Almighty God** for our freedom, in order to secure its blessings..."

NORTH CAROLINA 1868: "We, the people of the State of North Carolina, grateful to **Almighty God**, the **Sovereign Ruler of Nations**, for...our civil, political, and religious liberties, and acknowledging our dependence upon Him for the continuance of those..."

NORTH DAKOTA 1889: "We, the people of North Dakota, grateful to **Almighty God** for the blessings of civil and religious liberty..."

OHIO 1852: "We, the people of the State of Ohio, grateful to **Almighty God** for our freedom.."

OKLAHOMA 1907: "Invoking the guidance of **Almighty God,** in order to secure and perpetuate the blessing of liberty...we, the people of Oklahoma, do ordain and establish this Constitution..."

OREGON 1857: "All men shall be secure in the Natural right, to worship **Almighty God** according to the dictates of their consciences..."

PENNSYLVANIA 1776: "We, the people of Pennsylvania, grateful to **Almighty God** for the blessings of civil and religious liberty, and humbly invoking His guidance..."

RHODE ISLAND 1842: "We, the people of the State of Rhode Island, grateful to **Almighty God** for the civil and religious liberty which He hath so long permitted us to enjoy, and looking to Him for a blessing..."

SOUTH CAROLINA 1778: "We, the people of the State of South Carolina, grateful to **God** for our liberties..."

SOUTH DAKOTA 1889: "We, the people of South Dakota, grateful to **Almighty God** for our civil and religious liberties..."

TENNESSEE 1796: "All men have a natural and indefeasible right to worship **Almighty God** according to the dictates of their conscience..."

TEXAS 1845: "We, the people of the Republic of Texas, acknowledging, with gratitude, the grace and beneficence of **God**..."

UTAH 1896: "Grateful to **Almighty God** for life and liberty, we, the people of Utah, in order to secure and perpetuate the principles of free government..."

VERMONT 1777: "Whereas all government ought to...enable the individuals who compose it to enjoy their natural rights, and other blessings which the **Author of Existence** has bestowed on man..."

VIRGINIA 1776: "Religion, or the Duty which we owe our **Creator**...can be only directed only by Reason...and that it is the mutual duty of all to practice Christian Forbearance, Love and Charity towards each other..."

WASHINGTON 1889: "We, the people of the State of Washington, grateful to the **Supreme Ruler of the Universe** for our liberties..."

WEST VIRGINIA 1872: "Since through **Divine Providence** we enjoy the blessings of civil, political and religious liberty, we, the people of West Virginia...reaffirm our faith in and constant reliance upon **God**..."

WISCONSIN 1848: "We, the people of Wisconsin, grateful to **Almighty God** for our freedom, domestic tranquillity and to promote the general welfare..."

WYOMING 1890: "We, the people of the State of Wyoming, grateful to **God** for our civil, political, and religious liberties..."

FIRST EXPRESSION OF AMERICANISM

In a National Day of Prayer Proclamation, December 5, 1974, President Gerald R. Ford, quoted President Dwight David Eisenhower's 1955 statement:

> Without God there could be no American form of government, nor an American way of life. Recognition of the Supreme Being is the first - the most basic - expression of Americanism.[218]

The Episcopal Churchnews Magazine asked President Dwight D. Eisenhower to write a summary of his ideas on religion. He responded with comments on America's founding principles and the invasion of Normandy in June of 1944:

The founding fathers had to refer to the **Creator** in order to make their revolutionary experiment make sense; it was because "all men are endowed by their Creator with certain inalienable rights" that men could dare to be free.

They wrote their religious faith into our founding documents, stamped their trust in God on the face of our coins and currency, put it boldly at the base of our institutions, and when they drew up their bold Bill of Rights, where did they put freedom to worship? First, in the cornerstone position!

That was no accident. Our forefathers proved that only a people strong in Godliness is a people strong enough to overcome tyranny and make themselves and others free....What is our battle against communism if it is not a fight between anti-God and a belief in the Almighty?[219]

President Dwight D. Eisenhower stated to the National Co-Chairmen of the Commission on Religious Organizations, National Conference of Christians and Jews, July 9, 1953:

The churches of America are citadels of our faith in individual freedom and human dignity. This faith is the living source of our spiritual strength. And this strength is our matchless armor in our world-wide struggle against the forces of **Godless** tyranny and oppression. [220]

President Ronald Reagan addressed the annual National Religious Broadcasters Convention, January 31, 1983:

Let us come together, Christians and Jews, let us pray together, march, lobby, and mobilize every force we have, so that we can end the tragic taking of unborn children's lives....

"Thou shalt love the Lord thy God with all thy heart, and with all thy soul, and with all thy might" and "Thou shalt love they neighbor as thyself."

When Americans reach out for values of faith, family, and caring for the needy, they're saying, "We want the Word of God. We want to face the future with the Bible." ...Within the covers of that single Book are all the answers to all the problems that face us today, if we'd only look there.

"The grass withereth, the flower fadeth, but the word of our God shall stand forever." It's my firm belief that the enduring values, as I say, presented in its pages have a great meaning for each of us and for our nation.

The Bible can touch our hearts, order our minds, refresh our souls. Now, I realize it's fashionable in some circles to believe that no one in government should...encourage others to read the Bible....

We're told that will violate the constitutional separation of church and state established by the founding fathers in the *First Amendment.*

Well, it might interest those critics to know that none other than the father of our country, George Washington, kissed the Bible at his inauguration.

And he also said words to the effect that there could be no real morality in a society without religion. John Adams called it "the best book in the world," and Ben Franklin said,

"...the longer I live, the more convincing proofs I see of this truth, that God governs in the affairs of men...without His concurring aid, we shall succeed in this political building no better than the builders of Babel; we shall be divided by our little, partial, local interests, our projects will be confounded, and we ourselves shall become a reproach, a bye-word down to future ages."...

All of us, as Protestants, Catholics, and Jews, have a special responsibility to remember our fellow believers who are being persecuted in other lands. We're all children of Abraham. **We're children of the same God....**

This year, for the first time in history, the Voice of America broadcast a religious service worldwide - Christmas Eve at the National Presbyterian Church in Washington, D.C.

Now, these broadcasts are not popular with government of totalitarian power. But make no mistake, we have a duty to broadcast. Aleksandr Herzen, the Russian writer, warned, "To shrink from saying a word in defense of the oppressed is as bad as any crime."

Well, I pledge to you that America will stand up, speak out, and defend the values we share. To those who would crush religious freedom, our message is plain:

You may jail your believers. **You may close their churches, confiscate their Bibles, and harass their rabbis and priests, but you will never destroy the love of God and freedom that burns in their hearts.**

They will triumph over you. Malcolm Muggeridge, the brilliant English commentator, has written, "The most important happening in the world today is the resurgence of Christianity in the Soviet Union, demonstrating that the whole effort sustained over sixty years to brainwash the Russian people into accepting materialism has been a fiasco."

Think of it: the most awesome military machine in history, but it is not match for that one single man, hero, strong yet tender, Prince of Peace. His name alone, Jesus, can lift our hearts, soothe our sorrows, heal our wounds, and drive away our fears....

With His message and with your conviction and commitment, we can still move mountains. Before I say goodbye, I wanted to leave with you these words from an old Netherlands folk song, because they made me think of our meeting here today:

"We gather together to ask the Lord's blessing; We all do extol Thee, Thou Leader triumphant, And pray that Thou still our Defender wilt be. Let Thy congregation escape tribulation: Thy name be ever praised! O Lord, make us free!"

To which I would only add a line from another song: **"America, America, God shed His grace on thee."** [221]

SPIRIT OF TOLERANCE...SPIRIT OF GOD

President Harry S Truman, in addressing a Conference of the Federal Council of Churches in Columbus, Ohio, March 6, 1946, pointed out that belief in God was the foundation for tolerance - "a spirit of tolerance...in the spirit of God":

We have just come through a decade in which the **forces of evil** in various parts of the world have been lined up in a bitter **fight to banish from the face of the earth religion and democracy**...

In that long struggle between these two doctrines, the cause of decency and righteousness has been victorious. The right of every human being to live in dignity and freedom, the right to worship **God** in his own way, the right to fix his own relationship to his fellow men and to his **Creator** - these again have been saved for mankind....

Now that we have preserved our freedom of conscience and religion, our right to live by a decent moral and spiritual code of our own choosing, let us make full use of that freedom...

Let us determine to carry on in a **spirit of tolerance**, and understanding for all men and for all nations **in the spirit of God** and religious unity.[222]

New Jersey State Court, in *Doremus v. Board of Education of Borough of Hawthorne*, 1950, stated:

We consider that the Old Testament, because of its antiquity, its contents, and its wide acceptance, **is not a sectarian book** when read without comment. Cf. *Vidal v. Girard's Executors.* [223]

ENLIGHTENED BY A BENIGN RELIGION

President Thomas Jefferson stated in his *First Inaugural Address*, March 4, 1801, that "intolerance" was banished, yet he went on to applaud "a benign religion...proffessed...and practiced" and "adoring an overruling Providence":

And let us reflect that **having banished from our land that religious intolerance** under which mankind so long bled and suffered, we have yet gained little if we countenance [support] a political intolerance as despotic, as wicked, and capable of as bitter and bloody persecutions....

Enlightened by a benign religion, professed, indeed, and practiced in various forms, yet all of them inculcating [teaching] honesty, truth, temperance, gratitude, and the love of man; **acknowledging and adoring an overruling Providence**, which by all its dispensations proves that it delights in the happiness of man here and his greater happiness hereafter...

And may that **Infinite Power** which rules the destinies of the universe, lead our councils to what is best, and give them a favorable issue for your peace and prosperity. [224]

New Jersey State Court, in *Doremus v. Board of Education of Borough of Hawthorne*, 1950, stated:

> The adherents of those religions (Jewish, Catholic, Protestant) constitute the great bulk of our population. **There are other religious groups**...but in this country they are numerically small and, in point of impact upon our national life, negligible....
>
> And it is not to say that because **a religious group is small**, it thereby loses its constitutional rights or that it is not entitled to the protection of those rights.
>
> The application is that some of our national incidents are developments from the almost **universal belief in God** which so strongly shaped and nurtured our people during the colonial period and the formative years of our constitutional government, with the result that we accept as a commendable part of our public life certain conditions and practices which in a country of different origins would be rejected....
>
> Again, **take the instance of an atheist:** - he has all the protection of the *Constitution*...but he lives in a country where theism is in the warp and woof of the social and governmental fabric and **he has no authority to eradicate from governmental activities every vestige of the existence of God.**
>
> With reference to saying the Lord's Prayer, this court found "nothing in the Lord's Prayer that is controversial, ritualistic or dogmatic. It is a prayer to "God, our Father." It does not contain Christ's name and makes no reference to Him. It is, in our opinion, in the same position as is the Bible reading. [225]

While it is necessary that there be a separation between church and state, **it is not necessary that the state should be stripped of religious sentiment....**

The American people are and always have been to our origins and the direction which it has given to our progress are beyond calculation. It may be of the theistic,...that belief in God shall abide....

The day the children should pause to hear a few words from the wisdom of the ages [Scriptures] and to bow the head in humility before the Supreme Power. No rights, no ceremony, no doctrinal teachings; just a brief moment with eternity.[226]

But it is clear, we think that the sense of **the** *First Amendment* **does not serve to prohibit government from recognizing the existence and sovereignty of God** and that the motives which inspired the *Amendment* and the interpretation given by the several departments of the Federal Government concurrently with and subsequent to the submission and adoption of the *Amendment* are inconsistent with any other conclusion....

The fact is that **the** *First Amendment* **does not say**, and so far as we are able to determine was not intended to say, **that God shall not be acknowledged by our government as God.** [227]

In his effort to broaden tolerance to monotheistic Muslims, George W. Bush was the first President to mention the Koran in an Inaugural Address, January 20, 2005, celebrate Muslim Ramadan in the White House, November 19, 2001, speak at an Islamic Center, December 5, 2002, and have an Islamic postage stamp, *"Eid mubarak,"* issued during his Administration, August 1, 2001.

TOLERANCE
FOR POLYTHEISTS
& NEW RELIGIONS

Beginning in the 1840's and continuing into the 1900's, some States forbade citizenship to Chinese, Japanese, and those of the "Mongolian" race, in part because they were polytheists. They were not allowed to give testimony in court, not allowed access to schools, not allowed to marry other races, required to carry a certificate of residence, and even had a special tax.

This was eventually stopped and tolerance was extended to people of any religion, whether believing in a deity or in deities. In the early 1900's tolerance extended to new religions, such as Mormons and Jehovah's Witnesses.

Dr. Benjamin Rush, a signer of the *Declaration of Independence*, wrote in his *Thoughts Upon the Mode of Education Proper in a Republic*, 1786:

> I proceed to inquire what mode of education we shall adopt so as to secure to the state all of the advantages that are to be derived from the proper instruction of the youth; and here I beg leave to remark that the only foundation for a useful education in a republic is to be laid on the foundation of religion.
>
> Without this there can be no virtue, and without virtue there can be no liberty, and liberty is the object and life of all republican governments.

Such is my veneration for every religion that reveals the attributes of the Deity, or a future state of rewards and punishments, that I had rather see the opinions of Confucius or Mohamed inculcated [impressed] upon our youth than to see them grow up wholly devoid of a system of religious principles.

But the religion I mean to recommend in this place is that of the New Testament.

It is not my purpose to hint at the arguments which establish the truth of the Christian revelation. My only business is to declare that all its doctrines and precepts are calculated to promote the happiness of society and the safety and well-being of civil government.

A Christian cannot fail of being a republican...for every precept of the Gospel inculcates [teaches] those degrees of humility, self-denial, and brotherly kindness which are directly opposed to the pride of monarchy....

A Christian cannot fail of being useful to the republic, for his religion teaches him that no man "liveth to himself." And lastly a Christian cannot fail of being wholly inoffensive, for his religion teaches him in all things to do to others what he would wish, in like circumstances, they should do to him. [228]

In his *Annual Message*, December 4, 1854, President Franklin Pierce spoke of a "universal religious toleration":

We have to...harmonize a sincere and ardent devotion to the institutions of religious faith with **the most universal religious toleration**....

whilst exalting the condition of the Republic, to assure to it the legitimate influence and the benign authority of a great example amongst all the powers of Christendom. [229]

In his *Inaugural Address*, March 4, 1869, President Ulysses Grant requested "forbearance one toward another":

> In conclusion I ask **patient forbearance one toward another** throughout the land... and I ask the prayers of the nation to Almighty God in behalf of this consummation. [230]

President Theodore Roosevelt's term 'Gentile" in his *Annual Message,* December 5, 1905, alluded to other religions:

> It is unwise to discriminate for or against any man who desires to come here and become a citizen, if the man is from the moral and social standpoint of such a character as to add value to the community he should be heartily welcomed.
>
> We cannot afford to pay heed to whether he is of one creed or another, of one nation, or another. We cannot afford to consider whether he is Catholic or Protestant, Jew or **Gentile**. [231]

President Theodore Roosevelt stated in his *Sixth Annual Message* to Congress, December 3, 1906:

> Not only must we treat all nations fairly, but we must treat with justice and good will all immigrants who come here under the law. Whether they are Catholic or Protestant, Jew or **Gentile**." [232]

Justice Robert Houghwout Jackson cited "other faiths" in U.S. Supreme Court *McCollum v. Board of Education,* 1948:

> I think it remains to be demonstrated whether it is possible, even desirable,...to isolate and cast out

of **secular education** all that some people may reasonably regard as religious instruction....

It would not seem practical to teach...appreciation of the arts if we are to forbid exposure of youth to any religious influences. Music without sacred music, architecture minus the cathedral, or painting without the Scriptural themes would be eccentric and incomplete, even from a secular point of view....

Even such a 'science' as biology raises the issue between evolution and creation as an explanation of our presence on this planet. Certainly a course on English literature that omitted the Bible and other powerful uses of our mother tongue for religious ends would be pretty barren.

And I suppose it is a proper, if not indispensable, part of the preparation for a worldly life to know the roles that religion and religions have played in the tragic story of mankind.

The fact is that, for good or ill, **nearly everything in our culture worth transmitting, everything which gives meaning to life, is saturated with the influences derived from paganism, Judaism, Christianity - both Catholic and Protestant - and other faiths accepted by a large part of the world's people....**

One can hardly respect a system of education that would leave a student wholly ignorant of the currents of religious thought that moved the world society for a part in which he is being prepared. [233]

TOLERANCE FOR ATHEISTS & ANTI-RELIGIOUS

The common denominator of tolerance evolved into any form of a "belief system."

The definition of the word "religion" has changed from Webster's 1828 Dictionary, "belief in the being and perfections of God," to today's definition of "any specific system of belief."

This new definition includes worldviews that mean little more that "a state of mind or way of life," and has been advanced contrary to national tradition.

Based on the founders' Christian concept of "doing unto others as you would have them do undo you," the circle of tolerance expanded in an attempt to find common ground with the waves of immigrants that arrived and the new beliefs that were invented. The common denominator went from:

Everyone who was Puritan, to
Everyone who was Protestant, to
Everyone who was Christian, to
Everyone believing in a Judeo-Christian God, to
Everyone believing in a Supreme Being, to
Everyone believing in Theism – God or gods, to
Everyone believing or not believing.

The problem is that in order to find common ground with atheists, belief in a "Supreme Being" must be excluded. Those not believing do not want to allow tolerance to those believing. Inclusion of atheism implies exclusion of theism.

This is similar to, as seen on Nature television programs, the introduction of a foreign plant or animal aggressively over-running the habitat of a more docile domestic plant or animal. This rival dynamics of this broadening of tolerance in seen in the following historical citations;

New Jersey State Court, in *Doremus v. Board of Education of Borough of Hawthorne*, 1950, stated:

> Again, take the instance of **an atheist:** - he has all the protection of the *Constitution*...but he lives in a country where theism is in the warp and woof of the social and governmental fabric and h**e has no authority to eradicate from governmental activities every vestige of the existence of God.**[234]

The Massachusetts Supreme Court heard the case of *Commonwealth v. Abner Kneeland*, 1838, in which a **Universalist** claimed the right of "freedom of the press" as a defense for publishing libelous and defamatory remarks about God.

> "If any person shall willfully blaspheme the holy name of God, by denying, cursing, or contumeliously [insultingly] reproaching God, his creation, government, or final judging of the world..."
>
> In general, blasphemy [libel against God] may be described, as consisting in speaking evil of the Deity...to alienate the minds of others from the love and reverence of God. It is purposely using words concerning God...to impair and destroy the reverence, respect, and confidence due him....

It is a wilful and malicious attempt to lessen men's reverence of God by denying his existence, of his attributes as an intelligent creator, governor and judge of men, and to prevent their having confidence in him....

But another ground for arresting the judgement, and one apparently most relied on and urged by the defendant, is, that this statute itself is repugnant to the *Constitution*...and therefore wholly void....

[This law] was passed very soon after the adoption of the *Constitution*, and no doubt, many members of the convention which framed the *Constitution*, were members of the legislature which passed this law....

In New Hampshire, the *Constitution* of which State has a similar declaration of [religious] rights, the open denial of the being and existence of God or of the Supreme Being is prohibited by statute, and declared to be blasphemy.

In Vermont, with a similar declaration of rights, a statute was passed in 1797, by which it was enacted, that if any person shall publicly deny the being and existence of God or the Supreme Being, or shall contumeliously [insultingly] reproach his providence and government, he shall be deemed a disturber of the peace and tranquility of the State, and an offender against the good morals and manners of society, and shall be punishable by fine....

The State of Maine also, having adopted the same constitutional provision with that of Massachusetts, in her declaration of rights, in respect to religious freedom, immediately after the adoption of the *Constitution* reenacted, the Massachusetts statue against blasphemy....

In New York the universal toleration of all religious professions and sentiments, is secured in the most ample manner. It is declared in the *Constitution*...that the free exercise and enjoyment of religious worship, without discrimination or preference, shall for ever be allowed in this State to all mankind....

Notwithstanding this constitutional declaration carrying the doctrine of unlimited toleration as far as the peace and safety of any community will allow, the courts have decided that blasphemy was a crime at common law and was not abrogated by the *Constitution* [*People v. Ruggles*]. [235]

The *First Amendment* embraces all who believe in the existence of God, as well...as Christians of every denomination....

This provision does not extend to atheists, because they do not believe in God or religion; and therefore...their sentiments and professions, whatever they may be, cannot be called religious sentiments and professions. [236]

A New York State Court referenced "nonbelievers in God" in *Lewis v. Board of Education of City of New York,* 1935:

In this land where all races and creeds are equal before the law, regardless of color or religion, the doors of the schools should not be shut in the faces of those who by birth or otherwise belong to a particular race or adhere to a particular religion.

Indeed, by opening the doors to all, the school authorities more honestly and faithfully cling to the enduring principles of our free institutions, and more sincerely and indiscriminately sustain the constitutional guarantees, than do those who would deny admission to certain persons because of creed or racial solidarity.

The sanctified principle of freedom of religious belief does not distinguish between believers and **nonbelievers**.

It embraces both, and accords one as much protection and freedom as the other. A sect or tenet which is intolerant of those of a different sect or tenet is the precise antithesis of religious liberty.

Freedom is negated if it does not comprehend freedom for those who believe as well as **those who disbelieve**. The law is astute and zealous in seeing to it that all religious beliefs or **disbeliefs** be given unfettered expression.

Authentic free thinking involves the indubitable [unquestionable] right to believe in God as well as the unfettered **license not to believe or to disbelieve in a Deity**.

To examine into the sectarianism of those seeking access to public school buildings would make a travesty of our glorified liberty of conscience. Liberty for **nonbelievers in God**, but denial to believers in a Deity, would be a mock liberty.

Rather than inimical [unfriendly] to the educational policy of the state, or subversive of legitimate use, it is a wholesome thing to have the school buildings, which are maintained at large expense by the taxpayers, used for the purposes and by the groups whose exclusion is here sought.

[The plaintiff sought to exclude religious groups, including the YMCA, Hi-Y clubs, Hebrew Menorah and Junior Hadassah Clubs from the use of public schools for assembly.]

It is the use to which the school buildings are put, and not the identity of the users that is decisive of the lawfulness of the use.

Manifestly, therefore, the defense set forth in paragraph X of the answers, to the effect that the school buildings are being used for the purpose of giving and receiving instruction in education learning, and the arts is legally sufficient. [237]

The U.S. Supreme Court in *School District of Abington Township v. Schempp*, 1963, referred to this emergence of "no-belief religions" and "religion of secularism":

> **Secularism is unconstitutional**.... preferring those who do not believe over those who do believe....It is the duty of government to deter no-belief religions.... Facilities of government cannot offend religious principles....
>
> The State may not establish a '**religion of secularism**' in the sense of affirmatively opposing or showing hostility to religion, thus 'preferring those who believe in no religion over those who do believe.[238]

Courts have struggled with toleration's evolution to include atheism as it effectively excludes theism, as cited in the Minnesota case of *Kaplan v. Independent School District*, 1927:

> The legislature has, however, seen the need of moral training and of instruction in the care of body and mind.
>
> What is more natural than turning to that book for moral precepts which for ages has been regarded by the majority of the peoples of the most civilized nations as the fountain of moral teachings?
>
> [Quoting *Vidal v. Girard's Executor's*]....It may be truthfully asserted that no more exacting rules of obedience to constituted civil authority and of right living conducive to good will among men exists

anywhere than those found in the New Testament of the Bible - rules to which neither Jew nor atheist can reasonably take exception.

We shall not stop to discuss whether or not this is a Christian nation; it is enough to refer to such discussion in the decisions hereinafter cited.

However, we think it cannot be successfully controverted that this government was founded on the principles of Christianity by men either dominated by or reared amidst its influence....

This intolerance touching religion, the Bible, or certain scientific lines of study...seems to grip the atheist and the disbeliever as intensely.

Speaking for myself only, I think that instead of fostering **this spirit of intolerance** by a strained construction of the *Constitution* so as to exclude from use by public schools of any book proclaiming great moral precepts,

it is more desirable that a liberal construction be adopted to the end that even in the public school the pupils perceive that there is that in our principles of government which recognizes the religious element of man and guarantees protection to its free exercise.[239]

Supreme Court Justice Antonin Scalia commented in his dissenting opinion of *Lee v. Weisman*, 1992:

Nothing, absolutely nothing, is so inclined to foster among religious believers of various faiths a **toleration** no, an affection for one another than voluntarily joining in prayer together, to God whom they all worship and seek....

The Baptist or Catholic who heard and joined in the simple and inspiring prayers of Rabbi Gutterman on this official and patriotic occasion was inoculated from religious bigotry and prejudice in a manner that can not be replicated. [240]

Early thinkers, though considered opened minded by previous standards, would not have taken this last step in the evolution of tolerance. In his treatise titled, *Of Atheism*, Sir Francis Bacon declared:

A little philosophy inclineth man's mind to **atheism**, but depth in philosophy bringeth men's minds about to religion. [241]

Referencing atheism, Benjamin Franklin wrote:

That I may be preserved from **atheism** and infidelity, impiety and profaneness, and in my addresses to Thee carefully avoid irreverence and ostentation, formality and odious hypocrisy, Help me, O Father. [242]

In 1754, in a pamphlet titled *Information to Those Who Would Remove to America*, Benjamin Franklin wrote to Europeans interested in immigrating or sending their youth to this land:

Hence bad examples to youth are more rare in America, which must be a comfortable consideration to parents. To this may be truly added, that serious religion, under its various denominations, is not only tolerated, but respected and practised. **Atheism is unknown there**; Infidelity rare and secret; so that persons may live to a great age in that country without having their piety shocked by meeting with either **an Atheist or an Infidel**.

And the Divine Being seems to have manifested his approbation of the mutual forbearance and kindness with which the different sects treat each other; by the remarkable prosperity with which he has been pleased to favor the whole country. [243]

Edmund Burke (1729-1797), a Britain leader during the Revolutionary War, stated in his *Second Speech on the Conciliation with America-The Thirteen Resolutions*, March 22, 1775:

Freedom and not servitude is the cure of anarchy; as religion, and **not atheism**, is the true remedy for superstition. [244]

Timothy Dwight (1752-1817), grandson of Princeton President Jonathan Edwards, was president of Yale from 1795 to 1817. Dwight fostered a revival on campus with a large number of the Yale class professing Christ and entering the ministry. Timothy Dwight delivered an address in New Haven, titled *The Duty of Americans, at the Present Crisis*, July 4th, 1798:

About the year 1728, Voltaire, so celebrated for his wit and brilliancy and not less distinguished for his hatred of Christianity and his abandonment of principle, formed a systematical design to destroy Christianity and to introduce in its stead a general diffusion of **irreligion and atheism**. [245]

Henri Jean Fabre (1823-1915), "Father of Modern Entomology," was a French biologist who pioneered studies of insect habitats. A friend of Louis Pasteur, Fabre wrote:

Without Him I understand nothing; without Him all is darkness....Every period had its manias. I regard **Atheism** as a mania. It is the malady of the age. You could take my skin from me more easily than my faith in God. [246]

Henry Emerson Fosdick (1878-1969), popular pastor of First Presbyterian Church, New York City, and Park Avenue Baptist Church, New York City, commented:

Race prejudice is as thorough a denial of the Christian God as **atheism** is, and it is a much more common form of apostasy. [247]

In an effort to extend tolerance to Muslims, President **George W. Bush** was the first President to **mention the Qur'an in an Inaugural Address**, January 20, 2005; the first President to **celebrate Muslim Ramadan in the White House**, November 19, 2001; the first President to **speak at an Islamic Center**, December 5, 2002; the first President to **issue an Islamic postage stamp, "Eid mubarak,"** during his Administration, August 1, 2001; and the first President to **appoint a Muslim U.S. ambassador to the United Nations**, Zalmay Khalilzad, April 17, 2007.

Nancy Pelosi, the first woman Speaker of the U.S. House, stood next to **Keith Ellison** as he swore upon a Qur'an to become the **first Muslim U.S. Congressman** (5th District-MN), January 4, 2007. Nancy Pelosi is also the **first U.S. Speaker to submit to Islamic Law and cover her head with a Muslim Hijab (veil)** while visiting Syria, April 5, 2007.

Though intended to influence fundamental Muslims to be more tolerant by showing that America is tolerant, these actions may have actually encouraged radical Muslims that their hope of conquering the "infidel" West is imminent. Hadith Sahih al-Bukhari recorded:

Mohammed said, "No Muslim should be killed for killing a Kafir (infidel)." (Hadith Sahih al-Bukhari, Vol. 9, No. 50)

TOLERANCE ONLY FOR POLITICALLY CORRECT

"Religion begat prosperity, and the daughter devoured the mother."

-Cotton Mather, quoting St. Bernard of Clairvaux: Lat., Religio peperit divitias et filia devoravit matrem.[248]

Ironically, tolerance now seems to exist for every kind of belief system, except for traditional Judeo-Christian, the very ideology which gave birth to and fostered the idea of tolerance.

Today, some even regard the Bible as "hate speech" because it contains verses referring to adultery, homosexuality and sexual promiscuity as sinful.

Tolerance has broadened to encompass those who have a humanistic and atheistic system of belief, giving rise to a dilemma: in order to have equality among religions, all acknowledgments of deity or anything supernatural, must be removed. Indeed, favoritism seems to be given in schools, government agencies and courts to any belief system other than the founder's Judeo-Christian belief system.

To gain perspective on what has happened, picture two small round magnets stuck together. It is difficult to pull them apart, but as they are gradually separated and turned, the magnetic pull diminishes.

The more you turn them, the more the magnetic pull diminishes, until they are turned so much the opposite sides face, and the magnets repel each other.

So it has been with toleration. It was difficult for Puritans to tolerate other Protestants, and difficult for Protestants to tolerate Catholics, but as time went on those who gained tolerance granted it more easily until every belief was tolerated. Then gradually tolerance changed to repel and discriminate against the very ones who originally promoted it.

President Calvin Coolidge warned against this at the American Legion Convention in Omaha, Nebraska, 1925:

> It is not easy to conceive of anything that would be more unfortunate in a community based on the ideals of which Americans boast than any considerable development of **intolerance as regards religion**.[249]

Colorado State Court, in *Vollmar v. Stanley*, 1927, stated:

> **If all religious instruction were prohibited, no history could be taught.**
>
> Hume was an unbeliever and writes as such; Macaulay is accused of partiality to dissenters; Motely of injustice to Roman Catholics. Nearly all histories of New England and the United States, are bound up with religion, religious inferences, implications, and often prejudices.
>
> Modern New England histories take pains to correct some of these things, and some people object to the corrections. **Even religious toleration cannot be taught without teaching religion....**
>
> If we are to take the argument of plaintiff that sectarian means more than the sects of religion and say that it means religious, as we are asked to do, we must push it to its logical limit, and say that believers are a sect, and that, **in deference to atheists no reference to God may be made (unless to deny**

Him, which we suppose would not be regarded as sectarian) and this would bar the singing of America and the Star Spangled Banner;

and if we should say that sectarian means religious, we would bar not only the greatest of our poets, including Shakespeare and Milton, whose most inspiring passages have a religious basis, but the greatest of our orators, including Webster, Clay and Lincoln...

It is said that reading the Bible is intolerant and a form of religious persecution; but, if those who do not like it can stay away and yet say to those who do like it, "you shall not read it here," **who is intolerant?** Are those who stay away persecuted?

It is urged that to absent themselves for a religious reason "subjects the pupils to a religious stigma and places them at a disadvantage."

We cannot agree to that. The shoe is on the other foot. We have known many boys to be ridiculed for complying with religious regulations but never one for neglecting them or absenting himself from them.[250]

Chief Justice Burger wrote in *Lynch v. Donnelly* 1985:

There is an unbroken history of official acknowledgment by all three branches of government of the role of religion in America...

The *Constitution* does not require a complete separation of church and state. It affirmatively mandates accommodation, not merely tolerance, of all religions and forbids hostility towards any.[251]

President Ronald Reagan, in a National Day of Prayer ceremony at the White House, May 6, 1982, stated:

In recent years, well-meaning Americans in the name of freedom have taken freedom away. **For the sake of religious tolerance, they've forbidden religious practice in the classrooms.**

The law of this land has effectively removed prayer from our classrooms. How can we hope to retain our freedom through the generations if we fail to teach our young that our liberty springs from an abiding faith in our Creator?

Thomas Jefferson once said, "Almighty God created the mind free." But current interpretation of our *Constitution* holds that the minds of our children cannot be free to pray to God in public schools.

No one will ever convince me that a moment of voluntary prayer will harm a child or threaten a school or state. But I think it can strengthen our faith in a Creator who alone has the power to bless America.[252]

To get an idea of how things have changed, consider the role of a referee in football. He is to make sure one team is not preferred over another. But imagine if two hundred years go by and all the referees join together to ban football, and in addition, ban all sports.

This is what has happened with religion. Originally, a Federal judge's role was to make sure the Federal Government did not prefer one denomination over another, but two hundred years have gone by and now most Federal judges have joined together to ban public Judeo-Christian expression, and in addition, ban the very acknowledgment of God.

Proposed "Hate Crime" legislation has even led to criminalization of traditional Judeo-Christian views in Canada and Europe. Radical homosexuals and radical Muslims have joined in an unholy alliance. Now that they are tolerated, they both do not want to tolerate traditional Judeo-Christian beliefs. Not content with coming out of the closet, they want to push Christians into it.

TOLERANCE
ROLES REVERSED

"It does not happen by reducing our values
to the lowest common denominator. And friends, it
does not happen by asking Americans to accept what's
immoral and wrong in the name of tolerance."
– Rep. J.C. Watts, Jr., Feb. 5, 1997, *Response
to President Clinton's State of the Union* [253]

Today, the trend is for America to be intolerant of what
our founders were tolerant of, and tolerant of what our founders
were intolerant of. William Penn, in his *Fundamental Constitutions
of Pennsylvania*, 1682, noted that tolerance did not include
licentious immorality:

> Every Person shall enjoy the Free Possession
> of his or her faith...so long as every such Person
> useth not this Christian liberty to **Licentiousness,
> that is to say to speak loosely and prophainly of
> God, Christ or Religion, or to Committ any evil in
> their Conversation [behavior],** he or she shall be
> protected in the enjoyment of the aforesaid Christian
> liberty by the civil Magistrate.[254]

South Carolina Supreme Court resisted this effort to
include sexual lewdness in the definition of "tolerance" in *City
of Charleston v. S.A. Benjamin*, 1846:

But this toleration, thus granted, is a religious toleration; it is the free exercise and enjoyment of religious profession and worship, with the proviso which guards against **acts of licentiousness.**[255]

U.S. Supreme Court, 1889, in *Davis v. Beason,* agreed:

The *Constitution of New York* of 1777 provided: That the liberty of conscience, hereby granted, shall not be so construed as to excuse **acts of licentiousness.**...
Constitutions of California, Colorado, Connecticut, Florida, Georgia, Illinois, Maryland, Minnesota, Mississippi, Missouri, Nevada and South Carolina contain a similar declaration.[256]

Speaking of tolerating wrong things, President James Abram Garfield spoke at the 100th anniversary of the *Declaration of Independence*, July 4, 1876:

Now more than ever before, the people are responsible for the character of their Congress. If that body be ignorant, reckless, and corrupt, it is because **the people tolerate ignorance, recklessness, and corruption.**[257]

ATHEISTS DEMAND THERE IS NO GOD

Charles Hodge married the great-granddaughter of Ben Franklin, received his doctorate from Rutgers University and was a professor for fifty years at Princeton. In 1871, he anticipated the transformation of tolerance:

The proposition that the United States is a Christian nation, is not so much the assertion that the great majority of the people are Christians, but that the organic life, the institutions, laws, and official action of the government, is in accordance with the principles of Christianity....

If a man goes to China, he expects to find the government there administered according to the religion of the country. If he goes to Turkey, he expects to find the Koran supreme and regulating all public action. If he goes to a Christian country, he has no right to complain, should he find the Bible in the ascendancy and exerting its benign influence not only on the people, but also on the government....

In the process of time thousands have come who are not Christians **Some are Jews, some are infidels, and some atheists.**

All are welcomed; **all** are admitted to equal rights and privileges. **All** are allowed to acquired property, and to vote in every election. **All** are allowed to worship as they please, or not to worship at all....

No man is molested for his religion or for his want of religion. **No man** is required to profess any form of faith, or to join any religious association.

More than this cannot reasonably be demanded. More, however, is demanded.

The infidel demands that the government should be conducted on the principle that Christianity is false, the atheist demands that it should be conducted on the assumption that there is no God....

The sufficient answer to all this is that it cannot possibly be done.[258]

INTOLERANCE AGAINST RELIGION

According to the 2002 estimates posted on the U.S Government's www.CIA.gov World Factbook link, Americans are 78% Christian (52% Protestant, 24% Catholic, 2% Mormon), 1% Jewish, 1% Muslim, other 10%, none 10%.

It is certainly admirable for judges, politicians, educators and media to give believers in a moderate form of Islam and other religions encouragement, but this can be done without denying freedom of speech to the majority of Americans who are of traditional Judeo-Christian beliefs.

The intolerance of traditional American faith was demonstrated when, after the terrorist attacks of September 11, 2001, a Broken Arrow, Oklahoma, Public School ordered "God" removed from "God Bless America."[259]

In Washington, D.C., near the Lincoln, Jefferson and Washington Memorials, all of which acknowledge God, there is the new World War II Memorial, which is conspicuous in its complete absence of any mention of God.

In California, December 2004, a school superintendent did not allow a teacher to show the *Declaration of Independence* to students because he was pointing out the words "All men are endowed...by their Creator."

Even more disingenuous, after examining the Judeo-Christian origins of tolerance, is a political strategy described by *Newsweek* political reporter Howard Fineman to accuse those with Judeo-Christian beliefs as being intolerant.[260]

On February 25, 1984, President Reagan said the pendulum has swung to "intolerance against religious freedom":

> From the early days of the colonies, prayer in school was practiced and revered as an important tradition. Indeed, for nearly 200 years of our nation's history, it was considered a natural expression of our religious freedom.
>
> But in 1962, the Supreme Court handed down a controversial decision prohibiting prayer in public schools. Sometimes I can't help but feel the *First Amendment* is being turned on its head.

Ask yourselves: Can it really be true that the *First Amendment* can permit Nazis and Klu Klux Klansmen to march of public property, advocate the extermination of people of the Jewish faith and the subjugation of blacks, while the same *Amendment* forbids our children from saying a prayer in school?

When a group of students at the Guilderland High School in Albany, New York, sought to use an empty classroom for voluntary prayer meetings, the Second Circuit Court of Appeals said no.

The court thought it might be dangerous because students might be coerced into praying if they saw the football captain or student body president participating in prayer meetings....

Up to 80 percent of the American people support voluntary prayer. They understand what the founding fathers intended. The *First Amendment of the Constitution* was not written to protect the people from religion; that *Amendment* was written to protect religion from government tyranny.

The *Amendment* says, "Congress shall make no law respecting an establishment of religion or prohibiting the free exercise thereof." What could be more clear? The act that established our public school system called for public education to see that our children learned about religion and morality.

References to God can be found in the *Mayflower Compact* of 1620, the *Declaration of Independence*, the *Pledge of Allegiance*, and the *National Anthem*. Our legal tender states, "In God We Trust."

When the *Constitution* was being debated at the Constitutional Convention, Benjamin Franklin rose to say,

"The longer I live, the more convincing proofs I see that God governs in the affairs of men. Without His concurring aid, we shall succeed in this political building no better than the builders of Babel."

He asked: "Have we now forgotten this powerful Friend? Or do we imagine we no longer need His assistance?" Franklin then asked the Convention to begin its daily deliberations by asking for the assistance of Almighty God.

Washington believed that religion was an essential pillar of a strong society. In his *Farewell Address*, he said, "Reason and experience both forbid us to expect that national morality can prevail in exclusion of religious principle."

And when John Jay, the first Chief Justice of the United States Supreme Court, was asked in his dying hour if he had any farewell counsels to leave his children, Jay answered, "They have the Book."

But now we're told our children have no right to pray in school. Nonsense. **The pendulum has swung too far toward intolerance against genuine religious freedom. It is time to redress the balance.**

Former Supreme Court Justice Potter Stewart noted **if religious exercises are held to be impermissible activity in schools, religion is placed at an artificial and state-created disadvantage.**

Permission for such exercises for those who want them is necessary if the schools are truly to be neutral in the matter of religion. And a refusal to permit them is seen not as the realization of state neutrality, but rather as the establishment of a religion of secularism.[261]

COMPETING
WORLDVIEWS

At the beginning of this book, reference was made to the situation in Europe in the 1500-1700's where whatever the king believed, the kingdom had to believe.

In general, England was Anglican, Germany was Lutheran, Switzerland was Calvinist, Scotland was Presbyterian, Italy, Spain and France were Roman Catholic, Greece and Russia were Orthodox.

Those who disagreed with the king's chosen denomination were persecuted or fled. It was from these displaced peoples that immigrants came to North America and the concept of toleration developed, though at different rates in various regions.

If "toleration" were a life boat, as pictured on this book's cover, it was originally piloted by colonial "Puritan" Christians who first rescued out of the waters of persecution those of their own "Puritan" denomination.

Then were rescued members of other Protestant denominations, followed by Catholics, Unitarians and other "liberal" Christian denominations. Then, following Jesus' teaching to "do unto others as you would have them do unto you," they began pulling aboard Jewish survivors, followed by monotheists.

Those now in the boat decided to exhibit charity by picking up polytheists and those of unfamiliar religions, finally bringing aboard atheists, secular humanists and the anti-religious.

Ironically, with the plethora of lawsuits and court actions removing traditional acknowledgments of faith from the public arena, it appears that the last ones in the lifeboat feel it is overcrowded and want to push the first ones out. For the sake of equality, they are demanding that every acknowledgment of a Deity be removed.

So now we have an interesting scenario - every belief system is tolerated except the one that came up with the idea! The faith that gave birth to tolerance is no longer tolerated. The trend now is to only tolerate to those who are intolerant of traditional Judeo-Christian beliefs.

Roger Williams wrote in *Plea for Religious Tolerance,* 1644:

Magistrates judge and punish as they are persuaded in their own belief and conscience (be their conscience paganish, Turkish, or antichristian) -

What is this but to confound heaven and earth together, and not only to take away the being of Christianity out of the world, but to take away all civility, and the world out of the world, and to lay all upon heaps of confusion? [262]

Regarding reversed roles of tolerance, President Reagan asked the Ecumenical Prayer Breakfast, August 23, 1984:

The frustrating thing is that those who are attacking religion claim they are doing it in the name of tolerance and freedom and open-mindedness.

Question: Isn't the real truth that they are intolerant of religion? That they refuse to tolerate its importance in our lives? [263]

WHOSE BELIEF SYSTEM YOU VALUE MORE

An example of the new intolerant tolerance was seen when winning Nebraska football Coach Ron Brown was interviewed for a coaching job at Stanford University. *The Daily Nebraskan*, April 13, 2002, reported:

> It soon became apparent his religious views were incompatible with Stanford's liberal student body and active gay community.
>
> "His religion was definitely something that had to be considered," said Alan Glenn, Stanford's assistant athletic director."
>
> Stanford's gay student leaders were more blunt in voicing their opposition.
>
> "Wow, it would be really hard for him here," said Courtney Wooten, social director of Stanford's Queer Straight Social and Political Alliance...
>
> Does Stanford's view of Brown's religious beliefs as one reason for not hiring him constitute discrimination against Christians?...
>
> Is it ironic that a liberal university devoted to inclusion and diversity would refuse to hire a coach based in part on his Christian belief system?...
>
> "If I'd been discriminated against for being black, they would've never told me that," Brown said. "They had no problem telling me it was because of my Christian beliefs."...
>
> To some, this also suggests a double standard at the university, which changed its mascot from an Indian to the Cardinal in the early 1970s in response to claims of racial insensitivity...
>
> Stanford student leaders in the gay and gay-allied community admitted it was tricky to delineate between banning someone who might bring discriminatory tones to campus and discriminating

against that person based solely on beliefs he or she holds…

Pat Tetreault, co-chairwoman of the Committee of Gay, Lesbian, Bisexual and Transgender Concerns at UNL stated

"We shouldn't be discriminating on religion either, but you get into a slippery slope on whose belief system you value more."[264]

COMPETING WORLDVIEWS

Orthodox Rabbi Daniel Lapin, president of Towards Tradition, in his book *America's Real War* (Multnomah Publishers, 1999), examined the conflict between the secular belief system and the Judeo-Christian belief system:

It is disconcerting to human beings that we cannot scientifically measure whether there is a soul, whether there is life after death, where human beings came from, and if there is a God. What we have refused to acknowledge in America today is the concept that we cannot prove either side of the debate for all to agree.

Yet, in spite of being more difficult, some would say impossible, to answer, these questions frequently vex us because making important life decisions would be far easier if we knew the answers.

We would agonize less over dilemmas of whether to marry, whom to marry, whether to raise children and how many, how to balance career and family demands and how to respond to various crisis.

Questions about the natural sciences are more easily answered but have far less impact on serious life decisions. Nonetheless, life decisions must be made despite the fact that relevant questions are unanswered.

Often, the decision to await all relevant data is itself a decision to not act at all.

Upon becoming engaged, nobody knows for sure that the intended is the best possible choice for a spouse. Paradoxically, waiting for that data to become certain is the surest way to never marry. There is no way to determine whether the child being carried in the womb will later bring its mother pleasure or pain. Anyone requiring that certainty must assuredly remain childless.

The same is true when starting a business or embarking on a career. We invest our money without knowing every possible fact about the fiscal outcome of our decision. We plan for a career with no assurance that we will not find that it is really an unsuitable one for us.

Similarly, the decision regarding our ultimate origin and destiny must be made before we know for sure, which will not happen until we die. That we must choose before all relevant data is in does not negate the importance of the choice.

Whether we choose to accept or reject the God-centered approach defines the cosmic tug-of-war. Whichever side wins, it will have profound consequences for our society. Human nature seeks a unifying principle, something that explains and makes sense of life and its mysteries, and this unifying principle could well be one's view of God.

People are unified often without realizing it, into either one of the two available camps because there are really only two approaches from which to choose. Either we are here because God willed it or we are here by accident, the result of cosmic roulette.

Similarly, either death ends it all or it does not. These are questions we all have, and the answer determines our lives.

One is the pro-God view, the other is what I call the "anti-God view."

In using the term "anti-God view" rather than a less provocative one like "non-religious view," I am trying to clarify the point that to position one's self on the anti-God team, one need not be militantly or even consciously anti-God. In fact, one may very well be a church or synagogue member with a profession of deep faith.

However, by not understanding the connection between one's faith and public policies, the same person who does believe in God can be undermining that very faith by supporting policies that are actually anti-God.

One need only subscribe to a seductive canon of superficially appealing ideas. I am suggesting that just as there are only two answers to the question of where we came from and where we shall end up, there may be the same two ways to settle the question of what we should be doing during our life; namely, either following the pro-God worldview or the anti-God worldview.

The alternative, indifference to God, is unworthy of men or women and is therefore practiced chiefly by non-human life forms such as cows and carrots. In reality there are very few agnostics. I suspect that most of our cultural institutions are now firmly in the hands of those who reject the Almighty.

Those who run our entertainment and news media are consistently shown by polls to attend worship services far less, and to be less likely to have a religious affiliation, than the nation's population as a whole.

Those who run our schools, universities, and courts are constantly implementing anti-God doctrines no matter how often they might invoke His name.

I am not even too certain of many of our churches and synagogues. It is time for the rest of us to recognize that there is a war being waged and to fight back. There is a broad, loosely linked coalition of Americans who see it as axiomatic, that liberty and religion go hand in hand.

Many polls suggest that it is a majority of Americans, but there are of course those who believe just the opposite. They believe religion must be routed out in order for liberty to flourish. If we are to become one nation again, Americans must eventually choose one of these conflicting views.

As with the issue of slavery in the 19th century, it is too basic a question for one nation to disagree upon. In this great revolution over whether our culture is, at heart, derived from and linked to religious principles, the final decision will not be dictated by moral compromise.

Instead, it will be made on the basis of moral conviction and that gleaming flash of resolve which can capture the minds of men and which springs from the spiritual foundations of life itself. [265]

President Ronald Reagan, March 15, 1982, addressed the Alabama State Legislature:

To those who cite the *First Amendment* as reason for excluding God from more and more of our institutions and every-day life, may I just say:

The *First Amendment of the Constitution* was not written to protect the people of this country from religious values; it was written to protect religious values from government tyranny.[266]

REDEFINITION

"Diversity" - "Inclusion" - "Pluralism" - "Tolerance" These once friendly words have become code words of the activist agenda to remove traditional faith.

Is today's political left endeavoring to change the definition of words like "tolerance" to really mean "intolerance toward those of traditional values?"

From reading the news, especially during the Christmas season, one gets the distinct impression that those who intensely want to eradicate traditional beliefs have learned the art of using the word "tolerance" as a covering for spreading "intolerance" toward Judeo-Christian values.

ORWELLIAN DOUBLE-SPEAK

To show we are tolerant, we will not tolerate you. George Orwell's futuristic book titled *1984* described the government's "Ministry of Truth," which published a "Newspeak Dictionary" containing new definitions which were the exact opposite of the words original meaning. [267]

Has the definition of the word "tolerance" been changed to mean "intolerance" toward those who do not conform? Is this the realization of "double-speak."

People of traditional values are intimidated into accepting increased levels of immorality that the initial promoters of the idea of tolerance could never have imagined.

America's "taliban" of political correctness seems to have changed the definitions of "diversity" to mean "liberal uniformity," "inclusion" to mean "exclusion of commonly accepted morals," "pluralism" to mean promotion of any beliefs so long as they are not Judeo-Christian, and "tolerance" to mean "intolerance toward those of traditional values."

Conservatives are made to "be quiet" in order for there to be an "open dialogue," and "threatened" to create "non-threatening" environments.

President Bush commented that the Afghanistan Taliban attempted to hijack the religion of Muslims for their own terroristic agenda. Has the concept of "tolerance" been hijacked by a secular "Taliban" for their humanistic agenda?

In the U.S. Supreme Court case of *Lee v. Weisman,* 1992, by only a one-vote majority, Justice Kennedy wrote that a commencement prayer by a clergy is unconstitutional.

In a strong dissenting opinion, Justice Antonin Scalia, joined by Justices Byron White, Clarence Thomas and Chief Justice William Rehnquist, stated that invocations and benedictions may continue to be offered, provided a notice is included in the program that participation is voluntary:

> That obvious fact recited the graduates and their parents may proceed to thank God, as American have always done, for the blessings He has generously bestowed on them and their country. [268]
>
> From our Nation's origin, prayer has been a prominent part of governmental ceremonies and proclamations. *The Declaration of Independence*, the document marking our birth as a separate people, "appeal[ed] to the Supreme Judge of the World for the rectitude of our intentions" avowed "a firm reliance on the protection of divine Providence."
>
> In his first *Inaugural Address*, after swearing his oath of office on a Bible, George Washington deliberately made a prayer a part of his first official act as President....Such supplications have been a characteristic feature of *Inaugural Addresses* ever since.
>
> Thomas Jefferson, for example, prayed in his first *Inaugural Address*....In his second *Inaugural Address*, Jefferson acknowledged his need for divine guidance and invited his audience to join his prayer....
>
> Similarly, James Madison, in his first *Inaugural Address*, placed his confidence "in the guardianship

and guidance of that Almighty Being...[with] fervent supplications and best hopes for the future."...

The other two branches of the Federal Government also have a long-established practice of prayer at public events....There is simply no support for the proposition that the officially sponsored nondenominational invocation and benediction read by Rabbi Gutterman - with no one legally coerced to recite them - violated the *Constitution*.

To the contrary, they are so characteristically American they could have come from the pen of George Washington or Abraham Lincoln himself.[269]

As its instrument of destruction, the bulldozer of its social engineering, the Court invents a boundless, and boundlessly manipulable test of psychological coercion....

The opinion manifests that the Court itself has not given careful consideration to its test of psychological coercion. For if it had, how could it observe, with no hint of concern of disapproval, that students stood for the *Pledge of Allegiance*, which immediately preceded Rabbi Gutterman's invocation?....

Since the *Pledge of Allegiance*...included the phrase "under God," recital of the *Pledge* would appear to raise the same Establishment Clause issue as the invocation and benediction.

If students were psychologically coerced to remain standing during the invocation, they must also have been psychologically coerced, moments before, to stand for (and thereby, in the Court's view, take part in or appear to take part in) the *Pledge*.

Must the *Pledge* therefore be barred from the public schools (both from graduation ceremonies and from the classroom)?

Logically, that ought to be the next project for the Court's bulldozer. [270]

Nothing, absolutely nothing, is so inclined to foster among religious believers of various faiths a toleration - no, an affection - for one another than voluntarily joining in prayer together, to God whom they all worship and seek....

The Baptist or Catholic who heard and joined in the simple and inspiring prayers of Rabbi Gutterman on this official and patriotic occasion was inoculated from religious bigotry and prejudice in a manner that can not be replicated.

To deprive our society of that important unifying mechanism...is as senseless in policy as it is unsupported in law.[271]

The reader has been told...about the personal interest of Mr. Weisman and his daughter, and very little about the personal interests of the other side.

They are not inconsequential. Church and state would not be such a difficult subject if religion were, as the Court apparently thinks it to be, some purely personal avocation that can be indulged entirely in secret, like pornography, in the privacy of one's room.

For most believers it in not that, and has never been. Religious men and women of almost all denominations have felt it necessary to acknowledge and beseech the blessing of God as a people, and not just as individuals, because they believe in the "protection of divine Providence," as the *Declaration of Independence* put it, not just for individuals but for societies; because they believe God to be, as Washington's first *Thanksgiving Proclamation* put it, the "Great Lord and Ruler of Nations."

One can believe in the effectiveness of such public worship, or one can deprecate and deride it. But the longstanding American tradition of prayer at official ceremonies displays with unmistakable clarity that the Establishment Clause does not forbid the government to accommodate it.

The narrow context of the present case involves a community's celebration of one of the milestones in its young citizen's lives, and it is a bold step for this Court to seek to banish from that occasion, and from thousands of similar celebrations throughout this land, the expression of gratitude to God that a majority of the community wishes to make.[272]

The Court lays waste a longstanding American tradition of nonsectarian prayer to God at public celebrations.[273]

Our Nation's protection, that fortress which is our *Constitution,* cannot possibly rest upon the changeable philosophical predilections of the Justices of this Court, but must have deep foundations in the historic practices of our people.[274]

On March 8, 1983, at the National Association of Evangelicals in Orlando, Florida, President Reagan stated:

The *Declaration of Independence* mentions the Supreme Being no less than four times. "In God We Trust" is engraved on our coinage. The Supreme Court opens its proceedings with a religious invocation. And members of Congress open their sessions with a prayer. I just happen to believe that the school children of the United States are entitled to the same privileges as Supreme Court Justices and Congressmen.[275]

BACKFIRED

Intolerance of traditional Judeo-Christian values is increasing, as seen by a sampling of news headlines:

PRAYER

*New Orleans, LA- ACLU sued to stop student led prayer. (12/11/01 AP)

*Virginia- ACLU sued to stop student moment-of-silence. (10/29/01 FoxNews)

*Santa Fe, NM- ACLU sued to stop student-led prayer before a football game and, in Adler case, sued to stop a student-led message. (12/13/01 Liberty Counsel, lc.org)

*Virginia Military Institute- ACLU suit ended the 50-plus year tradition of meal prayer. (01/02 WND.com)

*New York- Kindergartener told she could not pray out loud before snack time. (4/12/02 CNSNews.com)

*Balch Springs, TX- Seniors told they could not pray over their meals at senior center. (9/03 libertylegal.org)

*Seward, NE- Superintendent threatened to fire teacher who asked for prayer at a private meeting because school was anticipating lay-offs. (7/02 Liberty Counsel lc.org)

*USA- The IRS said churches can't pray for Bush victory. (10/04 WorldNetDaily.com)

GOD BLESS AMERICA

*Rocklin, CA- ACLU demanded a God Bless America sign be taken down. (10/2/01 Washington Times)

*East Troy, WI- Less than a month after the September 11th attack, the Freedom from Religion Foundation threatened legal action against Prairie View Elementary School because of a sign reading "God Bless America." (10/11/01 Journal Sentinel, Liberty Counsel, lc.org)

*Cincinnati, OH- Free Inquiry Group opposed God Bless America signs after the 9-11 attack. (11/5/01 Scripps Howard)

*Anaheim, CA- Student told he could not wear pin with flag and God Bless America. (10/18/02 Pacific Justice Institute, PacificJustice.org)

*Broken Arrow, OK- State Superintendent of Schools had God taken out of God Bless America sign, so sign read Bless America. (9/25/01 Liberty Counsel, lc.org)

*Vermont- Student won contest to design yearbook cover but principal demanded God Bless America be removed or forfeit prize. (2/02 Christian Law Assoc.)

MOTTO

*ACLU opposed posting of *National Motto*, In God We Trust. (2/28/02 cwfpac.com)

*Spokane, WA- Teacher made student remove *National Motto*, In God We Trust, from artwork. (10/11/01 Pacific Justice Institute, PacificJustice.org)

*Cincinnati, OH- Free Inquiry opposed In God We Trust sign after 9-11 attack. (11/5/01 Scripps Howard)

UNDER GOD

*CA- ACLU sued in the 9th Circuit Court on behalf of Michael Newdow to remove "Under God" from the *Pledge of Allegiance*. (9/3/02 www.aclunc.org)

*Madison, WI- School Board voted to eliminate *Pledge of Allegiance* because of "under God." (10/16/02 AP)

OATHS

*Honolulu, HI- Hawaii Citizens for Separation of State & Church complaint resulted Police Chief Lee Donohue dropping "God" from the Honolulu Police Department oath. (9/24/02 Honolulu Star-Bulletin News)

TEN COMMANDMENTS

*Chester, PA- ACLU sued to remove 82 year-old *Ten Commandment* plaque. (3/6/02 Philadelphia Inquirer)

*Tennessee- ACLU sued to remove the *Ten Commandments* from Hamilton and Rutherford County court houses. (5/15/02 Newsday.com)

*Indiana- ICLU sued to stop Gov. O'Bannon from erecting a *Ten Commandment* monument to replace one that was vandalized. (2/19/02 www.law.com)

*Alabama- 11th Circuit Court orders Chief Justice Roy Moore's *Ten Commandment* Monument to be removed from the Alabama State Judicial Building. (8/5/02 VisionForum.com)

*Murfreesboro, TN- Judge Robert Exhols ordered *Ten Commandments* removed from a display of historical documents displayed in the Rutherford County Courthouse. (6/25/02 Liberty Counsel, www.lc.org)

LITERATURE

*Miami-Dade, FL- ACLU opposed teaching of a class titled The Bible as History and Literature. (6/21/2002 Miami Herald)

*San Francisco, CA- Stevens Creed School principal Patricia Vidmar barred fifth-grade teacher Steven Williams from showing students documents from American history that refer to God - including the *Declaration of Independence.* (11/24/04 Reuters)

BILLBOARDS

*New Orleans, LA- ACLU sued to remove billboard with Jesus is Lord outside of Franklinton. (1/29/02 tbo.com)

*Staten Island, NY- Local Government officials ordered billboards bought by Rev. Kristopher Okwedy of Keyword Ministries taken down because they had a scripture verse that was considered hate speech by homosexuals. (Beverly LaHaye, Concerned Women for America, www.cwfa.org)

BOY SCOUTS

*San Diego, CA- ACLU forced Boy Scouts to be evicted from using Balboa Park, which they had maintained for over 50 years. Clinton appointee Judge Napoleon Jones cited the reason was the Scout Oath, which says "Do my duty to God and my Country." (07/04 Fox News, NewsMax.com, AMOJ news group)

*Portland, OR- ACLU sued to prohibit Portland's public schools from letting the Boy Scouts use their facilities because the Scout oath states "do my duty to God and my Country." (02/02 cc.org, 12/3/04 advocate.com)

DISPLAYS

*Cranston, RI- ACLU sued to prohibit religious displays from being placed next to secular displays. (12/04 Conservative Petitions.com)

MEETINGS

*Waukesha, WI- Good News Club evicted from after-school meetings. (5/23/02 Liberty Counsel, lc.org)

*Orlando, FL- Rabbi fined for holding prayer gathering inside his home. (3/20/2002 AP, Local6.com)

*Pittsburgh, PA- Community room cancelled "We the People" event because some religious literature was displayed. (2/28/02 Liberty Counsel, lc.org)

*Baker City, OR- City Councilman Gary Dielman opposed opening council meetings with prayer, opposed "So help me God" in the oath, and opposed the *Pledge of Allegiance.* (He was defeated in a recall vote.) (2/02 Christian Coalition of America, www.cc.org)

*Rossford High, OH- Local rock band school concert cancelled because of groups controversial message-They are Christian. (12/04 www.faithandvalues.us)

*City of Terrell, TX- YMCA banned from renting their facility to a church. (10/04 Liberty Legal Institute)

*McKinney, TX- City code prohibits church members from meeting in their pastors home. (7/04 Liberty Legal Institute, libertylegal.org)

*Abilene, TX- Mitchell County Public Library denied application to use community room for a religious meeting (6/28/02 Liberty Counsel, www.lc.org)

*Philadelphia, PA- Christians faced 47 years in Prison because Judge Calls Bible Verses shared at Gay Outfest "Hateful." (12/04 American Family Association Center for Law & Policy, afa.net)

*Visalia, CA- City seizes downtown theater by eminent domain rather than permit a local church to purchase it for religious worship and community service. (2004 Pacific Justice Institute, www.pacificjustice.org)

*Sacramento, CA- City imposes illegal occupancy restrictions on a church of Russian immigrants, causing the worship service to split in half and meet in a local garage. (2004 Pacific Justice Institute, pacificjustice.org)

SYMBOLS

*Worldwide- In a partial surrender to ACLU lawsuit in Illinois 1999, the U.S. Defense Department announced military units worldwide would no longer sponsor Boy Scout troops. (02/05 American Legion, www.legion.org)

*Los Angeles, CA- ACLU's threat of suit results in City Supervisors voting to remove the cross from the City Seal, even though Los Angeles was founded by missionaries. (05/04 Los Angeles Daily News)

*Redlands, CA- ACLU pressured city officials elect to remove historical depictions of crosses from their municipal seals. (2004 Pacific Justice Institute, www.PacificJustice.org)

*Tallahassee, FL- State plan proposed to remove crosses and other vertical grave markers from a cemetery. (11/13/01 Liberty Counsel, lc.org)

*Logan Country, KY- Woman fired from public library for wearing cross pendant on necklace. (2/02 WND.com)

*Palm Beach, FL- Veterans Administration ordered Menorahs removed from Medical Center. (12/11/01 PalmBeachPost.com)

*Oxford, NC- Church not allowed to participate in school fund-raiser where groups purchased displays at athletic field. (9/25/02 WorldNetDaily.com)

*Comparing Christians to Terrorists: The Jihad Against Christian Symbols. (12/16/04 David Asman, Fox News)

*Judge's Religious Robes on Trial. (12/17/04 Kim Henderson, Andalusia Star-News)

EMPLOYMENT

*Univ. of Colorado fired Prof. Paul Mitchell, a Christian, yet kept Prof. Ward Churchill, who called 911 victims Nazi "little Eichmanns." (WorldNetDaily 3/9/05)

*West Michigan- Meijer fired cake decorator, Debra Kerkstra, for refusing to work Sundays for religious reasons. (12/01 The Grand Rapids Press)

*Detroit, MI- Meijer Inc. fired meat cutter, Pavle Doroslavac, for refusing to work Sundays for religious reasons. (12/27/02 The Grand Rapids Press)

*General Motors diversity initiative supports affinity groups of gay and lesbian employees, such as GM PLUS, but it refuses to recognize religious organizations, such as Christian Employee Network. (7/24/03 WND.com)

*Federated Department Stores - ordered its 450 stores, including Macy's and Bloomingdales, to replace "Merry Christmas" greeting with "Happy Holidays" and "SeasonsGreetings." (12/04 ConservativePetitions.com)

*Seattle, WA- Business owner played Christian radio in his office and had harassment charges filed against him by a homosexual employee. (Beverly LaHaye, Concerned Women for America, www.cwfa.org)

*Carroll County- School officials investigated whether a bus driver did anything wrong by reciting the Lord's Prayer the day after the September 11th attack and threaten her job if she continued saying it. (02/02 Carroll County Md. SunSpot.net, Christian Coalition, cc.org)

*California- State Supreme Court rules Catholic Charities must provide birth control to its employees despite their religious objection. (2004 Pacific Justice Institute, www.PacificJustice.org)

*California- Federal District Court rules that religious objectors to union membership are not entitled to the same benefits as political objectors. (2004 Pacific Justice Institute, www.PacificJustice.org)

*U.S. Senate-Charles Schumer D-NY pursues religious tests to keep those from being judges who have "deeply held personal beliefs" such as Pro-Life Catholics or Bible-believing Baptists. (5/14/2005 Washington Post)

SCHOOL

*Plano, TX- Young girl not allowed to pass out pencils with Jesus written on it, while other gifts with secular messages were permitted. (12/04 Liberty Legal Institute)

*Fort Worth, TX- School District did not allow student to pass out constitutionally protected material on public sidewalks. (2/04 Liberty Legal Institute, libertylegal.org)

*Liverpool, NY- Fourth grader Michaela Bloodgood at Perry Elementary School prohibited from distributing literature with religious message during non-instructional time. (10/28/04 Liberty Counsel, www.lc.org)

*Kettle Moraine School District- Second grader couldn't give Jesus Loves You Valentines, though Harry Potter and Star Wars "The Force be with You" were OK. (Liberty Counsel, www.lc.org).

*Texas Tech- speech code only permits free speech in certain designated areas, provided students obtain permission two days prior. (10/04 Liberty Legal.org)

*Jefferson County, CO- Elementary school student had her Bible confiscated from the playground when she was caught sharing some verses with a friend. (12/04 ConservativePetitions.com)

*Plano, TX- Girl forbidden from inviting friends to Easter event at her church. (12/04 LibertyLegal.org)

*Texas- Tyndale Seminary fined $173,000 for issuing theological degrees without a license from the State. (1998 Liberty Legal Institute, www.libertylegal.org)

*Plano, TX- Spurger Elementary School sponsored official cross-dressing day for students pre-K through 6th grade. (11/04 Liberty Legal Institute, libertylegal.org)

*Texas- South San Antonio ISD teacher used profane language to belittle the faith of high school student Charity Santa Cruz. (02/04 LibertyLegal.org)

*Political Correctness Running Amok on College Campuses. (12/16/04 Paul Strand, CBN)

*U.S. Supreme Court- Ruled that Washington State is allowed to deny scholarship funds to student studying devotional theology in precedent setting decision. (2004 Pacific Justice Institute, www.PacificJustice.org)

*Tangipahoa, Louisiana- ACLU asks for jail sentence for teachers who pray after court ban.(5/18/05 AP)

*Knox County, Tennessee-Karns Elementary Principal ordered 10-year-old to stop reading Bible on playground during recess. (Alliance Defense Fund 05/2005)

*St. Mary's County, Maryland-Public Schools have elimiated all references to God from Thanksgiving history of settlers. (Washington Times, 11/23/2004)

*Lexington, MA-Father arrested while gay agenda is promoted in kindergarten. (05/06/2005 www.ceai.org)

*Colorado Springs, CO-America's United for Separation of Church & State protest Air Force Academy's 50 year tradition of faith. (5/22/05 National Catholic Register)

CHRISTMAS

**Missouri- Kindergarteners told they could not sing Christmas carols in school during holidays. (12/04 Christian Law Association)

**East Bay, CA- School banned Christmas program. (11/20/02 Pacific Justice Institute, PacificJustice.org)

**Georgia- City officials told private owners of an amusement park they could not present holiday entertainment shows that mentioned the religious meaning of Christmas. (12/04 Christian Law Assoc.)

*Covington, GA- ACLU intimidated school board to remove the word "Christmas" from school calendar and replace it with "Winter Holiday." (10/05 www.LapTopAmerica.net)

*Baldwin, KS- Liberals barred Santa Claus from local public schools claiming he reflected the "Christmas Message." (10/05 www.LapTopAmerica.net)

**Madison, WI- Christmas Tree not allowed unless called a Holiday Tree. (10/1/01 Journal Sentinel)

*New York City, NY- Mayor removed nativity scenes from public places and declared the city's "Christmas Tree," as it had been known for over a hundred years, to be called a "Holiday Tree." (10/05 www.LapTopAmerica.net)

*King County, WA- County Executive memo to Salvation Army workers to say Happy Holidays instead of Merry Christmas. (12/11/01 komotv.com)

*Texas- First grader not allowed to mention Jesus when discussing origins of Christmas.(12/04 ChristianLaw.org)

*Tennessee- Teachers not allowed to include any religious material in a general holiday decorating theme in their classrooms. (12/04 Christian Law Association)

*King County, WA- Public library administrators banned Christmas trees in libraries. (12/04 Conservative Petitions.com)

*Texas- School teacher discontinued all Christmas celebrations and substituted Kwanzaa, where first graders were taught to worship ancestors. (12/04 Christian Law Association)

*Pennsylvania- Public High School Principal prohibited religious music at annual Christmas concert. (12/04 Christian Law Association)

*New Jersey & Pennsylvania- Students could not distribute candy canes, as packages had religious origins of the candy cane. (12/04 Christian Law Association)

*Illinois- Fourth grader who enjoyed hearing her public school teacher read a book about the origins of Hanukkah was told that the teacher would not read a book about the origins of Christmas. (12/04 Christian Law Association)

*Maplewood, NJ- School District banned singing and even instrumental playing of "Silent Night" or any other Christmas music. (12/23/04 Joe Scarborough, Scarborough Country MSNBC)

*Mustang, OK- ACLU attacked elementary school Christmas Pagent, removing nativity scene and banning the singing of "Silent Night." (10/05 www.LapTopAmerica.net)

*Plano, TX- Third grade boy not allowed to pass out candy canes with religious message at "winter" party. (12/04 Liberty Legal Institute,liberty legal.org)

*Denver, CO- Mayor John Hickenlooper decided to ban the words "Merry Christmas" from city and county buildings, replacing it with "Happy Holidays." (12/04 ConservativePetitions.com)

*Palm Beach County, FL- Teachers warned not to allow any Christmas decoration to be displayed. (12/04 Conservative Petitions.com)

*Maplewood, NJ- Elementary school class trip to see Broadway play "A Christmas Carol" cancelled due to threat of lawsuit citing play's "religious content." (12/04 ConservativePetitions.com, www.LapTopAmerica/net)

*Pennsylvania- Principal to public high school teacher he could not include religious music in school's annual Christmas concert. (12/04 Christian Law Association)

*Eugene, OR- Christmas trees were banished from the University of Oregon. (10/05 www.LapTopAmerica.net)

*Indiana- Principal banned any mention of the word "Christmas." (12/04 Christian Law Association)

*Oklahoma- School Superintendent ordered students and teachers at Lakehoma Elementary School to remove nativity scene and not sing "Silent Night" at the "holiday" play. (12/04 ConservativePetitions.com)

*South Orange/Mapelwood School District- Prohibited, for the first time, INSTRUMENTAL versions of Christmas carols, limiting their schools bands to playing "Winter Wonderland" and "Frosty the Snowman." (12/04 Conservative Petitions.com)

*Oklahoma- Public school banned all religious music and displays during Christmas season. (12/04 Christian Law Association)

*New Mexico- Church not allowed to put float with religious symbols in city's Christmas parade, nor distribute holiday tracts on sidewalk during parade. (12/04 Christian Law Association)

*Plano, TX- School changed "Christmas Break" to "Winter Holiday" and prohibited parents from bringing red and green plates and napkins to the "winter" party as these might remind children of Christmas. (12/04 Conservative Petitions.com)

*Mustang, OK- School superintendent removed nativity scene from elementary school. Incensed voters respond by voting down $11 million bond measure for school. (12/04 ConservativePetitions.com)

*Milford, CT- Privately funded nativity scene demonstrated against by American Atheist group (four people). (12/04 ConservativePetitions.com)

*French owned Target Stores (1,272 nationwide)- Salvation Army banned from placing their traditional red kettles and ringing their hand bells for donations for the poor because of the organization's Christian connections. (12/04 Conservative Petitions.com)

*Denver, CO- Traditional Christmas Parade changed to "Parade of Lights" and Christmas sign replaced with

"Happy Holidays." Faith Bible Church's nativity float not allowed to enter because of its religious theme, though "Two Spirit Society's float allowed, honoring homosexual American Indians as "holy people." (12/04 ConservativePetitions.com)

*Bay Harbor, FL- City's holiday display allows menorah but not nativity scene. (12/04 Conservative Petitions.com)

*ACLU Steals Much More Than Christmas. (12/17/04 Christopher G. Adamo, CNSNews)

*County Bans Christmas Trees in Public. (12/17/04 Jay Sekulow of ACLJ, AP)

*Northeastern, US- The Boscov Department Store chain removed all Christmas cards that mention "Christmas." (10/05 www.LapTopAmerica.net)

*US- Bloomingdales and Macy's Department Stores have eliminated "Merry Christmas" from holiday decorations. (10/05 www.LapTopAmerica.net)

*Mentioning Christmas in Workplace Attacked by Political Correctness Across US. (12/16/04 Lifesite)

*"White House Decries ACLU Assault on Christmas," (12/24/04 Jeff Gannon, Talon News):

The White House spoke out this week about lawsuits threatened against local governments, schools and community groups by the American Civil Liberties Union to remove religious symbols and songs from Christmas celebrations. Across the country, incidents have been reported where Christmas carols have been banned from school programs and community events.

President Bush's Press Secretary Scott McClellan told Talon News, "I think the president has made it very clear that people ought to be able to freely worship as they choose. And in terms of schools, he's talked about those issues, as well. He has been a strong supporter of voluntary efforts like voluntary student prayer. And so I think his views are very clear on these issues."

Americans have reacted strongly against the threats. In Maplewood, New Jersey, a crowd of more than 100 carolers sang Christmas and Hanukkah songs in front of Columbia High School in protest against the ban on religious songs in the South Orange/ Maplewood School District.

California Gov. Arnold Schwarzenegger reversed an executive order by former Democratic Gov. Gray Davis that referred to a "holiday tree." The Republican changed the name back to "Christmas tree" in time for the annual lighting ceremony in Sacramento.[279]

A CRIMINAL ACT?

Two Americans, Heather Mercer, 24, and Dayna Curry, 29, along with six others from Australia and Germany, were held prisoners for three months in Afghanistan. They were facing the death penalty, prior to their miraculous rescue, for the crime of preaching Christianity!

Afghanistan was ruled by the extremist Islamic government known as the Taliban. There, and in other strict Islamic countries, individuals are jailed, punished, or worse, if they publicly display Judeo-Christian beliefs.

Is there a "Taliban" of Political Correctness in America? Both activist courts' "Secular jihad" and wahhabi sect's "Islamic jihad" prohibit public Judeo-Christian expression.

LEGAL TERRORISM

Are groups like the ACLU, as judicial 'al-Qaida,' waging "legal terrorism" on communities with traditional values? *The American Legion Magazine* stated in an article subtitled **"FANATICAL *IN TERROREM* LITIGATION by the American Civil Liberties Union,"** February 2005:

> Elected and appointed officials at the local, state and federal levels have been literally terrorized from standing up to the ACLU in fear of enormous attorney fees being imposed by unelected judges not answerable to the taxpayers.

American Legion National Commander Thomas P. Cadmus expressed his outrage at the partial settlement of an ACLU 1999 Illinois lawsuit resulting in the Department of Defense ordering all its military bases worldwide to no longer sponsor Boy Scout troops. *The American Legion Magazine* reported:

> The [settlement] ignited a fiery national debate pitting the values of God and country against the constitutional interpretations of the ACLU, whose civil-rights activism was cast by some as a form of 'legal terrorism.'[276]

Even if schools or community organizations are operating completely within their rights under the law, they must spend enormous amounts of money, intended for other local or school projects, on legal bills defending themselves against the ACLU. And if they lose in court, the school or community is forced, not only to pay a fine, but to pay ACLU's legal bills, thus continuing to finance the secular jihad.

"The public generally does not know the ACLU is profiting in such cases by millions of dollars in taxpayer paid 'attorney fee awards'" reported *The American Legion*.[277]

On September 18, 1982, in a *Radio Address to the Nation*, President Ronald Reagan stated:

> At every crucial turning point in our history Americans have faced and overcome great odds, strengthened by spiritual faith.
>
> The Plymouth settlers triumphed over hunger, disease, and a cruel Northern wilderness because, in the words of William Bradford, "They knew they were Pilgrims, so they committed themselves to the will of God and resolved to proceed."
>
> George Washington knelt in prayer at Valley Forge and in the darkest days of our struggle for independence said that "the fate of unborn millions will now depend, under God, on the courage and conduct of this army."
>
> Thomas Jefferson, perhaps the wisest of our founding fathers, had no doubt about the source from which our cause was derived. "The God who gave us life," he declared, "gave us liberty."
>
> And nearly a century later, in the midst of a tragic and at times seemingly hopeless Civil War, Abraham Lincoln vowed that "this nation, under God, shall have a new birth of freedom."
>
> It's said that prayer can move mountains. Well, it's certainly moved the hearts and minds of Americans in their times of trial and helped them to achieve a society that, for all its imperfections, is still the envy of the world and the last, best hope of mankind.
>
> And just as prayer has helped us as a nation, it helps us as individuals. In nearly all our lives, there are moments when our prayers and the prayers of our friends and loved ones help to see us through and keep [us] on the right path.

In fact, prayer is one of the few things in the world that hurts no one and sustains the spirit of millions.

The founding fathers felt this so strongly that they enshrined the principle of freedom of religion in the *First Amendment of the Constitution.*

The purpose of that *Amendment* was to protect religion from the interference of government and to guarantee, in its own words, "the free exercise of religion."

Yet today we're told that to protect that *First Amendment,* we must suppress prayer and expel God from our children's classrooms. In one case, a court has ruled against the right of children to say grace in their own school cafeteria before they had lunch.

A group of children who sought, on their initiative and with their parents' approval, to begin the school day with a one-minute prayer meditation have been forbidden to do so.

And some students who wanted to join in prayer or religious study on school property, even outside of regular class hours, have been banned from doing so. A few people have been objected to prayers being said in Congress.

That's just plain wrong. The Constitution was never meant to prevent people from praying; its declared purpose was to protect their freedom to pray.

The time has come for this Congress to give a majority of American families what they want for their children - the firm assurance that children can hold voluntary prayers in their schools just as the Congress, itself, begins each of its daily sessions with an opening prayer.[278]

INSIDE-OUT, NOT OUTSIDE-IN

"Force makes hypocrites, 'tis persuasion only that makes converts." - William Penn, *England's Present Interest Considered,* 1675

In medieval Europe, religion was something forced from the outside-in. Kings were more concerned with a subject's outward compliance than with their inward personal experience.

In strict Islamic countries, rulers do not care if individuals have feelings in their heart for Allah, they insist on outward submission, sometimes even having police punish those who do not close their stores and bow to Mecca five times a day. In atheist countries, as the former Soviet Union, government tried to force denial of God from the outside-in.

In a strange irony, Christianity in America, in an effort to be truly Christian, allowed anti-Christian beliefs. Founder of Rhode Island and America's first Baptist Church, colonial leader Roger Williams wrote in his *Plea for Religious Liberty,* 1644:

An enforced uniformity of religion throughout a nation or civil state, confounds the civil and religious, denies the principles of Christianity and civility, and that Jesus Christ is come in the flesh. [280]

The doctrine of persecution for cause of conscience is most contrary to the doctrine of Christ Jesus the Prince of Peace.[281]

The blood of so many hundred thousand souls of Protestants and Papists, spilt in the wars of present and former ages, for their respective consciences, is not required nor accepted by Jesus Christ the Prince of Peace....

God requireth not a uniformity of religion to be enacted and enforced in any civil state; which enforced uniformity (sooner or later) is the greatest occasion of civil war, ravishing of conscience, persecution of Christ Jesus in his servants, and of the hypocrisy and destruction of millions of souls.[282]

The permission of other consciences and worships than a state professeth only can (according to God) procure a firm and lasting peace...

True civility and Christianity may both flourish in a state or kingdom, notwithstanding the permission of divers and contrary consciences, either of Jew or Gentile. [283]

It is as necessary, yea more honorable, godly, and Christian, to fight the fight of faith, with religious and spiritual artillery, and to contend earnestly for the faith of Jesus, once delivered to the saints against all opposers...

I add that a civil sword is so far from helping forward an opposite in religion to repentance that magistrates sin grievously against the work of God and blood of souls by such proceedings.[284]

If a parent forced their teenager to pray, it would not be pleasing to God, but if the teenager voluntary prayed, it would be meaningful. Founders called this the "Right of Conscience" where individuals could worship as they believed was most pleasing to the Lord without fear of punishment.

On September 25, 1982, at a candle-lighting ceremony for prayer in schools, President Ronald Reagan stated:

> Unfortunately, in the last two decades we've experienced an onslaught of such twisted logic that if Alice were visiting America, she might think she'd never left Wonderland.
>
> We're told that it somehow violates the rights of others to permit students in school who desire to pray to do so. Clearly this infringes on the freedom of those who choose to pray, the freedom taken for granted since the time of our Founding Fathers.
>
> **Now, no one is suggesting that others should be forced into any religious activity, but to prevent those who believe in God from expressing their faith is an outrage.**
>
> The relentless drive to eliminate God from our schools can and should be stopped...We can not and must not cut ourselves off from this indispensable source of strength and guidance....
>
> **I think it'd be a tragedy for us to deny our children what the rest of us, in and out of government, find so valuable.**
>
> If the President of the United States can pray with others in the Oval Office-and I have on a number of occasions-then let's make certain that our children have the same right as they go about preparing for their future and for the future of this country.[285]

Commenting on this Judeo-Christian concept of having a free choice, Oxford historian Arnold Joseph Toynbee wrote:

> The course of human history consists of a series of encounters...in which each man or woman or child...is challenged by God to make the free choice between doing God's will and refusing to do it.

When Man refuses, he is free to make his refusal and to take the consequences. [286]

The American Judeo-Christian idea is that religion springs from the inside-out, yet other countries and religions have the concept that religion is forced from the outside-in, as seen in a chapter of history of the persecution of Armenian Christians in Islamic Turkey at the end of the 19th century.

President Chester A. Arthur, wrote in his *First Annual Message to Congress,* December 6, 1881:

> The insecurity of life and property in many parts of Turkey has given rise to correspondence with the Porte looking particularly to the better protection of American missionaries in the Empire.
>
> The condemned **murderer of the eminent missionary Dr. Justin W. Parsons** has not yet been executed, although this Government has repeatedly demanded that exemplary justice be done. [287]

President Cleveland wrote December 11, 1894:

> Senate [requests] the President communicate information of alleged cruelties committed upon Armenians in Turkey, and especially whether any such **cruelties have been committed upon citizens** who have declared their intention to become naturalized in this country or upon persons **because of their being Christians**. And inform the Senate whether [protests] have been addressed to the Government of Turkey in regard to such matters or any proposals made by or to this Government to act in concert with other **Christian powers** regarding the same.[288]

President Grover Cleveland wrote in his *Seventh Annual Message to Congress*, December 2, 1895:

Occurrences in Turkey have continued to excite concern. The reported **massacres of Christians in Armenia** and the development there and in other districts of **a spirit of fanatic hostility** to Christian influences naturally excited apprehension for the safety of the devoted men and women who, as dependents of the foreign missionary societies in the United States, reside in Turkey under the guarantee of law and usage and in the legitimate performance of their educational and religious mission.

No efforts have been spared in their behalf, and their protection in person and property has been earnestly and vigorously enforced by every means within our power....Orders have been carried out, and our latest intelligence gives assurance of the present personal safety of our citizens and **missionaries.**

Though thus far no lives of American citizens have been sacrificed, there can be no doubt that serious loss and destruction of **mission** property have resulted from riotous conflicts and outrageous attacks.

By treaty several of the most powerful European powers have secured a right and have assumed a duty not only in behalf of their own citizens and in furtherance of their own interests, but as agents of the **Christian world.**

Their right to enforce such conduct of Turkish government as will refrain **fanatical brutality**, and if this fails their duty is to so interfere as to insure against such dreadful occurrences in Turkey as have lately shocked civilization. [289]

President Grover Cleveland wrote in his *Eighth Annual Message,* December 7, 1896:

> It would afford me satisfaction if I could assure the Congress that the disturbed condition in Asiatic Turkey had during the past year assumed a less **hideous and bloody** aspect and that, either as a consequence of the awakening of the Turkish Government to the demands of humane civilization or as the result of decisive action on the part of the great nations having the right by treaty to interfere for the protection of those exposed to the rage of **mad bigotry and cruel fanaticism**, the shocking features of the situation had been mitigated.
>
> Instead, however, of welcoming a softened disposition or protective intervention, we have been afflicted by continued and not infrequent **reports of the wanton destruction of homes and the bloody butchery of men, women, and children, made martyrs to their profession of Christian faith.**
>
> While none of our citizens in Turkey have thus far been killed or wounded, though often in the midst of dreadful scenes of danger, their safety in the future is by no means assured.
>
> Our Government at home and our minister at Constantinople have left nothing undone **to protect our missionaries** in Ottoman territory, who constitute nearly all the individuals residing there who have a right to claim our protection on the score of American citizenship.
>
> Our efforts in this direction will not be relaxed; but the deep feelings and sympathy that have been aroused among our people ought not to so far blind their reason and judgement as to lead them to demand impossible things.

The outbreaks of blind fury which lead to murder and pillage in Turkey occur suddenly and without notice....We have made claims against the Turkish Government for the pillage and **destruction of missionary property** at Harpoot and Marash during the uprisings at those places....

A number of Armenian refugees having arrived at our ports, an order has lately been obtained from the Turkish Government permitting the wives and children of such refugees to join them.

It is hoped that hereafter no obstacle will be interposed to prevent the escape of all those who seek to avoid the perils which threaten them in Turkish dominions....I do not believe that the present somber prospect in Turkey will be long permitted to offend the sight of **Christendom.**

It so mars the humane and enlightened civilization that belongs to the close of the nineteenth century that it seems hardly possible that the earnest demand of good people throughout **the Christian world** for its corrective treatment will remain unanswered. [290]

President William McKinley wrote in his *Second Annual Message to Congress,* December 5, 1898:

The newly accredited envoy of the United States to the Ottoman Porte carries instructions looking to the disposal of matters in controversy with Turkey for a number of years...especially to press for a just settlement of our claims for indemnity by reason of the **destruction of the property of American missionaries resident** in that country during the **Armenian troubles of 1895**. [291]

President Theodore Roosevelt wrote in his *Fourth Annual Message to Congress*, December 6, 1904:

It is inevitable that such a nation should desire eagerly to give expression to its horror on an occasion of...such **systematic and long-extended cruelty and oppression of which the Armenians** have been the victims, and which have won for them the indignant pity of the civilized world.[292]

President Woodrow Wilson addressed Congress regarding the League of Nations, May 24, 1920:

Testimony [cited] at the hearings conducted by the sub-committee of the Senate Committee on Foreign Relations has clearly established the truth of the **reported massacres and other atrocities from which the Armenian people have suffered....**

The people of the United States are deeply impressed by the deplorable conditions of insecurity, starvation and misery now prevalent in **Armenia**....

I received and read this document with great interest and with genuine gratification, not only because it embodied my own convictions and feelings with regard to **Armenia** and its people, but also, and more particularly, because it seemed to me **the voice of the American people expressing their genuine convictions and deep Christian sympathies** and intimating the line of duty which seemed to them to lie clearly before us....

I urgently...request that the Congress grant the Executive power to accept for the United States a mandate over **Armenia**...

The sympathy with **Armenia** has...come with extraordinary spontaneity and sincerity from **the**

whole of the great body of Christian men and women in this country, by whose free-will offerings **Armenia** has practically been saved at the most critical juncture of its existence.

At their hearts this great and generous people have made the cause of **Armenia** their own....

I am conscious that I am urging upon Congress a very critical choice, but I make the suggestion in the confidence that **I am speaking in the spirit and in accordance with the wishes of the greatest of the Christian peoples.**

The sympathy for **Armenia** among **our people has sprung from untainted consciences, pure Christian faith and an earnest desire to see Christian people everywhere succored in their time of suffering** and lifted from their abject subjection and distress and enabled to stand upon their feet and take their place among the free nations of the world. [293]

President Warren G. Harding wrote in a speech released for publication in San Francisco, July 31, 1923:

We were never technically at war with Turkey...which threatened to set the Near East aflame. But...we did not fail to voice American sentiment of behalf of **Christian minorities,** and we did assist in reaching a settlement calculated to assure their future protection.[294]

In the Wall Street Journal's Opinion Journal, May 20, 2005, Ali Al-Ahmed, director of the Saudi Institute in Washington, D.C., wrote an article titled: "Hypocrisy Most Holy-Muslims should show some respect to others' religions":

With the revelation that a copy of the Quran may have been desecrated by U.S. military personnel at Guantanamo Bay, Muslims and their governments—including that of Saudi Arabia—reacted angrily. This anger would have been understandable if the U.S. government's adopted policy was to desecrate our Quran. But even before the Newsweek report was discredited, that was never part of the allegations.

As a Muslim, I am able to purchase copies of the Quran in any bookstore in any American city, and study its contents in countless American universities. American museums spend millions to exhibit and celebrate Muslim arts and heritage. On the other hand, my Christian and other non-Muslim brothers and sisters in Saudi Arabia—where I come from—are not even allowed to own a copy of their holy books.

Indeed, the Saudi government desecrates and burns Bibles that its security forces confiscate at immigration points into the kingdom or during raids on Christian expatriates worshiping privately.

Soon after Newsweek published an account, later retracted, of an American soldier flushing a copy of the Quran down the toilet, the Saudi government voiced its strenuous disapproval. More specifically, the Saudi Embassy in Washington expressed "great concern" and urged the U.S. to "conduct a quick investigation."

Although considered as holy in Islam and mentioned in the Quran dozens of times, the Bible is banned in Saudi Arabia. This would seem curious to most people because of the fact that to most Muslims, the Bible is a holy book. But when it comes to Saudi Arabia we are not talking about most Muslims, but a tiny minority of hard-liners who constitute the Wahhabi Sect.

The Bible in Saudi Arabia may get a person killed, arrested, or deported. In September 1993, Sadeq Mallallah, 23, was beheaded in Qateef on a charge of apostasy for owning a Bible. The State Department's annual human rights reports detail the arrest and deportation of many Christian worshipers every year.

Just days before Crown Prince Abdullah met President Bush last month, two Christian gatherings were stormed in Riyadh. Bibles and crosses were confiscated, and will be incinerated.

(The Saudi government does not even spare the Quran from desecration. On Oct. 14, 2004, dozens of Saudi men and women carried copies of the Quran as they protested in support of reformers in the capital, Riyadh. Although they carried the Qurans in part to protect themselves from assault by police, they were charged by hundreds of riot police, who stepped on the books with their shoes, according to one of the protesters.)

As Muslims, we have not been as generous as our Christian and Jewish counterparts in respecting others' holy books and religious symbols. Saudi Arabia bans the importation or the display of crosses, Stars of David or any other religious symbols not approved by the Wahhabi establishment. TV programs that show Christian clergymen, crosses or Stars of David are censored.

The desecration of religious texts and symbols and intolerance of varying religious viewpoints and beliefs have been issues of some controversy inside Saudi Arabia. Ruled by a Wahhabi theocracy, the ruling elite of Saudi Arabia have made it difficult for Christians, Jews, Hindus and others, as well as dissenting sects of Islam, to visibly coexist inside the kingdom.

Another way in which religious and cultural issues are becoming more divisive is the Saudi treatment of Americans who are living in that country: Around 30,000 live and work in various parts of Saudi Arabia. These people are not allowed to celebrate their religious or even secular holidays. These include Christmas and Easter, but also Thanksgiving. All other Gulf states allow non-Islamic holidays to be celebrated.

The Saudi Embassy and other Saudi organizations in Washington have distributed hundreds of thousands of Qurans and many more Muslim books, some that have libeled Christians, Jews and others as pigs and monkeys. In Saudi school curricula, Jews and Christians are considered deviants and eternal enemies.

By contrast, Muslim communities in the West are the first to admit that Western countries—especially the U.S.—provide Muslims the strongest freedoms and protections that allow Islam to thrive in the West. Meanwhile Christianity and Judaism, both indigenous to the Middle East, are maligned through systematic hostility by Middle Eastern governments and their religious apparatuses.

The lesson here is simple: If Muslims wish other religions to respect tsheir beliefs and their Holy book, they should lead by example.[295]

Contrary to other countries, America's founders believed religion was not to be forced from the outside-in, but emanated from the inside-out, as Roger Williams observed:

That religion cannot be true which needs such instruments of violence to uphold it. [296]

LETTERS PRIOR TO JEFFERSON'S

Thomas Jefferson's phrase "separation of church and state" has been used by activist judges to remove religion from public expression. It originated from a letter he wrote to the Danbury Baptist Association of Connecticut, January 1, 1802. The background of this letter is important to understand.

When George Washington was elected as the first President, he received letters from a large number of the denominations in America, congratulating him on his election, and searching him out as to whether he might follow the example of Europe's leaders and choose a national denomination.

In general, the European monarchs had made England - Anglican; Germany - Lutheran; Switzerland - Calvinist; Scotland - Presbyterian; Italy, Spain, and France - Roman Catholic; Greece and Russia - Eastern Orthodox.

Washington wrote back to these various denominations, putting them at ease that he would do no such thing, that they would be free from government persecution.

President Washington addressed nearly all the churches in America: Episcopal, Congregational, Presbyterian, Society of Friends (Quaker), United Baptist, German Lutheran, German Reformed, Dutch Protestant, Dutch Reformed, Methodist, Swedenborgian, United Brethren (Moravian), Roman Catholic, and Hebrew. He attended not only the Episcopal Church, to which he was a member, but also visited churches that were Presbyterian, Dutch Reformed, Lutheran, German Reformed Churches and even Catholic.[297]

Just ten days after his swearing in, President George Washington wrote to the General Committee of the United Baptist Churches of Virginia, May 10, 1789:

> Gentlemen - I request that you will accept my best acknowledgments for your on my appointment to the first office in the nation. The kind manner in which you mention my past conduct equally claims the expression of my gratitude....
>
> **If I could have entertained the slightest apprehension that the *Constitution* framed by the Convention, where I had the honor to preside, might possibly endanger the religious rights of any ecclesiastical Society, certainly I would never have placed my signature to it;**
>
> If I could now conceive that the general Government might ever be so administered as to render liberty of conscience insecure, I beg you will be persuaded that no one would be more zealous than myself to establish effectual barriers against the horrors of spiritual tyranny, and every species of religious persecution;
>
> for you doubtless remember I have often expressed my sentiments, that **any man, conducting himself as a good citizen, and being accountable to God alone for his religious opinions, ought to be protected in worshipping the Deity according to the dictates of his own conscience.** [298]

The General Assembly of Presbyterian Churches in the U.S. sent a letter to President Washington, May 26, 1789:

> We derive a presage even more flattering from the piety of your character. Public virtue is the most certain means of public felicity, and religion is the surest basis of virtue.

We therefore esteem it a peculiar happiness to behold in our Chief Magistrate, a steady, uniform, avowed friend of the Christian religion; who has commenced his administration in rational and exalted sentiments of piety; and who, in his private conduct, adorns the doctrines of the gospel of Christ; and on the most public and solemn occasions, devoutly acknowledges the government of Divine Providence.[299]

In May of 1789, President Washington replied to the General Assembly of Presbyterian Churches:

Gentlemen: I receive with great sensibility the testimonial given by the General Assembly of the Presbyterian Church in the United States of America, of the lively and unfeigned pleasure experience by them on my appointment to the first office of the nation.

Although it will be my endeavor to avoid being elated by the too favorable opinion which your kindness for me may have induced you to express of the importance of my former conduct and the effect of my future services, yet, conscious of the disinterestedness of my motives, it is not necessary for me to conceal the satisfaction I have felt upon finding that my compliance with the call of my country and my dependence on the assistance of Heaven to support me in my arduous undertakings have, so far as I can learn, met the universal approbation of my countrymen.

While I reiterate the professions of my dependence upon Heaven as the source of all public and private blessings; I will observe that the general prevalence of piety, philanthropy, honesty, industry, and economy seems, in the ordinary course of human affairs, particularly necessary for advancing and conforming the happiness of our country.

While **all men within our territories are protected in worshipping the Deity according to the dictates of their consciences**; it is rationally to be expected from them in return, that they will be emulous of evincing the sanctity of their professions by the innocence of their lives and the beneficence of their actions; for no man who is profligate in his morals, or a bad member of the civil community, can possibly be a true Christian, or a credit to his own religious society.

I desire you to accept my acknowledgements for your laudable endeavors to render men sober, honest, and good citizens, and the obedient subjects of a lawful government, as well as for your prayers to Almighty God for His blessings on our common country, and the humble instrument which He has been pleased to make use of in the administration of its government. [300]

A month in office, President Washington wrote to the Methodist Episcopal Bishop of New York, May 29, 1789:

I return to you individually, and through you, to your society collectively in the United States, my thanks for the demonstrations of affection and the expressions of joy, offered in their behalf, on my late appointment.

It shall still be my endeavor to manifest by overt acts the purity of my inclinations for promoting the happiness of mankind, as well as the sincerity of my desires to contribute whatever may be in my power towards the preservation of the civil and religious liberties of the American people.

In pursuing this line of conduct, I hope, by the assistance of Divine Providence, not altogether to disappoint the confidence which you have been pleased to repose in me.

It always affords me satisfaction when I find a concurrence in sentiment and practice between all conscientious men in acknowledgements of homage to the great Governor of the Universe, and in professions of support to a just civil government.

After mentioning that **I trust the people of every denomination, who demean [behave] themselves as good citizens, will have every occasion to be convinced that I shall always strive to prove a faithful and impartial patron of genuine, vital religion,** I must assure you in particular, that I take in the kindest part the promise you make of presenting your prayers at the throne of grace for me, and that I likewise implore the divine benediction on yourselves and your religious community. [301]

In July of 1789, President Washington wrote to the Directors of the Society of the United Brethren for Propagating the Gospel among the Heathen:

Gentlemen: I received with satisfaction the congratulations of your society, and of the Brethren's congregations in the United States of America.

For you may be persuaded that the approbations and good wishes of such a peaceable and virtuous community cannot be indifferent to me.

You will also be pleased to accept my thanks for the treatise you presented, ("An account of the manner in which the Protestant Church of the Unitas

Fratrum, or United Brethren, preach the Gospel and carry on their mission among the Heathen,") and be assured of my patronage in your laudable undertakings.

In proportion as the general government of the United States shall acquire strength by duration, it is probable they may have it in their power to extend a salutary influence to the aborigines in the extremities of their territory. **In the meantime it will be a desirable thing, for the protection of the Union, to co-operate, as far as the circumstances may conveniently admit, with the disinterested endeavors of your Society to civilize and Christianize the Savages of the Wilderness.**

Under these impressions, I pray Almighty God to have you always in His Holy keeping. [302]

President Washington replied to the August 19, 1789, letter from the General Convention of Bishops, Clergy & Laity of the Protestant Episcopal Church of New York, New Jersey, Pennsylvania, Delaware, Maryland, Virginia & North Carolina:

Gentlemen: I sincerely thank you for your affectionate congratulations on my election to the chief magistracy of the United States....

On this occasion it would ill become me to conceal the joy I have felt in perceiving the fraternal affection, which appears to increase every day among friends of genuine religion.

It affords edifying prospects, indeed, to see Christians of different denominations dwell together in more charity, and conduct themselves in respect to each other with a more Christian-like spirit than ever they have done in any former age, or in any other nation.

I receive with the greater satisfaction your congratulations on the establishment of the new *Constitution* of government, because I believe its mild yet efficient operations will tend to remove every remaining apprehension of those with whose opinions it may not entirely coincide, as well as to confirm the hopes of its numerous friends; and because the moderation, patriotism, and wisdom of the present federal Legislature seem to promise the restoration of order and our ancient virtues, **the extension of genuine religion**, and the consequent advancement of our respectability abroad, and of our substantial happiness at home.

I request, most reverend and respected Gentlemen, that you will accept my cordial thanks for your devout supplications to the Supreme Ruler of the Universe in behalf of me.

May you, and the people whom you represent, be the happy subjects of the divine benedictions both here and hereafter. [303]

President George Washington wrote to the Synod of Dutch Reformed Churches in North America, October 9, 1789:

While just government protects all in their religious rights, **true religion affords to government its surest support.** [304]

President Washington addressed the Quakers at their yearly meeting for Pennsylvania, New Jersey, Delaware, and the western part of Virginia and Maryland, October of 1789:

Government being, among other purposes, instituted to protect the persons and consciences of men from oppression, it certainly is the duty of rulers, not only to abstain from it themselves, but according to their stations, to prevent it in others.

The liberty enjoyed by the People of these States of worshipping Almighty God agreeable to their consciences is not only among the choicest of their blessings, but also of their rights.

While men perform their social duties faithfully, they do all that society or the state can with propriety demand or expect; and **remain responsible only to their Maker for the religion, or modes of faith, which they may prefer or profess.**

Your principles and conduct are well known to me; and it is doing the people called Quakers no more than justice to say, (except their declining to share with others the burden of the common defense) there is no denomination among us, who are more exemplary and useful citizens. [305]

President Washington wrote to the elders of the Massachusetts and New Hampshire churches of the First Presbytery of the Eastward, Newburyport:, October 28, 1789:

I am persuaded that the path of true piety is so plain as to require but little political direction. To this consideration we ought to ascribe the absence of any regulation, respecting religion, from the Magna-Carta of our country.

To the guidance of the ministers of the gospel this important object is, perhaps, more properly committed.

It will be your care to instruct the ignorant, and to reclaim the devious. And in the progress of morality and science, to which our Government will give every furtherance, **we may confidently expect the advancement of true religion**, and the completion of our happiness.[306]

Less than a year after swearing in, President Washington wrote to the Hebrew Congregations of Philadelphia, Newport, Charlestown and Richmond, January of 1790:

The liberal sentiment towards each other which marks every political and religious denomination of men in this country stands unrivalled in the history of nations....

The power and goodness of the Almighty were strongly manifested in the events of our late glorious revolution and His kind interpositions in our behalf has been no less visible in the establishment on our present equal government. In war He directed the sword and in peace He has ruled in our councils. My agency in both has been guided by the best intentions, and a sense of the duty which I owe my country....

May the same temporal and eternal blessings which you implore for me, rest upon your congregations.[307]

President Washington wrote to the Hebrew Congregation in Newport, Rhode Island, August 17, 1790:

It is now no more that toleration is spoken of as if it were the indulgence of one class of people that another enjoyed the exercise of their inherent natural rights, for, happily, the Government of the United States, which gives to bigotry no sanction, to persecution no assistance, requires only that they who live under its protection should demean themselves as good citizens in giving it on all occasions their effectual support....

May the children of the stock of Abraham who dwell in this land continue to merit and enjoy the good will of the other inhabitants - while every one shall sit in safety under his own vine and fig tree and there shall be none to make him afraid.

May the Father of all mercies scatter light, and not darkness, upon our paths, and make us all in our several vocations useful here, and in His own due time and way everlastingly happy. [308]

President George Washington wrote to the Hebrew Congregations of the city of Savannah, Georgia:

Happily the people of the United States have in many instances exhibited examples worthy of imitation, the salutary influence of which will doubtless extend much farther if gratefully enjoying those blessings of peace which (under the favor of Heaven) have been attained by fortitude in war, they shall conduct themselves with reverence to the Deity and charity toward their fellow-creatures.

May the same wonder-working Deity, who long since delivering the Hebrews from their Egyptian Oppressors planted them in the promised land - whose Providential Agency has lately been conspicuous in establishing these United States as an independent Nation - still continue to water them with the dews of Heaven and to make the inhabitants of every denomination participate in the temporal and spiritual blessings of that people whose God is Jehovah. [309]

President George Washington wrote to the Roman Catholics, March 15, 1790:

> I feel that my conduct, in war and in peace, has met with more general approbation than could reasonably have been expected and I find myself disposed to consider that fortunate circumstance, in a great degree, resulting from the able support and extraordinary candour of my fellow-citizens of all denominations....
>
> America, under the smiles of a Divine Providence, the protection of a good government, and the cultivation of manners, morals, and piety, cannot fail of attaining an uncommon degree of eminence, in literature, commerce, agriculture, improvements at home and respectability abroad....
>
> I presume that your fellow-citizens will not forget the patriotic part which you took in the accomplishment of their Revolution, and the establishment of their government; or the important assistance which they received from a nation in which the Roman Catholic faith is professed....
>
> **May the members of your society in America, animated alone by the pure spirit of Christianity, and still conducting themselves as the faithful subjects of our free government, enjoy every temporal and spiritual felicity.** [310]

President Washington wrote to the congregation of New Church in Baltimore, January 27, 1793:

> We have abundant reason to rejoice that in this Land the light of truth and reason has triumphed over the power of bigotry and superstition, and that

every person may here worship God according to the dictates of his own heart.

In this enlightened Age and in this land of equal liberty it is our boast that a man's religious tenets will not forfeit the protection of the laws nor deprive him of the right of attaining and holding the highest offices that are known in the United States. [311]

President Washington addressed the Episcopalians:

That Government alone can be approved by Heaven, which promotes peace and secures protection to its Citizens in every thing that is dear and interesting to them. [312]

JEFFERSON'S SEPARATION OF CHURCH & STATE

The Supreme Court of New York, 1958, stated in the case of *Baer v. Kolmorgen,* 181 N. Y. S. 2d. 230, 237 (Sup. Ct. N. Y. 1958): "Much has been written in recent years concerning Thomas Jefferson's reference in 1802 to "a wall of separation between church and State."... Jefferson's figure of speech has received so much attention that one would almost think at times that it is to be found somewhere in our Constitution."

Indeed, the phrase "separation of church and state" is not in the Constitution, Declaration of Independence or Bill of Rights. It appears only one time in a personal letter written by Jefferson. For some unexplained reason, personal letters of other presidents advocating Bible reading, Sabbath observance, praise of Christian virtues and support of missionary work among the Indians are ignored.

There are two ways of changing laws. The first way is to get a majority of citizens to agree with your views and then elect politicians to enact those views into law.

The second way, if only a minority of citizens hold your views, is to have judges re-interpret existing laws to have new meanings. This can be subtly done by changing the definition of the words in the existing law.

It is ironic that Jefferson himself forsaw this temptation to "squeeze" new meanings out of a text. On June 12, 1823, Thomas Jefferson wrote to Supreme Court Justice William Johnson:

On every question of construction, carry ourselves back to the time when the Constitution was adopted, recollect the spirit manifested in the debates, and instead of trying what meaning may be squeezed out of the text, or invented against it, conform to the probable one in which it was passed.

At the time Jefferson wrote his phrase the definition of the word "church" was "church" - ie. Anglican Church, Catholic Church, Lutheran Church, Eastern Orthodox, etc. So "separation of church and state" meant "separation of the Anglican Church and the State"; "separation of the Catholic Church and the State"; "separation of the Lutheran Church and the state", etc. In other words, he simply wanted to prevent a repeat of Europe where each country had only one recognized church. Jefferson merely did not want one denomination to set up its headquarters in the White House.

Today, judges has re-defined the word "church" to mean "any and all religious activity or acknowledgment." So the new meaning of "separation of church and state" is "separation of any and all religious activity or acknowledgment and the state."

This action of judges was foreseen by Jefferson, as cited in his letter to William Jarvis, September 28, 1820:

You seem...to consider the judges as the ultimate arbiters of all constitutional questions; a very dangerous doctrine indeed, and one which would place us under the despotism of an oligarchy.

Our judges are as honest as other men, and not more so....and their power [is] the more dangerous, as they are in office for life and not responsible, as the other functionaries are, to the elective control.

The Constitution has erected no such single tribunal, knowing that to whatever hands confided, with corruptions of time and party, its members would become despots.

Thomas Jefferson warned Mr. Hammond in 1821:

The germ of dissolution of our federal government is in...the federal judiciary; an irresponsible body...working like gravity by night and by day, gaining a little today and a little tomorrow, and advancing its noiseless step like a thief, over the field of jurisdiction, until all shall be usurped from the States.

Jefferson wrote on September 6, 1819:

The Constitution is a mere thing of wax in the hands of the judiciary, which they may twist and shape into any form they please.

Jefferson wrote to Abigail Adams, September 11, 1804:

Nothing in the Constitution has given them [judges] a right to decide for the Executive, more than to the Executive to decide for them....

But the opinion which gives to the judges the right to decide what laws are constitutional, and what not, not only for themselves in their own sphere of action, but for the legislature and executive also, in their spheres, would make the judiciary a despotic branch.

Jefferson's "separation of church and state" phrase was not intended to erase all references to Judeo-Christian faith or prohibit all acknowledgements of God, as can be easily seen by examining Jefferson's actions while in public office.

In 1774, in the Virginia Assembly, Jefferson introduced a resolution calling for a Day of Fasting and Prayer:

To invoke the Divine interposition to give to the American people one heart and one mind to oppose by all just means every injury to American rights.

On July 6, 1775, in the Continental Congress, Jefferson composed The Declaration of the Causes and Necessity for taking up Arms, in which he stated:

With a humble confidence in the mercies of the Supreme and impartial God and Ruler of the Universe, we most devoutly implore His Divine goodness to protect us.

On July 4, 1776, Jefferson penned the Declaration of Independence, which referenced God 4 times:

Laws of Nature and of Nature's God....Endowed by their Creator with certain inalienable rights....Appealing to the Supreme Judge of the World for the rectitude of our intenions....With a firm reliance on the protection of Divine Providence.

On November 11, 1779, as Governor of Virginia, Jefferson issued a Proclamation Appointing a Day of Public and Solemn Thanksgiving and Prayer to Almighty God:

That He would in mercy look down upon us, pardon all our sins, and receive us into His favour; and finally that He would establish the Independence of these United States upon the basis of religion and virtue.

The Library of Congress' "Religion and the Founding of the American Republic" Exhibition (www.loc.gov/exhibits/religion/rel06-2.html) reported that just two days after Jefferson wrote his "separation of church and state" letter to the Danbury Baptists, he attended church services which met in the U.S. Capitol and heard popular Baptist minister John Leland preach:

In his diary, Manasseh Cutler (1742-1823), a Federalist Congressman from Massachusetts and Congregational minister, notes that on Sunday, January 3, 1802, John Leland preached a sermon on the text "'Behold a greater than Solomon is here.' Jefferson was present." Thomas Jefferson attended this church service in Congress, just two days after issuing the Danbury Baptist letter. Leland, a celebrated Baptist minister, had moved from Orange County, Virginia, and was serving a congregation in

Cheshire, Massachusetts, from which he had delivered to Jefferson a gift of a "mammoth cheese," weighing 1235 pounds.

Here is a description, by an early Washington "insider," Margaret Bayard Smith (1778-1844), a writer and social critic and wife of Samuel Harrison Smith, publisher of the *National Intelligencer,* of Jefferson's attendance at church services in the House of Representatives: "Jefferson during his whole administration was a most regular attendant. The seat he chose the first day sabbath, and the adjoining one, which his private secretary occupied, were ever afterwards by the courtesy of the congregation, left for him."

In a letter, Catherine Mitchill, wife of New York senator Samuel Latham Mitchill, describes stepping on Jefferson's toes at the conclusion of a church service in the House of Representatives. She was "so prodigiously frighten'd," she told her sister, "that I could not stop to make an apology, but got out of the way as quick as I could."...

The first woman to preach before the House (and probably the first woman to speak officially in Congress under any circumstances) was the English evangelist, Dorothy Ripley (1767-1832), who conducted a service on January 12, 1806. Jefferson and Vice President Aaron Burr were among those in a "crowded audience."

On April 30, 1802, President Jefferson signed the Enabling Act for Ohio, extending the Northwest Ordinance, which stated in Article III:

Religion, morality, and knowledge being necessary to good government and the happiness of mankind, school and the means of education **shall be forever encouraged.**

In December 3, 1803, President Jefferson approved a treaty with the Kaskaskia Indians which included the **annual**

support of a Catholic missionary priest of $100, to be paid out of the Federal treasury. Similar treaties were made in 1806 and 1807 with the Wyandotte and Cherokee tribes.

President Thomas Jefferson extended three times a 1787 act of Congress in which special lands were designated:

> For the sole use of **Christian Indians** and the Moravian Brethren missionaries for civilizing the Indians and **promoting Christianity.**

President Jefferson signed bills which appropriated financial support for **chaplains** in Congress and **chaplains** in the Armed Services. On April 10, 1806, President Jefferson signed the Articles of War, in which he:

> Earnestly recommended to all officers and soldiers, **diligently to attend divine services.**

President Jefferson chaired the school board for the District of Columbia, where he authored the first plan of education adopted by the city of Washington, which used Isaac **Watts' Hymnal and the Bible as the principle textbooks to teach reading!**

What was Jefferson's intent? Could it be that the way we understand his phrase today is different than what he intended? We may have to agree with Associate Justice William Rehnquist, who wrote in the 1985 U.S. Supreme Court case Wallace v. Jafree, 472 U. S., 38, 99:

> It is impossible to build sound constitutional doctrine upon a mistaken understanding of Constitutional history....
>
> The establishment clause had been expressly freighted with **Jefferson's misleading metaphor** for nearly forty years....
>
> **There is simply no historical foundation for the proposition that the framers intended to build a wall of separation....**
>
> The recent court decisions are in no way based on either the language or intent of the framers.

After reading President Washington letters to the various religious leaders upon taking office, assuring them they would not be persecuted under his administration, one can get a clearer understanding of the intention of President Jefferson's letter, written less than a year after he swore into office, to the Danbury Baptists, where he mentioned his now famous phrase "wall of separation between church and state."

Similar in style and intent to President Washington's letters is Thomas Jefferson's often quoted letter to Nehemiah Dodge, Ephraim Robbins, and Stephen Nelson of the Danbury Baptist Association, Danbury, Connecticut, January 1, 1802:

Gentleman, The affectionate sentiments of esteem and approbation which you are so good as to express towards me, on behalf of the Danbury Baptist Association, give me the highest satisfaction.

My duties dictate a faithful and zealous pursuit of the interests of my constituents, and in proportion as they are persuaded of my fidelity to those duties, the discharge of them becomes more and more pleasing.

Believing with you that religion is a matter which lies solely between man and his God, that he owes account to none other for his faith or his worship, that the legislative powers of government reach actions only, and not opinions, I contemplate with sovereign reverence that act of the whole American people which declared that their legislature should "make no law respecting an establishment of religion, or prohibiting the free exercise thereof," **thus building a wall of separation between church and State.**

Adhering to this expression of the supreme will of the nation in behalf of the rights of conscience, I shall see with sincere satisfaction the progress of those sentiments which tend to restore to man all his natural rights, convinced he has no natural right in opposition to his social duties.

I reciprocate your kind prayers for the protection and blessing of the common Father and Creator of man, and tender you for yourselves and your religious association, assurances of my high respect and esteem. Thomas Jefferson. [313]

Who would know what Thomas Jefferson meant by his phrase "separation of church and state" better than Thomas Jefferson himself.

Thomas Jefferson's view of the *First Amendment* was to prevent the Federal or "General" government from interfering in church affairs as King George III did. Imagine the dismay if an IRS agent showed up at the Southern Baptist Convention or the American Catholic Bishops' Convention and attempted to "prescribe the religious exercises."

In his *Second Inaugural Address*, March 4, 1805, President Thomas Jefferson explained:

> **In matters of religion I have considered that its free exercise is placed by the *Constitution* independent of the powers of the General Government.**
>
> I have therefore undertaken, on no occasion, to prescribe the religious exercise suited to it; but have left them, as the *Constitution* found them, under the direction and discipline of state and church authorities by the several religious societies. [314]

Jefferson's letter to Samuel Miller, January 23, 1808, makes clear his understanding that the *First Amendment* was to simply keep the Federal Government from "intermeddling with religious institutions, their doctrines, discipline, or exercises":

> **I consider the [federal] government of the United States as interdicted [prohibited] by the *Constitution* from intermeddling with religious institutions, their doctrines, discipline, or exercises..**
>
> This results not only from the provision that no law shall be made respecting the establishment or free exercise of religion, but from that also which reserves to the states the powers not delegated to the United States [*10th Amendment*].
>
> **Certainly no power to prescribe any religious exercise, or to assume authority in religious discipline, has been delegated to the**

General government. It must then rest with the States as far as it can be in any human authority....
I do not believe it is for the interest of religion to invite the civil magistrate to direct its exercises, its discipline, or its doctrines....Every religious society has a right to determine for itself the times for these exercises, and the objects proper for them, according to their own particular tenets.[315]

Jefferson's statement that the government of the United States is "interdicted [prohibited] by the *Constitution* from intermeddling with religious institutions" is similar to James Madison's Journal entry, June 12, 1788:

There is not a shadow of right in the general [federal] government to intermeddle with religion...The subject is, for the honor of America, perfectly free and unshackled. The government has no jurisdiction over it.[316]

Jefferson's concept of the *First Amendment* keeping the Federal Government from intermeddling with church affairs is consistent with that of early colonial Baptist leader, Roger Williams, who responded to Massachusetts Puritan leader John Cotton in his work "The Bloody Tenet of Persecution for Conscience Sake" and "Mr. Cotton's Letter, Lately Printed, Examined and Answered," published in London, 1644:

Mr. Cotton...hath not duly considered these following particulars.
First, the faithful labors of many witnesses of **Jesus Christ**, existing in the world, abundantly proving, that the **Church of the Jews under the Old Testament in the type** and **the Church of the Christians under the New Testament in the antitype**, were both **separate from the world**; and that when they have **opened a gap** in the **hedge**, or **wall of separation,** between **the garden of the Church and the wilderness of the world, God hath ever broken down the wall** itself, **removed the**

candlestick, &c. and **made his garden a wilderness**, as at this day.

And that therefore if **He** will ever please to **restore His garden and paradise again**, it must of necessity be **walled in** peculiarly unto **Himself** from the **world**, and that all that shall be saved out of the world are to be transplanted out of the **wilderness of the world** and added unto **His Church or garden**...a **separation** of **Holy** from **unHoly**, penitent from impenitent, **Godly** from **unGodly**.

In his *Plea for Religious Liberty,* 1644, Roger Williams wrote:

All civil states with their officers of justice in their respective constitutions and administrations are proved essentially civil, and therefore **not judges,** governors, or defenders **of the spiritual or Christian state and worship...Magistrates, as magistrates, have no power of setting up the form of church government,** electing church officers, punishing with church censures. [317]

Thomas Cooley, Professor of Law at the University of Michigan, appointed to State Supreme Court and elected President of the American Bar Association, 1893, wrote in his Treatise on Constitutional Limitations:

While thus careful to establish, protect, and defend religious freedom and equality, **the American constitutions contain no provisions which prohibit the authorities from such solemn recognition of a superintending Providence** in public transactions and exercises as the general religious sentiment of mankind inspires, and as seems meet and proper infinite and dependent beings.

Whatever may be the shades of religious belief, **all must acknowledge the fitness of recognizing in important human affairs the superintending care and control of the great Governor of the Universe,** and of acknowledging with thanksgiving His boundless favors, of bowing in contrition when visited with the penalties of His broken laws. [318]

FIRST AMENDMENT

"The *First Amendment* is to protect not government from religion, but religion from government tyranny."
- Ronald Reagan, May 10, 1982, Briefing with Midwest Editors[319]

With all the debate over the intended meaning of the *First Amendment*, it only makes sense that one should look at the person who introduced it. On June 7, 1789, James Madison introduced the *First Amendment* in the first session of Congress with the wording:

The civil rights of none shall be abridged on account of religious belief or worship.[320]

To understand his intent, other *Bills* introduced by him should be examined. On Oct. 31, 1785, in the Virginia Assembly, James Madison introduced a bill *Appointing Days of Public Fasting & Thanksgiving*, and a bill for *Punishing Disturbers of Religious Worship & Sabbath Breakers*, passed in 1789. [321]

As referred to in an earlier chapter, while debating a *Bill* for state supported teachers of religion in the Virginia Assembly, 1785, James Madison delivered his *Memorial & Remonstrance*, warning of the temptation that would come to those in charge of hiring religious teachers to hire individuals of their own denomination, thus setting up a state denomination de facto.

Madison's abbreviated notes, written in November 1784, reveal he opposed the *Bill* for government support of religious teachers in Virginia, not because he was against religion, but because he did not want a judge deciding which version of the Bible was correct, what doctrines were accurate, was salvation by faith or works also, what was orthodox and heresy:

v. Probable effects of the Bill,

1. limited
2. in particular.
3. What is Christianity? Courts of law to judge.
4. What edition: Hebrew, Septuagint, or Vulgate? What copy? What translation?
5. What books canonical, what apocryphal? the papists holding to be the former what protestants the latter, the Lutherans the latter what the protestants & papists ye former.
6. In what light are they to be viewed, as dictated every letter by inspiration, or the essential parts only? Or the matter in general not the words?
7. What sense the true one for if some doctrines be essential to Christianity those who reject these, whatever name they take are no Christian in Society.
8. Is it Trinitarianism, Arianism, Socinianism? Is it salvation by faith or works also, by free grace or by will, &c, &c.
9. What clue is to guide a Judge thro' this labyrinth when ye question come before them whether any particular society is a Christian society?
10. Ends in what is orthodoxy, what heresy,. Dishonors christianity. panegyric on it, on our side. Decl. Rights. [322]

The Library of Congress Exhibition "Religion and the Founding of the Ameircan Republic" (www.loc.gov/exhibits/religion/rel06-2.html) stated:

> The first services in the Capitol, held when the government moved to Washington in the fall of 1800, were conducted in the "hall" of the House in the north wing of the building.
>
> In 1801 the House moved to temporary quarters in the south wing, called the "Oven," which it vacated in 1804, returning to the north wing for three years. Church services were held in what is now called Statuary Hall from 1807 to 1857. Services were conducted in the House until after the Civil War. The Speaker's podium was used as the preacher's pulpit...

Abijah Bigelow, a Federalist congressman from Massachusetts, describes President James Madison at a church service in the House on December 27, 1812...

Madison thought the only abuse to guard against was what took place in Europe, where whatever the King believed, the kingdom had to believe. He never imagined in the future there would be a ditch to avoid on the other side of the road, namely, the attempt to prohibit all public recognition of God.

Madison's intent was not to lessen the spread of religion, but to increase it, as he stated to the Virginia Assembly in his *Memorial & Remonstrance*, 1785:

> The policy of the bill is adverse to the diffusion of the **light of Christianity.** The first wish of those who ought to enjoy this precious gift, ought to be, that it may be imparted to the whole race of mankind.
>
> Compare the number of those who have as yet received it, with the number still remaining under the **dominions of false religions,** and how small is the former!
>
> Does the policy of the bill tend to lessen the disproportion? No; it at once discourages those who are **strangers to the Light of Truth**, from coming into the regions of it.[323]

Though Madison acknowledged the importance of spreading "the light of Christianity" as a "precious gift" to those "remaining under the dominions of false religions," he reasoned the Government's role was not to evangelize, but simply to provide an unbiased environment so churches could.

Madison identified two spheres of influence: civil and religious. Civil influence belonged to the Government, which was responsible to *provide* an equal, level playing field for religious activity; and Religious influence belonged to Churches, which were responsible to *perform* the religious activity.

This categorizing of responsibilities was quite a contrast to the situation in Europe during the Middle Ages, where Governments thought it was their responsibility to "evangelize" through forced compliance.

President James Madison enlarged on his views during the War of 1812 in a *Proclamation of a National Day of Public Humiliation & Prayer,* July 23, 1813:

> If the public homage of a people can ever be worthy of the favorable regard of the Holy and Omniscient Being to whom it is addressed, it must be...guided only by their free choice, by the impulse of their hearts and the dictates of their consciences;
>
> and such a spectacle must be interesting to all Christian nations as proving that religion, that gift of Heaven for the good of man [is] freed from all coercive edicts. [324]

Far from removing God from public recognition, Madison's aim was to make the public's worship more "worthy" to God by having it be voluntary and freewill, as expressed in his *Proclamation of a National Day of Public Humiliation, Fasting & Prayer,* November 16, 1814:

> I have deemed it proper...a day on which all may have an opportunity of voluntarily offering at the same time in their respective religious assemblies, their humble adoration to the Great Sovereign of the Universe, of confessing their sins and transgressions, and of strengthening their vows of repentance. [325]

When the War of 1812 ended, President Madison emphasized "freewill offering" in a *Proclamation of Thanksgiving & of Devout Acknowledgments to Almighty God,* March 4, 1815:

> No people ought to feel greater obligations to celebrate the goodness of the Great Disposer of Events and of the Destiny of Nations than the people of the United States....
>
> Every religious denomination may in their solemn assemblies unite their hearts and their voices in a freewill offering, to their Heavenly Benefactor, of their homage of thanksgiving and their songs of praise. [326]

Madison demonstrated there was a common set of religious beliefs in America from the Holy Scriptures by using the phrase "our holy religion" in a *Proclamation,* July 9, 1812:

> With a reverence for the unerring precept of our holy religion, to do to others as they would require that others should do to them.[327]

James Madison not only introduced the *First Amendment* in the first session of Congress, but he was called the "Chief Architect of the Constitution" because his influence on its formation was so great.

In an act that revealed his intent, perhaps better than any other, was when President Madison appointed Joseph Story to be a Justice on the U.S. Supreme Court in 1811. Joseph Story was the son of a Boston Tea Party "Indian," graduated second in his class from Harvard, was a Massachusetts Legislator, Speaker of the Massachusetts House, and served as a U.S. Representative.

Joseph Story was on the Supreme Court for 34 years, serving with Chief Justice John Marshall, and is considered the founder of the Harvard Law School, being its Professor of Law from 1829 till his death in 1845.

In his *Familiar Exposition of the Constitution of the United States*, 1840, U.S. Supreme Court Justice Joseph Story wrote:

> We are not to attribute this prohibition of a national religious establishment *First Amendment* to an indifference to religion in general, and especially to Christianity (which none could hold in more reverence than the framers of the *Constitution*)....
>
> Probably, at the time of the adoption of the *Constitution*, and of the *Amendment* to it now under consideration, the general, if not the universal, sentiment in America was, that Christianity ought to receive encouragement from the State so far as was not incompatible with the private rights of conscience and the freedom of religious worship.

An attempt to level all religions, and to make it a matter of state policy to hold all in utter indifference, would have created universal disapprobation, if not universal indignation.

But the duty of supporting religion, and especially the Christian religion, is very different from the right to force the consciences of other men or to punish them for worshipping God in the manner which they believe their accountability to Him requires. [328]

Justice Joseph Story continued:

The rights of conscience are, indeed, beyond the just reach of any human power. They are given by God, and cannot be encroached upon by human authority without a criminal disobedience of the precepts of natural as well as of revealed religion.

The real object of the *First Amendment* was not to countenance [favor], much less to advance Mohammedanism, or Judaism, or infidelity, by prostrating Christianity, but to exclude all rivalry among Christian sects and to prevent any national ecclesiastical establishment which should give to a hierarchy the exclusive patronage of the national government. [329]

THREE MONTHS
OF DEBATE

What was James Madison's intention for introducing the *First Amendment*? After reviewing some of the actions he performed in public office, it can be seen that he was a man who considered religion, "that gift of Heaven for the good of man," a vital part of American life and welcomed the acknowledgment of God in official government capacities.

He supported *Bills* appointing days of "public fasting & thanksgiving" and "punished disturbers of religious worship and Sabbath breakers." He opposed *Bills* that kept "strangers to the Light of Truth from coming into the regions of it."

James Madison's intent of his *First Amendment* was not to remove religion from the public arena, nor to promote irreligion, pornography or alternative sexual behavior, but simply to cause the public's worship of God to be more meaningful by being "guided only by their free choice, by the impulse of their hearts and the dictates of their consciences," a voluntary "freewill offering to their Heavenly Benefactor."

The intentions of the other delegates who helped write the *First Amendment,* which was primarily a limit on the Federal Government's power, can be easily understood by reading the *Journals of Congress* the three month it was debated. The initial draft of the *First Amendment* was made by James Madison, of Virginia, on June 8, 1789. His wording was:

> The civil rights of none shall be abridged on account of religious belief or worship, nor shall any national religion be established, nor shall the full and equal rights of conscience be in any manner, or on any pretext, infringed. [330]

George Mason, the author of the *Virginia Declaration of Rights* and a member of the Constitutional Convention, was largely responsible for the States' insistence that the powers of Congress be limited by a *Bill of Rights*. He had previously suggested the *First Amendment* wording be:

> All men have an equal, natural and unalienable right to the free exercise of religion, according to the dictates of conscience; and that no particular sect or society of Christians ought to be favored or established by law in preference to others.[331]

On August 15, 1789, the House Select Committee revised the proposed wording to:

> No religion shall be established by law, nor shall the equal rights of conscience be infringed.[332]

Peter Sylvester, Representative of New York, had some doubts as to the Select Committee's version, as:

> It might be thought to have a tendency to abolish religion altogether. [333]

Elbridge Gerry, Massachusetts, said it should read:

> No religious doctrine shall be established by law.[334]

James Madison said he:

> ...apprehended the meaning of the words to be, that Congress should not establish a religion and enforce the legal observation of it by law, nor compel men to worship God in any manner contrary to their conscience.[335]

Representative Benjamin Huntington, son of the prestigious governor of Connecticut, protested that:

> The words might be taken in such latitude as to be extremely hurtful to the cause of religion.[336]

Representative Huntington then suggested that:

> The *Amendment* be made in such a way as to

secure the rights of religion, but not to patronize those who professed no religion at all. [337]

James Madison responded agreeably to Representative Huntington and Representative Peter Sylvester, that he:

> ...believes that the people feared one sect might obtain a preeminence, or two [Anglican and Congregational] combine and establish a religion to which they would compel others to conform.[338]

Roger Sherman did not even want an amendment, realizing that the federal government was not to have any say in what was under the individual States' jurisdictions. James Madison then proposed the insertion of the word "national" before religion, thereby pointing the amendment directly to the object it was intended to prevent. [339]

On August 15, 1789, Samuel Livermore of New Hampshire proposed the wording:

> Congress shall make no laws touching religion, or infringing the rights of conscience. [340]

The House agreed and accepted the first five words of this version. On August 20, 1789, Fisher Ames of Massachusetts introduced the language:

> Congress shall make no law establishing religion, or to prevent the free exercise thereof, or to infringe the rights of conscience. [341]

This proposal was accepted by the House, which then sent it to the Senate for discussion. On September 3, 1789, the Senate proposed several versions in succession:

> Congress shall not make any law infringing the rights of conscience, or establishing any religious sect or society. [342]

> Congress shall make no law establishing any particular denomination of religion in preference to another, or prohibiting the free exercise thereof, nor shall the rights of conscience be infringed. [343]

> Congress shall make no law establishing one
> religious society in preference to others, or to infringe
> on the rights of conscience. [344]

The version accepted by the Senate at the end of the
day, September 3, 1789 was:

> Congress shall make no law establishing
> religion, or prohibiting the free exercise thereof.[345]

On September 9, 1789, the Senate agreed on:

> Congress shall make no law establishing
> articles of faith or a mode of worship, or prohibiting
> the free exercise of religion. [346]

This proposal was then sent to a joint committee of
both the House and the Senate to reconcile the differences.
The final wording agreed upon was:

> Congress shall make no law respecting an
> establishment of religion, or prohibiting the free
> exercise thereof. [347]

On December 15, 1791, *The Bill of Rights* was finally
ratified by the states. This was a declaration of what the federal
government could not do, leaving the States free within the
controls of their own constitutions.

The *First Amendment* in its entirety, states:

> Congress shall make no law respecting an
> establishment of religion, or prohibiting the free
> exercise thereof; or abridging the freedom of speech,
> or of the press; or the right of the people peaceably
> to assemble, and to petition the Government for a
> redress of grievances. [348]

ON THE FIRST AMENDMENT

On March 8, 1983, at the National Association of
Evangelicals in Orlando, Florida, President Reagan stated:

When our founding fathers passed the *First Amendment*, they sought to protect churches from government interference. They never intended to construct a wall of hostility between government and the concept of religious belief itself." [349]

President Bill Clinton, in an address at James Madison High School in Vienna, Virginia, July 12, 1995, stated:

The *First Amendment* does not require students to leave their religion at the schoolhouse door....It is especially important that parents feel confident that their children can practice religion....We need to make it easier and more acceptable for people to express and to celebrate their faith....

If students can wear T-shirts advertising sports teams, rock groups or politicians, they can also wear T-shirts that promote religion....Religion is too important to our history and our heritage for us to keep it out of our schools....It shouldn't be demanded, but as long as it is not sponsored by school officials and doesn't interfere with other children's rights it mustn't be denied....

Nothing in the *First Amendment* converts our public schools into religion-free zones or requires all religious expression to be left behind at the schoolhouse door....

While the government may not use schools to coerce the consciences of our students, or to convey official endorsement of religion, the government's schools also may not discriminate against private religious expression during the school day. [350]

U.S. Congress, January 19, 1853, recorded the report of Mr. Badger of the Senate Judiciary Committee as part of a Congressional investigation:

The *First Amendment* clause speaks of "an establishment of religion." What is meant by that expression? It referred, without doubt, to that establishment which existed in the mother-country, and its meaning is to be ascertained by ascertaining what that establishment was.

It was the connection, with the state, of a particular religious society, by its endowment at the public expense, in exclusion of, or in preference to, any other, by giving to its members exclusive political rights, and by compelling the attendance of those who rejected its communion upon its worship or religious observances.

These three particulars constituted that union of Church and State of which our ancestors were so justly jealous and against which they so wisely and carefully provided....

If Congress has passed, or should pass, any law which, fairly construed, has in any degree introduced, or should attempt to introduce, in favor of any church, or ecclesiastical association, or system of religious faith, all or any one of these obnoxious particulars, -endowment at the public expense, peculiar privileges to its members, or disadvantages or penalties upon those who should reject its doctrines or belong to other communions,- such law would be a "law respecting an establishment of religion," and, therefore, in violation of the *Constitution*.

But no law yet passed by Congress is justly liable to such an objection....We have chaplains in the army and navy, and in Congress; but these are officers chosen with the freest and widest range of selection, -the law making no distinction whatever between any of the religions, Churches, or professions of faith known to the world.

Of these, none by law is excluded, none has any priority of legal right. True, selections, in point of fact, are always made from some one of the denominations into which Christians are distributed; but that is not in consequence of any legal right or privilege, but by the voluntary choice of those who have the power of appointment.

This results from the fact that we are a Christian people, - from the fact that almost our entire population belongs to or sympathize with some one of the Christian denominations which compose the Christian world.

And Christians will of course select, for the performance of religious services, one who professes the faith of Christ. This...it should be carefully noted, is not by virtue of provision, but voluntary choice.

We are Christians, not because the law demands it, not to gain exclusive benefits or to avoid legal disabilities, but from choice and education; and in a land thus universally Christian, what is to be expected, what desired, but that we shall pay a due regard to Christianity, and have a reasonable respect for its ministers and religious solemnities?...

They intended, by this *Amendment*, to prohibit "an establishment of religion" such as the English Church presented, or any thing like it.

But they had no fear or jealousy of religion itself, nor did they wish to see us an irreligious people; they did not intend to prohibit a just expression of religious devotion by the legislators or the nation, even in their public character as legislators; they did not intend to send our armies and navies forth to do battle for their country without any national recognition of that God on whom success or failure depends; they did not intend to spread over all the public authorities and the whole public action of the nation the dead and revolting spectacle of atheistical apathy.

Not so had the battles of the Revolution been fought and the deliberations of the Revolutionary Congress been conducted. On the contrary, all had been done with a continual appeal to the Supreme Ruler of the World, and an habitual reliance upon His protection of the righteous cause which they commended to His care.[351]

The U.S. Congress received the report of Mr. Meacham of the House Committee on the Judiciary, March 27, 1854:

"Congress shall make no law respecting an establishment of religion." Does our present practice violate that article? What is an establishment of religion? It must have a creed, defining what a man must believe; it must have rites and ordinances, which believers must observe; it must have ministers of defined qualifications, to teach the doctrines and administer the rites; it must have tests for the submissive and penalties for the non-conformist.

There never was as established religion without all these. Is there now, or has there ever been, anything of this in the appointment of chaplains in Congress, or army, or navy?

The practice before the adoption of the *Constitution* does not seem to have changed... Chaplains were appointed for the Revolutionary army on its organization; rules for their regulation are found among the earliest of the articles of war.

Congress ordered, on May 27, 1777, that there should be one chaplain to each brigade of the army, nominated by the brigadier-general, and appointed by Congress, with the same pay as colonel, and, on the 18th of September following, ordered chaplains to be appointed to the hospitals in the several departments, with the pay of $60 per month, three rations per day, and forage for one horse.

When the *Constitution* was formed...we find provision for chaplains in the acts of 1791, of 1812, and of 1838....there is to be one to each brigade in the army. The chaplain is also to discharge the duties of schoolmaster...Is there any violation of the *Constitution* in these laws for the appointment of chaplains? [352]

WHOSE RELIGION IS PREFERRED

The ACLU, Americans United for the Separation of Church and State, and similar groups, want "under God" taken out of the *Pledge of Allegiance, Ten Commandments* removed, prayer prohibited in schools, and teachers fired for wearing cross necklaces. At the same time, the ACLU defends pornography, abortion, polygamy, North American Man-Boy Love Association, and printed "Getting Hitched in Canada" guide for gay marriage.

These groups say they want government "neutral," but is this a disguise for promoting their own agenda, their own belief system, their own religion?

RELIGION OF SECULARISM

Random House Unabridged Dictionary defines "religion" as: "a set of beliefs." Webster's New World Dictionary defines "religion" as: "a system of belief."

The word "belief" is defined as opinions, convictions - thoughts upon which one bases their actions. Thus, it follows, that as long as a person is doing "actions," they have thoughts preceding those actions - and that collection of thoughts is that person's "system of belief" or "religion."

As long as the government does "actions," the government has thoughts preceding those actions - and that collection of thoughts is the government's "system of belief" or "religion." There can never really be a separation of belief and government - as long as the government is doing "actions" there are thoughts or beliefs underlying those actions.

The ACLU is not trying to be "religion" neutral, but it is, in fact, promoting a "non-deity-based" belief system - its own "religion of secularism." The U.S. Supreme Court, in *Abington Township v. Schempp*, 1963, wrote:

> The state may not establish a "religion of secularism" in the sense of affirmatively opposing or showing hostility to religion, thus "preferring those who believe in no religion over those who do believe"...Refusal to permit religious exercises thus is seen, not as the realization of state neutrality, but rather as the establishment of a **religion of secularism**. [353]

Ronald Reagan referred to this decision in a radio address, February 25, 1984:

Former Supreme Court Justice Potter Stewart noted if religious exercises are held to be impermissible activity in schools, religion is placed at an artificial and state-created disadvantage.

Permission for such exercises for those who want them is necessary if the schools are truly to be neutral in the matter of religion.

And a refusal to permit them is seen not as the realization of state neutrality, but rather as the establishment of a **religion of secularism.** [354]

U.S. District Court, *Crockett v. Sorenson,* W.D. Va,. 1983:

The *First Amendment* was never intended to insulate our public institutions from any mention of God, the Bible or religion. When such insulation occurs, **another religion, such as secular humanism**, is effectively established. [355]

WHAT'S SUPERIOR - SECULAR OR SPIRITUAL?

Noah Webster's original 1828 *American Dictionary of the English Language* gives the definition:

SEC'ULAR, a. 1. Pertaining to the present world, or to things not spiritual or holy; relating to things not immediately or primarily respecting the soul, but the body; worldly. The **secular** concerns of life respect making provision for the support of life, the preservation of health, the temporal prosperity of men, of states, &c. Secular power is that which superintends and governs the temporal affairs of men, the civil or political power; and is contradistinguished from spiritual or ecclesiastical power. [356]

Did past leaders think secular or spiritual was superior? On March 6, 1799, President John Adams issued a *Proclamation of a National a Day of Humiliation, Fasting & Prayer:*

That the citizens on that day abstain, as far as may be, from their **secular** occupation, and devote the time to the sacred duties of religion, in public and in private.[357]

President Zachary Taylor issued a *Proclamation of a National Day of Prayer*, July 3, 1849, due to a cholera epidemic:

All business will be sustained in the various branches of the public service on that day; and it is recommended to persons of all religious denominations to abstain as far as practical from **secular** occupations and to assemble in their respective places of public worship, to acknowledge the Infinite Goodness which has watched over our existence as a nation. [358]

On October 26, 1867, President Andrew Johnson issued a *Proclamation of a National Day of Thanksgiving & Praise:*

Resting and refraining from **secular** labors on that day, let us reverently and devoutly give thanks to our Heavenly Father for the mercies and blessings with which He has crowned the now closing year. [359]

On March 30, 1863, President Abraham Lincoln issued a *Proclamation appointing a National Day of Fasting & Prayer:*

I do hereby request all the people to abstain on that day from their ordinary **secular** pursuits, and to unite, at their several places of public worship and their respective homes, in keeping the day holy to the Lord.[360]

On October 27, 1875, President Ulysses S. Grant issued a *Proclamation of a National Day of Thanksgiving:*

I do recommend that on...the 25th day of November, the people of the United States, abstaining from all **secular** pursuits and from their accustomed avocations, do assemble in their respective places of worship, and, in such form as may seem most appropriate in their own hearts, offer to Almighty God their acknowledgments and thanks for all His mercies. [361]

On October 26, 1876, President Ulysses S. Grant issued a *Proclamation of a National Day of Thanksgiving:*

I do recommend to the people of the United States to devote the 30th day of November next to the expression of their thanks and prayers to Almighty God, and, laying aside their daily avocations and all **secular** occupations, to assemble in their respective places of worship. [362]

On October 29, 1877, President Rutherford B. Hayes issued a *Proclamation of a National Day of Thanksgiving & Prayer:*

I do appoint Thursday, the 29th day of November, as a day of national thanksgiving and prayer; and I earnestly recommend that, withdrawing themselves from **secular** cares and labors, the people of the United States do meet together on that day in their respective places of worship, there to give thanks and praise to Almighty God. [363]

On October 30, 1878, President Rutherford B. Hayes issued a *Proclamation of a National Day of Thanksgiving & Prayer:*

I earnestly recommend that, withdrawing themselves from **secular** cares and labors, the people of the United States do meet together on that day in their respective places of worship, there to give thanks and praise to Almighty God for His mercies. [364]

On November 3, 1879, President Rutherford B. Hayes issued a *Proclamation of a National Day of Thanksgiving & Prayer:*

I earnestly recommend that, withdrawing themselves from **secular** cares and labors, the people of the United States do meet together on that day in their respective places of worship, there to give thanks and praise to Almighty God. [365]

On November 4, 1881, President Chester A. Arthur issued a *Proclamation of a National Day of Thanksgiving & Prayer:*

I recommend that all the people observe Thursday, the 24th day of November instant, as a day of national thanksgiving and prayer, by ceasing, so far as may be, from their **secular** labors and meeting in their several places of worship, there to join in ascribing honor and praise to Almighty God.[366]

On November 2, 1885, President Grover Cleveland issued a *Proclamation of a National Day of Thanksgiving & Prayer:*

On that day let all **secular** business be suspended, and let people assemble in their usual places of worship and with prayer and songs of praise devoutly testify their gratitude to the Giver of Every Good and Perfect Gift for all that He has done.[367]

On October 25, 1887, President Grover Cleveland issued a *Proclamation of a National Day of Thanksgiving & Prayer:*

On that day let all **secular** work and employment be suspended, and let our people assemble in their accustomed places of worship and with prayer and songs of praise give thanks to our Heavenly Father for all that He has done for us, while we humbly implore the forgiveness of our sins and a continuance of His mercy.[368]

In the U.S. Supreme Court case of *School District of Abington Township v. Schempp,* 1963, Justice Tom Clark delivered the Court's opinion, Justice Brennan concurring:

Nothing we have said here indicates that such study of the Bible or of religion, when presented objectively as part of a **secular** program of education, may not be effected consistently with the *First Amendment.*[369]

U.S. District Court, Western District of Virginia, in *Crockett v. Sorenson,* 1983, stated:

The *First Amendment* was never intended to insulate our public institutions from any mention of God, the Bible or religion. When such insulation occurs, another religion, such as **secular** humanism, is effectively established. Clearly, the Establishment Clause can be violated in this regard without a showing of outright hostility to traditional theistic religions...

The modern university intends to be, and supposes that it is, neutral, but it is not...It neither implicates nor expressly repudiates belief in God. But it does what is far more deadly than open rejection; it ignores Him....It is in this sense that the university today is atheistic....It is a fallacy to suppose by omitting a subject you teach nothing about it. On the contrary, you teach that it is to be omitted, and that it is therefore a matter of secondary importance.

And you teach this not openly and explicitly, which could invite criticism, you simply take it for granted and thereby insinuate it silently, insidiously, and albeit irresistibly. Moberly, *The Crisis in the University,* 55-56 (1949) (Whitehead and Conlin, *The Establishment of Religion of Secular Humanism & Its First Amendment Implications,* 10 Tex. Tech. L. Rev. 1, 19 n. 104, 1978).

In art, one cannot truly appreciate such great works as da Vinci's Last Supper, Michelangelo's work in the Sistine Chapel, or Albrecht Durer's woodcuts without some basic understanding of what the Bible contains.

Without some introduction to the book of Isaiah, Handel's *Messiah* loses much of its force and importance. Literature is replete with biblical allusion. Some of the better known works which rely heavily on allusions from the Bible include Milton's *Paradise Lost;* the plays of Shakespeare, especially *Measure for Measure*; Blake's *Marriage of Heaven and Hell*; Melville's *Moby Dick*; Faulkner's *Absalom, Absalom;* T.S. Eliot's *The Wasteland;* and C.S. Lewis' *The Screwtape Letters.*

Our language and popular culture are also replete with biblical allusions. The symbol for the American Medical Association, a staff with a serpent on it, is drawn from an episode in the book of Numbers, when Moses, at God's suggestion, raised a bronze serpent on a staff and all the children of Israel who looked upon it were healed of snakebites.

The phrase "handwriting on the wall" comes from a passage in the book of Daniel in which handwriting on the wall foretold rough time ahead for Babylonian King Belshazzar. The popular phrase "the apple of my eye" is used in the Old Testament as one of God's descriptions for His people Israel. And, of course, the term "Armageddon" is the site where the battle will take place which will mark the end of the age, as described in the Book of Revelations.

Anglo-American law as we know it today is also heavily indebted to the principles and concepts found in the Bible. William Blackstone, one of the most influential figures in the development of the common law, explained:

"The doctrine thus delivered we call the revealed or divine law and they are to be found only in the Holy Scriptures....Upon these two foundations, the law of nature and the law of revelation, depend all human laws, that is to say, no human law should be suffered to contradict these."

Blackstone posited [put] that the law of nature as well as the law of revelation, was derived from God. Further, biblical influences pervade many specific areas of the law. The "good Samaritan" laws use a phrase lifted directly out of one of Jesus' parables.

The concept of the "fertile octogenarian," applicable to the law of wills and trusts, is in a large part derived from the book of Genesis where we are told that Sarah, the wife of the patriarch Abraham, gave birth to Isaac when she was "past age."

In addition, the *Ten Commandments* have had immeasurable effect on Anglo-American legal development. Moreover, we as Americans, should especially be aware of the influence that the Bible and its principles have had on the founding and development of our nation.

In this regard it is significant that Former President Ronald Reagan, on February 3, 1983, issued a proclamation declaring 1983 the "year of the Bible" in recognition of the Bible's fundamental and enduring influence on our country.

Secular education imposes immediate demands that the student have a good knowledge of the Bible. Two defense exhibits vividly illustrate this point. Defendants Exhibit 14 is a summary of references to the Bible in a 1980 edition of the Scholastic Aptitude Manual, used by high school students to prepare for the Scholastic Aptitude Test....

Defendants' Exhibit 15, a summary of Bible references found in textbooks used in the Bristol public schools, is based on selected books from elementary, junior high and high school classes....In light of the above, it becomes obvious that a basic background in the Bible is essential to fully appreciate and understand both Western culture and current events. [370]

DON'T ASK DON'T TELL

The movie Black Hawk Down depicted the 1993 horror in Somalia after President Clinton's Administration denied equipment requested by the troops. General Boykin was commander of the downed Special Forces, which were surrounded by warlord fighters. He probably still hears his soldiers' desperate radio calls for backup. The enemy not only killed the U.S. Soldiers but stripped them, tied cables around their necks and dragged their naked bodies through the streets of Mogadishu.

Lt. General Boykin was accused of being "insensitive" in his remarks about these Somalian warlords when he stated at a prayer breakfast that this treatment of U.S. Soldiers was demonic and whatever god those who perpetrated it serve, it was not the same as his.

Lt. General William G. 'Jerry' Boykin, recipient of the Purple Heart, Bronze Star, and Legion of Merit, was criticized by Reps. Dennis Kucinich (D-OH), Sheila Jackson Lee (D-TX) and Maxine Waters (D-CA) who introduced House Resolution 419, calling for, in essence, a new military policy of "Don't Ask-Don't Tell if you are Christian."

NPR's Nina Totenberg stated regarding the General "I hope he's not long for this world." When her shocked co-panelist reacted to what sounded like a death wish, she quickly responded "In his job, in his job, in his job, please, please, please, in his job." If she had made this slip about another religion or sexual persuasion she probably would have lost her job. Has tolerance backfired, where even what someone says at a prayer breakfast may be used against them?

FREEDOM "OF"
NOT "FROM" RELIGION

"**I** hope we will also recognize the true meaning of the *First Amendment*. Its words were meant to guarantee freedom of religion to everyone. But I believe the *First Amendment* has been twisted to the point that freedom of religion is in danger of becoming freedom from religion."
- President Ronald Reagan, in a Q & A session, October 13, 1983.[371]

One is reminded of Robespierre during the French Revolution, who accused thousands of being disloyal to the beliefs of the new atheistic French Regime and brought them before a mob court which sent them to the guillotine. Hitler's SS, Stalin's KGB, or Mao Tse-Tung's PRC also punished thousands who expressed thoughts contrary to their godless governments.

Jefferson wrote to Benjamin Rush, September 21, 1800:

I have sworn upon the altar of God eternal hostility against every form of tyranny over the mind of man. [372]

It is ironic that Jefferson's quote acknowledged God in his fight against tyranny, yet activist judges are now using Jefferson's quotes in a tyrannical effort to prevent acknowledgment God.

THE LIGHT THAT SHINES THE FARTHEST

Catherine the Great of Russia would dress up the peasants along the road to give visitors from other countries the illusion of prosperity, when in reality her people were suffering in poverty.

It is said, "the light that shines the farthest - shines the brightest at home." If America is serious about spreading tolerance around the world, it must start at home with tolerance toward people of traditional Judeo-Christian faith.

Wouldn't it be ironic if after defeating Saddam's tyrannical regime in Iraq, America set up a secular tyrannical regime? Wouldn't it be ironic, that after defeating the atheistic empire of the Soviet Union, the United States gradually adopt the former Soviet policies of intolerance toward religion.

On January 26, 1984, in a Salute to Free Enterprise, President Ronald Reagan stated:

> Today we're told that to protect the *First Amendment* we must expel God, the source of all knowledge, from our children's classrooms.
>
> Well, pardon me, but the *First Amendment* was not written to protect the American people from religion; the *First Amendment* was written to protect the American people from government tyranny. [373]

AN IDEA WHOSE TIME HAS COME

If there can be days, weeks or months dedicated to acknowledging the contributions to American life from various heritages, could there be a week acknowledging the contributions to American life from those of Christian heritage?

In 1992, U.S. Rep. Nick Joe Rahall II introduced legislation in the 102nd U.S. Congress to declare November 22-28, 1992, as "America's Christian Heritage Week." The *Congressional Record*, Vol 138, No. 1, August 12, 1992, reads:

I rise today to introduce a House joint resolution calling for the designation of Thanksgiving week as "America's Christian Heritage Week." This year, the proclamation would cover the week of November 22 through November 28. It proclaims that America does, indeed, have a Christian heritage.

Mr. Speaker, one of the first things we, our parents before us, and our children after us, learned in school was that the settlement of America came about because of the desire of oppressed peoples to have the freedom to worship as they please.

At this time in history we as Americans-free men and women-are being called upon to witness emerging democracies struggle with the same potentially politically divisive questions as our Founding Fathers struggled with more than 200 years ago.

Questions such as: To what extent should public schools recognize and teach religion? How much should the State regulate a church's charitable activities? Should churches be exempt from general laws? To what extent should church and State be separated?

And while we watch and wait for those emerging democracies to turn from the long held atheism of communism to true religious freedoms, we find ourselves, with heavy hearts, watching our own Government succumb to pressures to distant itself from God and religion.

All because of a simple constitutional prohibition of a State-sponsored church, our own Government and higher court has allowed it to evolve into bans against the simple freedom as:

First, representation of the *Ten Commandments* on government buildings; Second, Christmas manger scenes on public property; Third, prayer in schools;

and Fourth, prayer at public meetings - including high school graduation ceremonies.

We seem to be bowing to pressure to seek a blind standard of legislative amorality, with a total exclusion of the mention of God in the public square, instead of a national morality based on religious principles of which Washington spoke.

Such a standard of religious exclusion is absolutely and unequivocally counter to the intention of those who designed our Government. It was not, in my view, mere chance that placed the freedom to worship according to individual conscience among the first freedoms specified in the *Bill of Rights* - freedoms that must flourish together or perish separately.

The Founding Fathers understood this country's religious heritage. But as Samuel Adams said: "I thank God that I have lived to see my country independent and free. She may long enjoy her independence and freedom if she will. It depends upon her virtue."

In other words, it depends upon us. When Abraham Lincoln sat apart a day for national prayer and humiliation, he cried out: "We have grown in numbers, wealth and power as no other nation has ever grown. But we have forgotten God."

At a time of increasing focus on family values by us as individuals, as political parties, as religious groups, as communities, let us set aside an occasion of celebration to help us make our families truly free by teaching them that God holds us all accountable.

It depends upon all of us whether America long enjoys her independence and freedom-and it depends upon our virtue.

As legislators let us each try never to support legislation that sponsors laws contrary to the laws of God.

The freedom we give thanks for daily, and the freedom we especially celebrate on Thanksgiving day, is at stake when we can no longer hear a child's prayer in school, or a benediction at a high school students' graduation ceremony.

Let us all be wise and remember the source of our many blessings, and never be timid or apologetic in sharing this knowledge with others. There is no better place than this great land of America for people to embrace and declare that our trust is in God, and that we look to His commandments and teachings for values that fortify and give direction to our families.

This resolution I introduce today is like many others we have voted on in this body - in celebration of prayer, of Bible reading, of our trust in God. We as Members of Congress begin our session in the House Chamber with a prayer and we follow it by a *Pledge of Allegiance* which contains the words, "one Nation under God, indivisible..." a change brought about at President Eisenhower's bidding, approved by Congress on June 14, 1956.

At that time, President Eisenhower said, "In this way we are reaffirming the transcendence of religious faith in America's heritage and future, in this way we shall constantly strengthen those spiritual weapons which forever will be our country's most powerful resource in peace and in war."

As Members we are deeply familiar with George Washington's Thanksgiving Proclamation, acknowledging the Providence of Almighty God.

In October 1982 President Ronald Reagan signed a joint resolution of Congress proclaiming the year 1983 as the "Year of the Bible."

More recently in 1990, President George Bush proclaimed 1990 as "International Year of Bible Reading." President Bush issued another proclamation in 1991, calling for a National Day of Prayer on February 3, 1991, to keep our fighting men and women safe while they sought the liberation of Kuwait.

My colleagues, we are not strangers to resolutions recognizing, observing, proclaiming this Government's belief in and reliance in Almighty God, and the power of prayer to strengthen us and guide us as a nation in all that we do here and throughout the world.

I invite each of you to cosponsor the resolution I have introduce today, proclaiming the week of November 22 through November 28, 1992, as "America's Christian Heritage Week." I pray that it will be given the support and cosponsorship it deserves and that it will become law in time for our prayerful observances, each in our own ways, at Thanksgiving time this year. [374]

CANNOT ENJOY RESULT
IF ABANDON CAUSE

"Unless the faith of the American in these religious convictions is to endure, the principles of our *Declaration* will perish. We can not continue to enjoy the result if we neglect and abandon the cause."
- President Calvin Coolidge, July 5, 1926 [375]

America has been a beacon of hope and freedom to peoples from around the world, no matter what their religion is. The City University of New York's American Religious Identification Survey, conducted in 2001, divides the U.S. Population into the religious groups: 76.5% Christian (52% Protestant, 24.5% Catholic), 13.2% Secular, 1.3% Jewish, 0.5% Muslim, 0.5% Buddhist, 0.5% Agnostic, 0.4% Atheist, 0.4% Hindu, 0.3% Unitarian Universalist, 0.1% Wiccan Pagan Druid, with the remaining as Spiritualist, Native American, Baha'i, New Age, Scientology, Humanist, Deist, Taoist, Eckankar, and Other.

As well intended as promoters of Pluralism are, it must be understood that all other faiths have freedom in America because of the Judeo-Christian foundation laid by the nation's founders. President Reagan said in a radio address, February 25, 1984:

Sometimes I can't help but feel the *First Amendment* is being turned on its head....Can it really be true that the *First Amendment* can permit Nazis and Klu Klux Klansmen to march of public property, advocate the extermination of people of the Jewish faith and the subjugation of blacks, while the same *Amendment* forbids our children from saying a prayer in school?...Up to 80 percent of the American people support voluntary prayer. They understand what the founding fathers intended.

The *First Amendment of the Constitution* was not written to protect the people from religion; that *Amendment* was written to protect religion from government tyranny....

But now we're told our children have no right to pray in school. Nonsense. The pendulum has swung too far toward intolerance against genuine religious freedom. It is time to redress the balance...

By reasserting their liberty of free religious expression, we will be helping our children understand the diversity of America's religious beliefs and practices. If ever there was a time for you, the good people of this country, to make your voices heard, to make the mighty power of your will the decisive force in the halls of Congress, that time is now.[376]

If activist courts continue dismantling the country's Judeo-Christian foundations in the name of tolerance, then all the contributions to freedom that that foundation has made will also be dismantled, including the very concept of tolerance itself. "We cannot enjoy the result if we abandon the cause."

The Christian umbrella in America has allowed tolerance to all. The danger, though, is that the Golden Rule - "do unto others as you would have them do unto you," might be replaced with "whoever has the gold rules," whoever gets power in the courts, media, education and commerce. President Calvin Coolidge said at the 150th anniversary of the *Declaration of Independence,* Philadelphia, July 5, 1926:

The *Declaration of Independence* [has] three very definite propositions set out in its preamble regarding the nature of mankind and therefore of government...that all men are created equal, that they are endowed with certain inalienable rights, and that therefore the source of just powers of government must be derived from the consent of the governed....

The principles of our declaration had been under discussion in the Colonies for nearly two generations....

Rev. Thomas Hooker of Connecticut as early as 1638...said in a sermon before the General Court that: "The foundation of authority is laid in the free consent of the people. The choice of public magistrates belongs unto the people by God's own allowance."...

Rev. John Wise, of Massachusetts...was one of the leaders of the revolt against the royal governor Andros in 1687, for which he suffered imprisonment....His works...reprinted in 1772...have been declared to have been...a textbook of liberty for our Revolutionary father....

That these ideas were prevalent in Virginia is further revealed by the *Declaration of Rights*, which was prepared by George Mason and presented to the general assembly on May 27, 1776.

This document asserted popular sovereignty and inherent natural rights, but confined the doctrine of equality to the assertion that "All men are created equally free and independent." It can scarcely be imagined that Jefferson was unacquainted with what had been done in his own Commonwealth of Virginia when he took up the task of drafting the *Declaration of Independence*....

John Wise...in 1710...said, "Every man must be acknowledged equal to every man." Again, "The end of all good government is to cultivate humanity and promote the happiness of all and the good of every man in all his rights, his life, liberty, estate, honor, and so forth..." And again, "For as they have a power every man in his natural state, so upon combination they can and do bequeath this power to others and settle it according as their united discretion shall determine."

And again, "Democracy is Christ's government in church and state." Here was the doctrine of equality, popular sovereignty, and the substance of the theory of inalienable rights clearly asserted by Wise at the opening of the 18th century, just as we have the principle of the consent of the governed stated by Hooker as early as 1638.

When we take all these circumstances into consideration, it is but natural that the first paragraph of the *Declaration of Independence* should open with a reference to Nature's God and should close in the final paragraphs with an appeal to the Supreme Judge of the world and an assertion of a firm reliance on Divine Providence...

It is no wonder that Samuel Adams could say, "The people seem to recognize this revolution as though it were a decree promulgated from heaven."

No one can examine this record and escape the conclusion that in the great outline of its principles the *Declaration* was the result of the religious teachings of the preceding period.

The profound philosophy which Jonathan Edwards applied to theology, the popular preaching of George Whitefield, had aroused the thought and stirred the people of the Colonies in preparation for this great event....

The principles of human relationship which went into the *Declaration of Independence*...are found in the texts, the sermons, and the writings of the early colonial clergy who were earnestly undertaking to instruct their congregations in the great mystery of how to live.

They preached equality because they believed in the fatherhood of God and the brotherhood of man. They justified freedom by the text that we are all created in the divine image, all partakers of the divine spirit....Placing every man on a plane where he acknowledged no superiors, where no one possessed any right to rule over him, he must inevitably choose his own rulers through a system of self-government.

This was their theory of democracy. In those days such doctrines would scarcely have been permitted to flourish and spread in any other country. This was the purpose which the fathers cherished. In order that they might have freedom to express these thoughts and opportunity to put them into action, whole congregations with their pastors had migrated to the colonies.

In its main feature the *Declaration of Independence* is a great spiritual document. It is a declaration not of material but of spiritual conceptions. Equality, liberty, popular sovereignty, the rights of man - these are not elements which we can see and touch. They are ideals. They have their source and their roots in the religious convictions. They belong to the unseen world.

Unless the faith of the American in these religious convictions is to endure, the principles of our *Declaration* will perish. We can not continue to enjoy the result if we neglect and abandon the cause....

We come back to the theory of John Wise that "Democracy is Christ's government..." The ultimate sanction of law rests on the righteous authority of the Almighty....

Ours is a government of the people. It represents their will. Its officers sometimes go astray, but that is not a reason for criticizing the principles of our institutions. The real heart of the American Government depends upon the heart of the people. It is from that source that we must look for all genuine reform...

It was in the contemplation of these truths that the fathers made their *Declaration* and adopted their *Constitution*. It was to establish a free government, which must not be permitted to degenerate into the unrestrained authority of a mere majority or the unbridled weight of a mere influential few...

We must think the thoughts which they thought. Their intellectual life centered around the meeting-house. They were intent upon religious worship....They were a people who came under the influence of a great spiritual development and acquired a great moral power....We live in an age of science and of abounding accumulation of material things. These did not create the *Declaration*.

Our *Declaration* created them. The things of the spirit come first. Unless we cling to that, all our material prosperity, overwhelming though it may appear, will turn to a barren sceptre in our grasp. If we are to maintain the great heritage which has been bequeathed to us, we must be like-minded as the fathers who created it.

We must not sink into a pagan materialism. We must cultivate the reverence which they had for the things that are holy. We must follow the spiritual and moral leadership which they showed. We must keep replenished, that they may glow with a more compelling flame, the altar fires before which they worshipped.[377]

Calvin Coolidge's words "unless the faith of the American in these religious convictions is to endure, the principles of our *Declaration* will perish. We can not continue to enjoy the result if we abandon the cause," echo Thomas Jefferson's warning engraved on walls of the Jefferson Memorial in Washington, D.C.:

God who gave us life gave us liberty. And can the liberties of a nation be thought secure when we have removed their only firm basis, a conviction in the minds of the people that these liberties are of the Gift of God? That they are not to be violated but with His wrath? Indeed, I tremble for my country when I reflect that God is just; that His justice cannot sleep forever.[378]

Harvard Professor James Russell Lowell was once asked by French historian Francois Guizot (1787-1874), "How long will the American Republic endure?" Lowell replied: "As long as the ideas of the men who founded it continue dominant."[379]

ENDNOTES

[1] U.S. Congress. Aug. 11, 1992, U.S. Rep. Nick Joe Rahall introduced legislation in 102nd Congress to declare Nov. 22-28, 1992, America's Christian Heritage Week. (103rd Cong. Res. H.J. 113), Cong. Record, Vol 138, No. 1, 8/12/92.

[2] Webster, Noah. 1828, American Dictionary of the English Language 1828 (reprinted San Francisco: Foundation for American Christian Education, 1967), definition of "religion."

[3] Coolidge, Calvin. May 3, 1925, laying the cornerstone of the Jewish Community Center, Washington, D.C. Calvin Coolidge, Foundations of the Republic Speeches & Addresses (NY: Charles Scribner's Sons, 1926), pp. 209-218.

[4] Bradford, William. 1650, *The History of Plymouth Plantation 1608-1650* (Boston, Massachusetts: Mass. Historical Society, 1856; Boston, Mass.: Wright & Potter, 1898, 1901, from Original Manuscript, Library of Congress Rare Book Collection, Wash, D.C.

[5] Reagan, Ronald. Mar. 19, 1985, National Day of Prayer Proclamation. Public Papers of the Presidents.

[6] Mather, Cotton. 1702. Cotton Mather, Magnalia Christi Americana, (The Great Achievement of Christ in America), 2 vols. (Edinburgh: The Banner of Truth Trust, 1702, 1979), 1:26.

[7] Higginson, John. 1663. Puritan author (1616 - 1708) in his Election Sermon-The Cause of God and His People in New England.

[8] Wilson, Henry. 1866, at Natick, Massachusetts to the Young Men's Christian Assoc. Thomas Russell, Life of Henry Wilson. Stephen Abbott Northrop, D.D., A Cloud of Witnesses (Portland, OR: American Heritage Ministries, 1987; Mantle Ministries, 228 Still Ridge, Bulverde, TX), pp. 509-510.

[9] Bancroft, George. 1834, *History of the United States of America,* Vol. I, p. 318. Stephen Abbot Northrop, D.D., A Cloud of Witnesses (Portland, OR: American Heritage Min., 1987; Mantle Ministries, 228 Still Ridge, Bulverde, TX), p. 24.

[10] Lowell, James Russell. 1810-1890, Literary Essays, Vol. II, New England Two Centuries Ago. Charles Fadiman, ed., The American Treasury (NY: Harper & Brothers, Pub., 1955), p. 119. John Bartlett, Bartlett's Familiar Quotations (Boston: Little, Brown & Co., 1855, 1980), p. 569.

[11] President Oakes, Election Sermon, 1673. Catholic Encyclopedia: "New Hampshire" - http://www.newadvent.org/cathen/10785a.htm

[12] Mather, Cotton. Sept. 15, 1682, to Mr. John Higginson. F.L. Yost, *Let Freedom Ring,* p. 56.

[13] Coolidge, (John) Calvin. May 3, 1925, laying cornerstone of Jewish Community Center, Washington, D.C. Calvin Coolidge, Foundations of the Republic Speeches & Addresses (NY: Charles Scribner's Sons, 1926), pp. 209-218.

[14] Congress, Continental. Sept. 1774, Article X, Articles of Association.

[15] Burke, Edmund. Mar. 22, 1775, address to Parliament: *Second Speech on the Conciliation with America-The Thirteen Resolutions*. Sidney Carelton Newsom, ed., Burke's Speech on Conciliation with America (NY: Macmillan Co., 1899; 1913), pp. 28-29. John Bartlett, Bartlett's Familiar Quotations (Boston: Little, Brown & Co, 1855, 1980), p. 372. Ernest R. Clark, ed., Burke's Speech on the Conciliation with America (NY: American Book Co., 1895; 1911) p. 34.

[16] Jay, John. 1887, message to Westchester County Bible Society, titled "National Perils & Opportunities," pp. 8-9. Stephen Abbott Northrop, D.D., A Cloud of Witnesses (Portland, OR: American Heritage Ministries, 1987; Mantle Ministries, 228 Still Ridge, Bulverde, TX), p. 250.

[17] Adams, Samuel. Aug. 1, 1776, addressing Continental Congress at State House, Philadelphia. Frank Moore, ed., American Eloquence (NY: D Appleton & Co., 1876), pp. 324-330. Charles Hurd, ed., A Treasury of Great American Speeches (NY: Hawthorne Books, 1959), p. 32.

[18, 19] Bancroft, George. Population of America during Revolutionary period indirectly influenced by John Calvin. Dr. Loraine Boettner, Reformed Doctrine of Predestination (Philadelphia: Presbyterian & Reformed, 1972), p. 382. John Eidsmoe, Christianity & the Constitution-The Faith of Our Founding Fathers (Grand Rapids, MI: Baker Book, Mott Media, 1987; 1993), p. 18-9.

[20] Madison, James. March 2, 1819, in a letter to Robert Walsh. Gaillard Hunt, ed., Writings of James Madison, for the first time printed, 9 vols. (NY: G.P. Putnam's Sons, 1900-1910). Norman Cousins, In God We Trust - The Religious Beliefs and Ideas of the American Founding Fathers (NY: Harper & Brothers, 1958), pp. 319-320.

[21] Morris, Gouverneur. Apr. 29, 1789, to George Washington. Jared Sparks, ed., The Life of Gouverneur Morris, with Selections from His Correspondence & Misc. Papers, 3 vols. (Boston: Gray & Bowen, 1832), Vol. II, pp. 68-69.

[22] Winthrop, John. May 19, 1643, Constitution of New England Confederation. Benjamin Franklin Morris, The Christian Life & Character of the Civil Institutions of the United States (Philadelphia, PA: L. Johnson & Co., 1863; George W. Childs, 1864), p. 56. William McDonald, ed., Documentary Source Book of American History 1606-1889 (NY: Macmillan Co., 1909), p. 46. Henry Steele Commager, ed., Documents of American History, 2 vols. (NY: F.S. Crofts & Co., 1934; Appleton-Century-Crofts., 1948, 6th edition, 1958; Englewood Cliffs, NJ: Prentice Hall, Inc., 9th ed., 1973), p. 26.

[23] Charter of Georgia, June 9, 1732, www.yale.edu/lawweb/avalon/states/ga01.htm

[24] New Jersey, State of. 1776, Constitution, Article XVIII. The Constitutions of the Several Independent States of America (Boston: Norman & Bowen, 1785), p. 73, Sec. 19. Benjamin Franklin Morris, The Christian Life & Character of the Civil Institutions of the United States (Philadelphia, PA: L. Johnson & Co., 1863; George W. Childs, 1864), p. 234. Frances Newton Thorpe, ed., Federal & State Constitutions, Colonial Charters, & Other Organic Laws of the States, Territories, & Colonies now or heretofore forming the United States, 7 vols. (Wash.: Gov. Printing Office, 1905; 1909; St. Clair Shores, MI: Scholarly Press, 1968). Edwin S. Gaustad, Neither King nor Prelate Religion & the New Nation, 17761826 (Grand Rapids, MI: William B. Eerdmans, 1993), p. 17-8.

[25] North Carolina, State of. 1776, Constitution, Article XXXII. The Constitutions of the Several Independent States of America, Pub. by Order of Congress (Boston: Norman & Bowen, 1785) p. 138. The Constitutions of All the United States According to the Latest Amendments (Lexington, KY: Thomas T. Skillman, 1817), p. 224. Benjamin Franklin Morris, The Christian Life & Character of the Civil Institutions of the United States (Philadelphia, PA: L. Johnson & Co., 1863; George W. Childs, 1864), p. 233. Supreme Court Justice David Josiah Brewer, who served 1890-1910, in his work, The United States-Christian Nation (Philadelphia: The John C. Winston Co., 1905, Supreme Court Collection).

Frances Newton Thorpe, ed., Federal & State Constitutions, Colonial Charters, & Other Organic Laws of the States, Territories, & Colonies now or heretofore forming the United States, 7 vols. (Washington: Government Printing Office, 1905; 1909; St. Clair Shores, MI: Scholarly Press, 1968).

[26] Vermont, State of. 1777, Constitution, Declaration of Rights, III. Perley Poore, ed., Federal & State Constitutions, Colonial Charters, & Other Organic Laws of the United States (Washington, 1877). Frances Newton Thorpe, ed., Federal & State Constitutions, Colonial Charters, & Other Organic Laws of the States, Territories, & Colonies now or heretofore forming the United States, 7 vols. (Washington: Gov. Printing Office, 1905; 1909; St. Clair Shores, MI: Scholarly Press, 1968). Annals of America, 20 vols. (Chicago, IL: Encyclopedia Britannica, 1968), Vol. 2, p. 485.

[27] South Carolina, State of. 1778, Constitution, Article XXXVIII. Benjamin Franklin Morris, The Christian Life & Character of the Civil Institutions of the United States (Philadelphia, PA: L. Johnson & Co., 1863; George W. Childs, 1864), pp. 230-231. Frances Newton Thorpe, ed., Federal & State Constitutions, Colonial Charters, & Other Organic Laws of the States, Territories, & Colonies now or heretofore forming the United States, 7 vols. (Washington: Government Printing Office, 1905; 1909; St. Clair Shores, MI: Scholarly Press, 1968), Vol. V, p. 3264. Edwin S. Gaustad, Neither King nor Prelate-Religion & the New Nation 1776-1826 (Grand Rapids, MI: William B. Eerdmans Pub. Co., 1993), pp. 170-172. John J. McGrath, ed., Church & State in American Law: Cases & Materials (Milwaukee: The Bruce Pub. Co., 1962), p. 375. Anson Phelps Stokes & Leo Pfeffer, Church & State in the United States (NY: Harper & Row, 1950, revised edition, 1964), p. 79. South Carolina, State of. 1778, Constitution, Art. XII. The Constitutions of the Several Independent States of America (Boston: Norman & Bowen, 1785), S. Carolina, 1776, Sec. 13, p. 146.

[28] Massachusetts, State of. 1780, Constitution, Part I, Article II. The Constitutions of All the United States According to the Latest Amendments (Lexington, KY: Thomas T. Skillman, 1817), pp. 60, 62. Frances Newton Thorpe, ed., Federal & State Constitutions, Colonial Charters, & Other Organic Laws of the States, Territories, & Colonies now or heretofore forming the United States, 7 vols. (Washington: Gov. Printing Office, 1905; 1909; St. Clair Shores, MI: Scholarly Press, 1968), Vol. V, p. 38. Henry Steele Commager, ed., Documents of American History, 2 vols. (NY: F.S. Crofts & Co., 1934; Appleton-Century-Crofts, Inc., 1948, 6th edition, 1958; Englewood Cliffs, NJ: Prentice Hall, Inc., 9th edition, 1973), Vol. I, pp. 107-108. Annals of America, 20 vols. (Chicago, IL: Encyclopedia Britannica, 1968), Vol. I, pp. 322-333. Jacob C. Meyer, Church & State in Massachusetts from 1740-1833 (Cleveland: Western Reserve Press, 1930) pp. 234-235. Anson Phelps Stokes & Leo Pfeffer, Church & State in the United States (NY: Harper & Row, Pub., 1950, revised one-vol. ed., 1964), p. 77. The Constitutions of the Several Independent States of America (Philadelphia: Bailey, pub. by order of the U.S. Continental Congress, 1781, in the Evans Collection, #17390), p. 138.

[29] New Hampshire, State of. 1784, 1792, Constitution, in effect till 1877. Supreme Court Justice David Josiah Brewer, 1890-1910, The United States-Christian Nation (Philadelphia: The John C. Winston Co., 1905, Supreme Court Collection). The Constitutions of the Several Independent States of America, Pub. by Order of Congress (Boston: Norman & Bowen, 1785) p. 3-4. Frances Newton Thorpe, ed., Federal & State Constitutions, Colonial Charters, & Other Organic Laws of the States, Territories, & Colonies now or heretofore forming the United States, 7 vols. (Washington: Gov. Printing Office, 1905; 1909; St. Clair Shores, MI: Scholarly Press, 1968). Edwin S. Gaustad, Neither King nor Prelate-Religion & the New Nation, 1776-1826 (Grand Rapids, MI: Eerdmans Pub. Co., 1993), p. 166. New Hampshiire Constitution, June 2, 1784, Article I, Section VI, "Bill of Rights." The Constitutions of All the United States According to the Latest Amendments (Lexington, KY: Thomas T. Skillman, 1817), pp. 27, 29, 37, 38. The Constitutions of the United States of America with the Latest Amendments (Trenton: Moore & Lake, 1813), p. 37-38. Richard L. Perry, ed., Sources of Our Liberties-Documentary Origins of Individual Liberties in the United States Constitution & Bill of Rights (Chicago: American Bar Foundation, 1978; NY: 1952), p. 382.

[30] Vermont, State of. 1786, Constitution, Frame of Government, Section IX. Edwin Gaustad, Faith of Our Fathers (San Francisco: Harper & Row, 1987), p. 173-4. Anson Phelps Stokes, Church & State in the United States (NY: Harper & Brothers, 1950), Vol. I, p. 441. Frances Newton Thorpe, ed., Federal & State Constitutions, Colonial Charters, & Other Organic Laws of the States, Territories, & Colonies, 7 vols. (Wash.: Gov. Printing Office, 1905; 1909; St. Clair Shores, MI: Scholarly Press, 1968). Anson Phelp Stokes & Leo Pfeffer, Church & State in U.S., (NY: Harper & Bros, 1950), Vol. I, p. 441.

[31] Georgia, State of. 1777, Constitution, Arti. VI. Benjamin Franklin Morris, The Christian Life & Character of the Civil Institutions of the U.S. (Philadelphia, PA: L. Johnson & Co., 1863; George W. Childs, 1864), p. 235. Frances Newton Thorpe, ed., Federal & State Constitutions, Colonial Charters, & Other Organic Laws of the States, Territories, & Colonies, 7 vols. (Wash.: Gov. Printing Office, 1905; 1909; St. Clair Shores, MI: Scholarly Press, 1968).

[32] Jefferson, Thomas. Dec. 3, 1803, treaty with Kaskaskia Indians, 1806 with Wyandotte Indians, and 1807 Cherokee Indians. Daniel L. Driesbach, Real Threat & Mere Shadow: Religious Liberty & the First Amendment (Westchester, IL: Crossway Books, 1987), p. 127. Richard Peters, ed., The Public Statutes at Large of the United States of America (Boston: Charles C. Little & James Brown, 1846), A Treaty Between United States and Kaskaskia Tribe of Indians, 23 Dec. 1803, Art. III, Vol. VII, p. 78-9., Treaty with Wyandots, etc., 1805, Vol. VII, Art. IV, p. 88, Treaty with Cherokees, 1806, Vol.VII, Art,II, p. 102. Robert L. Cord, Separation of Church & State (NY: Lambeta Press, 1982), p. 39.

[33] Texas, Declaration of Independence. Mar. 2, 1836, General Convention, Town of Washington. Printed by Baker & Bordens, San Felipe de Austin. Historical Doc.s Co, (8 N. Preston St., Philadelphia, PA. 19104), 1977.

[34] Maryland, Toleration Act of. Apr. 21, 1649. W.H. Browne, ed., The Archives of Maryland, I:244ff. Henry Steele Commager, ed., Documents of American History, 2 vols. (NY: F.S. Crofts & Co., 1934; Appleton CenturyCrofts, Inc., 1948, 6th edition, 1958; Englewood Cliffs, NJ: Prentice Hall, Inc., 9th edition, 1973), Vol. I, p. 31. Lillian W. Kay, ed., The Ground on Which We Stand Basic Documents of American History (NY: Franklin Watts., Inc, 1969), (portions), pp. 45. Samuel Wilberforce, A History of the Protestant Episcopal Church in America (Oxford, London: 1853). Verna M. Hall, The Christian History of the American Revolution (San Francisco: Foundation for Christian Education, 1976), p. 159. "An Act concerning Religion" issued by Maryland Colonial Assembly. Anson Phelps Stokes & Leo Pfeffer, Church & State in U.S. (NY: Harper & Row, 1950, 1964), p. 12.

[35] Penn, William. The World Book Encyclopedia, 18 vols. (Chicago, IL: Field Enterprises, Inc., 1957; W.F. Quarrie & Co., 8 vols., 1917; World Book, Inc., 22 vols., 1989), Vol. 13, pp. 6181-6183, 6192-6195.

[36] Penn, William. Verna M. Hall, Christian History of the Constitution of the United States of America (San Francisco: Foundation for American

Christian Education, 1966), p. 262A. George Bancroft, Bancroft's History of the United States (Boston: Little, Brown & Co., 1859), Vol. II, p. 385. Mason Locke Weems, The Life of William Penn (Philadelphia: Uriah Hunt, 1836), p. 121

[37] Johnson, Samuel. 1763. James Boswell, Life of Johnson (1791, edited by G.B. Hill, revised by L.F. Powell, 1934). John Bartlett, Bartlett's Familiar Quotations (Boston: Little, Brown & Co., 1855, 1980), p. 354.

[38] Washington, George. Aug. 15, 1787, to the Marquis de Lafayette. Jared Sparks, ed., The Writings of George Washington 12 vols. (Boston: American Stationer's Co., 1837; NY: F. Andrew's, 1834-1847), Vol. IX, p. 262. William J. Johnson, George Washington The Christian (St. Paul, MN: William J. Johnson, Merriam Park, Feb. 23, 1919; Nashville, TN: Abingdon Press, 1919; reprinted Milford, MI: Mott Media, 1976; reprinted Arlington Heights, IL: Christian Liberty Press, 502 W. Euclid Ave., Arlington Heights, IL, 60004, 1992), pp. 153154.

[39] John Carroll Univ., 20700 North Park Blvd, University Heights, OH 44118, (216) 397-1886. jcu.edu/library/johncarr/jced.htm

[40] Washington, George. Mar. 15, 1790, addressing Roman Catholic Churches in America. William Barclay Allen, ed., George Washington A Collection (Indianapolis: Liberty Classics, Liberty Fund, Inc., 7440 N. Shadeland, Indianapolis, IN 46250, 1988; from The Writings of George Washington original manuscripts, 1745-99/John Clement Fitzpatrick, ed.), pp. 546-7. John Clement Fitzpatrick, ed., The Writings of George Washington, 1749-99, 39 vols. (Wash., D.C.: U.S. Gov. Printing Office, 1931-44).

[41] Washington, George. May 26, 1787, diary entry. William S. Baker, Washington after the Revolution, 1784-1799 (1897), p. 77. William J. Johnson, George Washington-The Christian (St. Paul, MN: William J. Johnson, Merriam Park, Feb. 23, 1919; Nashville, TN: Abingdon Press, 1919; reprinted Milford, MI: Mott Media, 1976; reprinted Arlington Heights, IL: Christian Liberty Press, 502 W. Euclid Ave., Arlington Heights, IL, 60004, 1992), p. 152.

[42] Adams, John. Jan. 21, 1810, to Dr. Benjamin Rush. Norman Cousins, In God We Trust-The Religious Beliefs & Ideas of the American Founding Fathers (NY: Harper & Brothers, 1958), p. 101.

[43] Jefferson, Thomas. Sept. 26, 1814, to Miles King. Compiled for Senator A. Willis Robertson, Letters of Thomas Jefferson on Religion (Williamsburg, VA: The Williamsburg Foundation, Apr. 27, 1960).

[44] Carroll, Charles. Oct. 9, 1827, to Rev. John Stanford. Kate Mason Rowland, The Life of Charles Carroll of Carrollton, 1737-1832, With His Correspondence & Public Papers (NY: G.P. Putnam's Sons, 1898), Vol. II, p. 357-8.

[45] Carroll, Charles. November 4, 1800, to James McHenry. Bernard C. Steiner, The Life & Correspondence of James McHenry (Cleveland: The Burrows Brothers, 1907), 475.

[46] U.S. Congress. Mar. 27, 1854, Mr. Meacham giving report of House Committee on Judiciary. Reports of Committees of House of Representatives made during 1st Session, 33rd Congress (Washington: A.O.P. Nicholson, 1854), pp. 1, 6, 8-9. Benjamin Franklin Morris, The Christian Life & Character of the Civil Institutions of the United States (Philadelphia, PA: L. Johnson & Co., entered, according to Act of Congress, in Clerk's Office of U.S. District Court for E. Dist. PA., 1863; George W. Childs, 1864), pp. 317-324.

[47] Jefferson, Thomas. Dec. 3, 1803, Kaskaskia Indian Treaty, Wyandotte Indians, 1806, and Cherokee Indians, 1807. Costanzo, Federal Aid to Education & Religious Liberty, 36 U. of Det. L.J., 1, 15 (1958). Charles E. Rice, The Supreme Court & Public Prayer (NY: Fordham Univ. Press, 1964), p. 64. Daniel L. Driesbach, Real Threat & Mere Shadow: Religious Liberty & the First Amendment (Westchester, IL: Crossway Books, 1987), p. 127. Richard Peters, ed., Public Statutes at Large of the United States of America (Boston: Charles C. Little & James Brown, 1846), A Treaty Between the United States and the Kaskaskia Tribe of Indians, 23 Dec. 1803, Art. III, Vol. VII, pp. 78-79., Treaty with the Wyandots, etc., 1805, Vol. VII, Art. IV, p. 88, Treaty with the Cherokees, 1806, vol.VII, Art. II, p. 102. Robert L. Cord, Separation of Church & State (NY: Lambeta Press, 1982), p. 39. "A Treaty Between the United States of America and the Kaskaskian Tribe of Indians." 7 Stat. 78-9 (1846). Daniel L. Driesbach, Real Threat & Mere Shadow-Religious Liberty & the First Amendment (Westchester, IL: Crossway Books, 1987), p. 127.

[48] Jackson, Andrew. Mar. 25, 1835, in a letter. Robert V. Remini, Andrew Jackson & the Course of American Freedom, 1822-1832 (NY: Harper & Row, 1981), Vol. 2, p. 251.

[49] Hayes, Rutherford Birchard. In his diary. Edmund Fuller & David E. Green, God in the White House-The Faiths of American Presidents (NY: Crown Pub., Inc., 1968), p. 137.

[50] Cleveland, (Stephen) Grover. Nov. 14, 1896, Proclamation. James D. Richardson (U.S. Rep.-TN), ed., A Compilation of the Messages & Papers of the Presidents 1789-1897, 10 vols. (Wash., D.C.: U.S. Gov. Printing Office, pub. by Authority of Congress, 1897, 1899; Wash, D.C.: Bureau of National Literature & Art, 1789-1902, 11 vols., 1907, 1910), Vol. IX, pp. 696-7.

[51] Roosevelt, Theodore. Dec. 5, 1905, Fifth Annual Message to Congress. A Compilation of the Messages & Papers of the Presidents 20 vols. (NY: Bureau of National Literature, Inc., prepared under the direction of the Joint Committee on Printing, of the House & Senate, 1893, 1923), Vol. XIV, pp. 6973, 6975-6, 6980, 6984-6, 6992-4, 7003, 7008, 7015-6.

[52] Smith, Alfred E. May 1927. Alfred E. Smith, Atlantic Monthly, May 1927. Annals of America, 20 vols. (Chicago, IL: Encyclopedia Britannica, 1968), Vol. 14, p. 536. The National Experience, (second edition), p. 655.

[53] Pennsylvania State Court. 1894, Hysong v. School Dist. Gallitzin Borough, 164 Pa. St. 629, 30 A. 482 (1894), p. 483.

[54] Roosevelt, Theodore. Dec. 5, 1905, in his 5th Annual Message. A Compilation of the Messages & Papers of the Presidents 20 vols. (NY: Bureau of National Literature, Inc., prepared under the direction of the Joint Committee on Printing, of the House & Senate, 1893, 1923), Vol. XIV, pp. 6973, 6975-6, 6980, 6984-6, 6992-4, 7003, 7008, 7015-6.

[55] Johnson, Lyndon Baines. Nov. 22, 1963, approx. 2:40 p.m. CST, repeated oath of office, administered by Judge Sarah Hughes,, stateroom, Air Force One, Love Field, Dallas, TX, after President John F. Kennedy was assassinated a few hours prior. Lyndon Baines Johnson, The Vantage Point-Perspectives of the Presidency 1963-69 (NY: Holt, Rinehart & Winston, 1971), p. 15.

[56] Grund, Francis J. 1837. Francis J. Grund, The Americans in Their Moral, Social & Political Relations, (1837), Vol. I, pp. 281, 292, 294. Anson Phelps Stokes & Leo Pfeffer, Church & State in the United States (NY: Harper & Row, Pub., 1950, 1964), p. 210.

[57] Tocqueville, Alexis de. The Republic of the United States of America & Its Political Institutions, Rvd & Exmd, 2 vols. (NY: Alfred A. Knopf, 1945), Vol. I, p. 303. Alexis de Tocqueville, Democracy in America (NY: Vintage Books, 1945), Vol. I, pp. 314-315.

[58] Beaumont, Gustave de. 1835, in his work titled, Marie ou l'Esclavage aux E'tas-Unis (Paris: 1835), Vol. II, pp. 183. Annals of America, 20 vols. (Chicago, IL: Encyclopedia Britannica, 1968), Vol. 6, p. 150.

[59] Jefferson, Thomas. Mar. 4, 1801, *Inaugural Address*, Public Papers of the Presidents.

[60] Tocqueville, Alexis de. Alexis de Tocqueville, The Republic of the United states of America & Its Political Institutions, Reviewed & Examined, Henry Reeves, trans., (Garden City, NY: A.S. Barnes & Co., 1851), Vol. I, p. 334.

[61] Lincoln, Abraham. Mar. 5, 1865, *Inaugural Address*, Public Papers of the Presidents.

[62] U.S. Congress. Mar. 27, 1854, Mr. Meacham giving report of House Committee on Judiciary. Reports of Committees of House of Representatives made during 1st Session, 33rd Congress (Washington: A.O.P. Nicholson, 1854), pp. 1, 6, 89. Benjamin Franklin Morris, The Christian Life & Character of the Civil Institutions of the United States (Philadelphia, PA: L. Johnson & Co., entered, according to Act of Congress, in Clerk's Office of U.S. District Court for E. Dist. PA, 1863; George W. Childs, 1864), p. 317-24.

[63,64,65] Adams, John Quincy. Dec. 24, 1814, in writing from London to Boston, after negotiating the Treaty of Ghent. Adams, Writings, Vol. VI, p. 329. Worthington Chauncey Ford, ed., Writings of John Quincy Adams (NY: Macmillan, 1915, 1916), Vol. 5, pp. 362, 431-3, Vol. 6, p. 135-6.

[66] Adams, John Quincy. In writing of Ralph Waldo Emerson. Edmund Fuller & David E. Green, God in the White House-The Faiths of American Presidents (NY: Crown Pub., Inc., 1968), p. 59.

[67] Rousseau, Jean Jacques. Emilius & Sophia (English Ed. 1767), Vol. III, Book IV, pp. 136-139. Stephen Abbott Northrop, D.D., A Cloud of Witnesses (Portland, OR: American Heritage Min., 1987; Mantle Ministries, 228 Still Ridge, Bulverde, TX), p. 385-6. Frank Ballard, The Miracles of Unbelief (Edinburgh: T & T Lark), p. 251. Tryon Edwards, D.D., The New Dictionary of Thoughts-A Cyclopedia of Quotations (Garden City, NY: Hanover House, 1852; revised by C.H. Catrevas, Ralph Emerson Browns & Jonathan Edwards, 1891; The Standard Book Co., 1955, 1963), p. 47.

[68] Madison, James. 1823, in a letter to Edward Everett. Gaillard Hunt, ed., Writings of James Madison, comprising his public papers and his private correspondence, for the first time printed, 9 vols. (NY: G.P. Putnam's Sons, 1900-1910), Vol. IX, pp. 24-30. Henry Steele Commager, ed., Freedom of Religion & Separation of Church and State (Mount Vernon, NY: A. Colish, Inc., 1985), p. 30.

[69] Washington, George. Aug. 19, 1789, to General Convention of Bishops, Clergy & the Laity of the Protestant Episcopal Church of NY, NJ, PA, Del, MD, VA & NC. Jared Sparks, ed., The Writings of George Washington 12 vols. (Boston: American Stationer's Co., 1837; NY: F. Andrew's, 1834-47), Vol. XII, pp. 162-3.

[70] Tocqueville, Alexis de. 1835, 1840. Alexis de Tocqueville, The Republic of the United States & Its Political Institutions, Reviewed & Examined, Henry Reeves, translator (Garden City, NY: A.S. Barnes & Co., 1851), Vol. I, p. 331-332. Alexis de Tocqueville, Democracy in America, 2 vols. (NY: Alfred A. Knopf, 1945), Vol. I, p. 303.

[71] Tocqueville, Alexis de. Statement. Democracy in America, Henry Reeve, translator, Francis Bowen ed., (Cambridge: 2nd edition, 1876). Alexis de Tocqueville, Democracy in America, George Lawrence, translator, (NY: Harper & Row, 1988) p. 291.

[72] Tocqueville, Alexis de. Democracy in America (NY: Vintage Books, 1945), Vol. I, p. 314-315. Alexis de Tocqueville, The Republic of the United States of America & Its Pol. Inst.s, Henry Reeves, trans., (Garden City, NY: A.S. Barnes & Co., 1851), Vol. I, p. 333.

[73,74] Brewer, David Josiah. 1905, in his work titled, The United States-A Christian Nation (Philadelphia, PA: John C. Winston Co., 1905, Supreme Court Collection), pp. 11-12, 31-32.

[75] *Cambridge Platform of the Massachusetts Bay Colony*, 1648, recorded in the *Plymouth Colony Records IX*, 1663, listed the proposal of William Vassall & others: CHAP: XVII: Of Civil Magistrates In Matters Ecclesiastical.

[76] Massachusetts, State of. 1780, Constitution, qualifications for the office of governor. Frances Newton Thorpe, ed., Federal & State Constitutions, Colonial Charters, & Other Organic Laws of the States, Territories, & Colonies now or heretofore forming the United States, 7 vols. (Wash.: Gov. Printing Office, 1905; 1909; St. Clair Shores, MI: Scholarly Press, 1968), Vol. III, pp. 1900, 1908.

[77] Massachusetts, State of. 1780, Constitution, Chapter VI, Article I. A Constitution or Frame of Government Agreed Upon By the Delegates of State of Massachusetts-Bay (Boston: Benjamin Edes & Sons, 1780), p. 44. Constitutions of All United States According to Latest Amendments (Lexington, KY: Thomas T. Skillman, 1817), p. 89.

[78] Massachusetts, State of. 1780, Massachusetts Constitution, Part I, Article III, "Declaration of Rights." A Constitution or Frame of Government Agreed Upon By the Delegates of the People of the State of Massachusetts-Bay (Boston: Benjamin Edes & Sons, 1780), pp. 7-8. The Constitutions of the Several Independent States of America (Philadelphia: Bailey, pub. by order of the U.S. Continental Congress, 1781, in the Evans Collection, #17390), p. 138. The Constitutions of All the United States According to the Latest Amendments (Lexington, KY: Thomas T. Skillman, 1817), pp. 60-62. Benjamin Franklin Morris, The Christian Life & Character of the Civil Institutions of the United States (Philadelphia, PA: L. Johnson & Co., 1863; George W. Childs, 1864), p. 229. Frances Newton Thorpe, ed., Federal & State Constitutions, Colonial Charters, & Other Organic Laws of the States, Territories, & Colonies now or heretofore forming the United States, 7 vols. (Washington: Government Printing Office, 1905; 1909; St. Clair Shores, MI: Scholarly Press, 1968), Vol. V, p. 38. Henry Steele Commager, ed., Documents of American History, 2 vols. (NY: F.S. Crofts & Co., 1934; Appleton-Century-Crofts, Inc., 1948, 6th edition, 1958; Englewood Cliffs, NJ: Prentice Hall, Inc., 9th edition, 1973), Vol. I, pp. 107-108. Jacob C. Meyer, Church & State in Massachusetts from 1740-1833 (Cleveland: Western Reserve Press, 1930) pp. 234-235. Anson Phelps Stokes & Leo Pfeffer, Church & State in the United States (NY: Harper & Row; Pub., 1950, revised one-vol. edition, 1964), p. 77. Annals of America, 20 vols. (Chicago, IL: Encyclopedia Britannica, 1968), Vol. I, p. 322-3.

[79] Massachusetts, State of. Tim LaHaye, Faith of Our Founding Fathers (Brentwood, TN: Wolgemuth & Hyatt, 1987), p. 74.

[80] Maryland, State of. Aug. 14, 1776, Constitution, Article XXXV. The Constitutions of All the United States According to the Latest Amendments (Lexington, KY: Thomas T. Skillman, 1817), p. 188. Benjamin Franklin Morris, The Christian Life & Character of the Civil Institutions of the United States (Philadelphia, PA: L. Johnson & Co., 1863; George W. Childs, 1864), p. 233. Frances Newton Thorpe, ed., Federal & State Constitutions, Colonial Charters, & Other Organic Laws of the States, Territories, & Colonies now or heretofore forming the United States, 7 vols. (Washington: Government Printing Office, 1905; 1909; St. Clair Shores, MI: Scholarly Press, 1968), Vol. III. Federal & State Constitutions, Colonial Charters, & Other Organic Laws of the States, Territories, & Colonies now or heretofore forming the United States, 7 vols. (Washington: Government Printing Office, 1909).

[81] Maryland, State of. 1776, Constitution, Article XIX, XXXIII. Benjamin Franklin Morris, The Christian Life & Character of the Civil Institutions of the United States (Philadelphia, PA: L. Johnson & Co., 1863; George W. Childs, 1864), p. 234. Frances Newton Thorpe, ed., Federal & State Constitutions, Colonial Charters, & Other Organic Laws of the States, Territories, & Colonies now or heretofore forming the United States, 7 vols. (Wash.: Gov. Printing Office, 1905; 1909; St. Clair Shores, MI: Scholarly Press, 1968).

[82] South Carolina, State of. 1778, Constitution, Article XXXVIII. The Constitutions of the Several Independent States of America, Pub. by Order of Congress (Boston: Norman & Bowen, 1785) p. 152.

[83] Virginia, State of. July 12, 1776; 1830; 1851; 1868; 1902; 1928, Constitution, Bill of Rights, Article I, Section 16. Frances Newton Thorpe, ed., Federal & State Constitutions, Colonial Charters, & Other Organic Laws of the States, Territories, & Colonies now or heretofore forming the United States, 7 vols. (Washington: Government Printing Office, 1905; 1909; St. Clair Shores, MI: Scholarly Press, 1968), Vol. VII, p. 3814. Benjamin Franklin Morris, The Christian Life & Character of the Civil Institutions of the United States (Philadelphia, PA: L. Johnson & Co., 1863; George W. Childs, 1864), p. 232. Henry Steele Commager, ed., Documents of American History, 2 vols. (NY: F.S. Crofts & Co., 1934; Appleton-Century-Crofts, Inc., 1948, 6th edition, 1958; Englewood Cliffs, NJ: Prentice Hall, Inc., 9th edition, 1973), pp. 103-104. Charles Fadiman, ed., The American Treasury (NY: Harper & Brothers, Pub., 1955), p. 121. Charles E. Rice, The Supreme Court & Public Prayer (NY: Fordham Univ. Press, 1964), pp. 175-176; "Hearings, Prayers in Public Schools & Other Matters," Committee on the Judiciary, U.S. Senate (87th Cong, 2nd Sess.), 1962, pp. 268 et seq. Annals of America, 20 vols. (Chicago, IL: Encyclopedia Britannica, 1968), Vol. 2, p. 433.

[84] North Carolina, State of. 1835, Constitution, Amendments to the North Carolina Constitution of 1776, Article IV, Section 2. The Constitutions of the Several States Composing the Union (Philadelphia: Hogan & Thompson, 1838), p. 202. Supreme Court Justice David Josiah Brewer, who served 1890-1910, in his work, The United States-Christian Nation (Philadelphia: John C. Winston Co., 1905, Supreme Court Collection). North Carolina, State of. 1776, Constitution, Article XXXII. The Constitutions of the Several Independent States of America, Pub. by Order of Congress (Boston: Norman & Bowen, 1785) p. 138. The Constitutions of All the United States According to the Latest Amendments (Lexington, KY: Thomas T. Skillman, 1817), p. 224. Benjamin Franklin Morris, The Christian Life & Character of the Civil Institutions of the United States (Philadelphia, PA: L. Johnson & Co., 1863; George W. Childs, 1864), p. 233. Frances Newton Thorpe, ed., Federal & State Constitutions, Colonial Charters, & Other Organic Laws of the States, Territories, & Colonies now or heretofore forming the United States, 7 vols. (Washington: Government Printing Office, 1905; 1909; St. Clair Shores, MI: Scholarly Press, 1968).

[85] Rhode Island & Providence Plantations, State of. July 8, 1663, Constitution & Charter, granted by King Charles II, in the 14th year of his reign, to Roger Williams, confirming the colonial patent of 1644; & continuing in effect until 1843. Benjamin Franklin Morris The Christian Life & Character of the Civil Institutions of the United States (Philadelphia, PA: L. Johnson & Co., 1863; George W. Childs, 1864), p. 236.

[86] Delaware, State of. 1776, Constitution, Article XXII, oath of office authored by George Read & Thomas McKean; until 1792. Constitutions of the Several Independent States of America, Pub. by Order of Congress (Boston: Norman & Bowen, 1785), pp. 99-100. Church of the Holy Trinity v. U.S. 143 US 457, 469-470 (1892). Benjamin Franklin Morris, The Christian Life & Character of the Civil Institutions of U.S. (Philadelphia, PA: L. Johnson., 1863; George W. Childs, 1864), pp. 233-4. Frances Newton Thorpe, ed., Federal & State Constitutions, Colonial Charters, & Other Organic Laws of the States, Territories, & Colonies now or heretofore forming U.S., 7 vols. (Wash.: Gov. Printing Office, 1905; 1909; St. Clair Shores, MI: Scholarly Press, 1968), Vol. I, p. 142.

[87] Pennsylvania, State of. 1776, Constitution, Frame of Government, Chapter 2, Section 10. The Constitutions of the Several Independent States of America (Boston: Norman & Bowen, 1785), p. 81. S.E. Morison, ed., Sources & Documents Illustrating the American Revolution 1764-1788 & the Formation of the Federal Constitution (NY: Oxford Univ. Press, 1923), p. 166. Benjamin Franklin Morris, The Christian Life & Character of the Civil Institutions of the United States (Philadelphia, PA: L. Johnson & Co., 1863; George W. Childs, 1864), p. 233.

[88] Adams, John. Mar. 4, 1797, *Inaugural Address*, Public Papers of the Presidents.

[89] Jefferson, Thomas. Apr. 21, 1803, to Benjamin Rush. William Linn, The Life of Thomas Jefferson (Ithaca, NY: Mack & Andrus, 1834), p. 265. Norman Cousins, In God We Trust-The Religious Beliefs & Ideas of American Founding Fathers (NY: Harper & Brothers, 1958), p. 170-1. Albert Ellery Bergh, ed., Writings of Thomas Jefferson (Wash., D.C.: Jefferson Mem. Ass., 1904), Vol. X, p. 380. Compiled for Sen. A. W. Robertson, Letters of Thomas Jefferson on Religion (Williamsburg, VA: Williamsburg Fnd, 1960).

[90] Adams, John Quincy. July 4, 1837, in his work titled, An Oration Delivered Before the Inhabitants of the Town of Newburyport at their Request on the 61st Anniversary of the Declaration of Independence (Newburyport: Charles Whipple, 1837), pp. 5-6.

[91] Harrison, William Henry. Mar. 4, 1841, *Inaugural Address*, Public Papers of the Presidents.

[92] Tyler, John. Apr. 13, 1841, in his first *Proclamation*, Public Papers of the Presidents

[93] Buchanan, James. Mar. 4, 1857, *Inaugural Address*, Public Papers of the Presidents.

[94] Lincoln, Abraham. Mar. 4, 1861, *Inaugural Address*, Public Papers of the Presidents.

[95] Johnson, Andrew. Apr. 29, 1865, regarding his first *Proclamation*, Public Papers of the Presidents.

[96] Roosevelt, Theodore. Sept. 14, 1901, in his first Proclamation, Public Papers of the Presidents.

[97] Coolidge, Calvin. May 31, 1923, Memorial Day, as Vice-President under President Harding, in his message titled "The Destiny of America." Calvin Coolidge, The Price of Freedom-Speeches & Addresses (NY: Charles Scribner's Sons, 1924), pp. 331-353. Annals of America, 20 vols. (Chicago, IL: Encyclopedia Britannica, 1968, 1977), Vol. XIV, pp. 410-4.

[98] Coolidge, Calvin. Mar. 4, 1925:, *Inaugural Address*, Public Papers of the Presidents.

[99] Maryland Supreme Court. 1799, Runkel v. Winemiller, 4 Harris & McHenry 276, 288 (Sup. Ct. Md. 1799). Runkel v. Winemiller, 4 Harris & McHenry (MD) 429 1 AD 411, 417, (Justice Chase).

[100] Massachusetts, Grand Jury of. 1802, appointed by Judge Nathaniel Freeman. "Our Christian Heritage," Letter from Plymouth Rock (Marlborough, NH: The Plymouth Rock Foundation), pp. 4-5.

[101] Kent, James. 1811, decision of Supreme Court of New York, People v. Ruggles, 8 Johns 545 (1811). James Kent, Commentaries on American Law (Boston: Little, Brown, 1826-1830, 1858), Vol. 2, pp. 35-36. (Emphasis original). Perry Miller, The Life of the Mind in America (London: Victor Gallanz, 1966), p. 66.

[102] Kent, James. 1811, opinion as Chief Justice of New York Supreme Court, People v. Ruggles, 8 Johns 545-547; cited by U.S. Supreme Court in Church of the Holy Trinity v. U.S., 143 US 457, 458, 465-471, 36 L ed 226, (1892), Justice David Josiah Brewer. James Kent, Commentaries on American Law (Boston: Little, Brown, 1826-1830, 1858), Vol. 2, pp. 35-36. Charles B. Galloway, Christianity & the American Commonwealth (Nashville, TN: Methodist Episcopal Church Pub. House, 1898), p. 169-70.

[103] Pennsylvania Supreme Court. 1824. Updegraph v. The Commonwealth, 11 Serg & Rawle, 393-394, 398-399, 400-401, 402-407; 5 Binn. R. 555; of New York, 8 Johns. R. 291; of Connecticut, 2 Swift's System. 321; of Massachusetts, Dane's Ab. vol. 7, c. 219, a. 2, 19. Church of the Holy

Trinity v. U.S., 143 US 457, 458, 465-471, 36 L ed 226, Justice David Josiah Brewer. Vide Cooper on the Law of Libel, 59 & 114, et seq.; & generally, 1 Russ. on Cr. 217; 1 Hawk, c. 5; 1 Vent. 293; 3 Keb. 607; 1 Barn. & Cress. 26. S. C. 8 Eng. Com. Law R. 14; Barnard. 162; Fitsgib. 66; Roscoe, Cr. Ev. 524; 2 Str. 834; 3 Barn. & Ald. 161; S. C. 5 Eng Com. Law R. 249 Jeff. Rep. Appx. See 1 Cro. Jac. 421 Vent. 293; 3 Keb. 607; Cooke on Def. 74; 2 How. S. C. 11-ep. 127, 197-201.

[104,105,106] Massachusetts Supreme Court. 1838. Commonwealth v. Abner Kneeland, 37 Mass. (20 Pick) 206, 216-217, 233-234.

[107,108] U.S. Supreme Court. 1844, Vidal v. Girard's Executors, 43 U.S. 126-143, 152-153, 170-175 (1844), pp. 198, 205-206.

[109] U.S. Supreme Court. Feb. 29, 1892, decided; Jan. 7, 1892, submitted. Justice David Josiah Brewer, Church of the Holy Trinity v. United States, 143 US 457-458, 465-471, 36 L ed 226. Cooley (Constitutional Limitations, 8th Ed., Vol. Two, p. 966, 974),

[110] Minnesota State Court. 1927, Kaplan v. Independent School Dist. of Virginia, 214 N.W. 18 (Minn. 1927), pp. 18 20.

[111] U.S. Supreme Court. 1948, Justice Frankfurter, McCollum v. Board of Ed. School District Number 71, 333 U.S. 203, 206 , 236.

[112] U.S. Congress. Mar. 27, 1854, Mr. Meacham's report of House Committee on Judiciary. Reports of Committees of House of Representatives, 1st Session, 33rd Congress (Wash.: A.O.P. Nicholson, 1854), pp. 1, 6, 89. Benjamin Franklin Morris, The Christian Life & Character of the Civil Institutions of the United States (Philadelphia, PA: L. Johnson & Co., Clerk's Office, U.S. District Court for Eastern Dist. of PA, 1863; George W. Childs, 1864), p. 317-24.

[113] U.S. Congress. Jan. 19, 1853, Mr. Badger giving report of Congressional investigations in U.S. Senate. Reports of Committees of U.S. Senate, 2nd Session, 32nd Congress, 1852-53 (Washington: Robert Armstrong, 1853), pp. 1, 6, 8-9. Benjamin Franklin Morris, The Christian Life & Character of the Civil Institutions of the United States (Philadelphia: George W. Childs, 1864), pp. 324-327.

[114] William M. Mallory, Treaties, Conventions, International Acts, Protocols and Agreements between the U.S. and Other Powers, 1776-1909, 4 vols. (NY: Greenwood Press, 1910, 1968) 2:1786. Gary DeMar, America's Christian History: The Untold Story (Atlanta, GA: American Vision, Inc., 1996) p. 131.

[115] September 3, 1783, Treaty of Paris ending War with Great Britain; ratified Congress January 14, 1784, under the Articles of Confederation. William M. Malloy, compiler, Treaties, Conventions, International Acts, Protocols and Agreements between the United States of America and Other Powers, 1776-1909, 4 vols. (New York: Greenwood Press, 1910, 1968), 2:1786.

[116] Richard Peters, ed., The Public Statutes at Large of the United States of America (Boston: Charles C. Little and James Brown, 1846), A Treaty Between the United States and the Kaskaskia Tribe of Indians, 23 December 1803, Art. III, Vol. VII, pp. 78-79., Treaty with the Wyandots, etc., 1805, Vol. VII, Art. IV, p. 88, Treaty with the Cherokees, 1806, Vol. VII, Art,II, p. 102. Robert L. Cord, Separation of Church and State (NY: Lambeta Press, 1982), p. 39.

[117] Jefferson, Thomas. December 3, 1803, Treaty with the Kaskaskia Indians, 1806 with the Wyandotte Indians, and 1807 Cherokee Indians. Richard Peters, ed., The Public Statutes at Large of the United States of America (Boston: Charles C. Little and James Brown, 1846), Art. III, Vol. VII, pp. 78-79, Treaty with the Wyandots, etc., 1805, Vol. VII, Art. IV, p. 88, Treaty with the Cherokees, 1806, vol.VII, Art. II, p. 102. Costanzo, Federal Aid to Education and Religious Liberty, 36 U. of Det. L.J., 1, 15 (1958). Charles E. Rice, The Supreme Court and Public Prayer (New York: Fordham University Press, 1964), p. 64. Robert L. Cord, Separation of Church and State (NY: Lambeta Press, 1982), p. 39. Daniel L. Driesbach, Real Threat and Mere Shadow: Religious Liberty and the First Amendment (Westchester, IL: Crossway Books, 1987), p. 127.

[118] U.S. Congress. 1822, both the House and Senate of the United States, along with Great Britain and Ireland, ratified the Convention for Indemnity under Award of Emperor of Russia as to the True Construction of the First Article of the Treaty of December 24, 1814. William M. Malloy, compiler, Treaties, Conventions, International Acts, Protocols and Agreements between the United States of America and Other Powers 1776-1909, 4 vols. (New York: Greenwood Press, 1910, 1968), 1:634.

[119] Jackson, Andrew. January 20, 1830, in a message to Congress. James D. Richardson (U.S. Representative from Tennessee), ed., A Compilation of the Messages and Papers of the Presidents 1789-1897, 10 vols. (Washington, D.C.: U.S. Government Printing Office, 1897, 1899; Wash, D.C.: Bureau of National Literature and Art, 1789-1902, 11 vols., 1907, 1910), Vol. II, p. 468.

[120] Jackson, Andrew. December 6, 1830, in his Second Annual Message to Congress. James D. Richardson (U.S. Representative from Tennessee), ed., A Compilation of the Messages and Papers of the Presidents 1789-1897, 10 vols. (Washington, D.C.: U.S. Government Printing Office, published by Authority of Congress, 1897, 1899; Washington, D.C.: Bureau of National Literature and Art, 1789-1902, 11 vols., 1907, 1910), Vol. II, pp. 500-501, 505, 520, 529.

[121] Jackson, Andrew. December 6, 1831, in his Third Annual Message to Congress. James D. Richardson (U.S. Representative from Tennessee), ed., A Compilation of the Messages and Papers of the Presidents 1789-1897, 10 vols. (Washington, D.C.: U.S. Government Printing Office, published by Authority of Congress, 1897, 1899; Washington, D.C.: Bureau of National Literature and Art, 1789-1902, 11 vols., 1907, 1910), Vol. II, pp. 544-549, 555-8.

[122] U.S. Congress. 1848, Peace Treaty with Mexico which ended the Mexican War; concluded at Guadalupe Hidalgo, February 2, 1848; ratified with amendments by U.S. Senate, March 10, 1848; ratified by President, March 16, 1848; ratifications exchanged at Queretaro, May 30, 1848; proclaimed July 4, 1848. Charles W. Eliot, LL.D., ed., American Historical Documents 1000-1904 (New York: P.F. Collier & Son Company, The Harvard Classics, 1910), Vol. 43, pp. 309-326.

[123] Lincoln, Abraham. December 3, 1863, in his Third Annual Message. James D. Richardson (U.S. Representative from Tennessee), ed., A Compilation of the Messages and Papers of the Presidents 1789-1897, 10 vols. (Wash., D.C.: U.S. Gov. Printing Office, 1897, 1899; Wash., D.C.: Bureau of National Literature and Art, 1789-1902, 11 vols., 1907, 1910), Vol. VI, pp. 179, 187.

[124] Cleveland, (Stephen) Grover. December 2, 1895, in his Third Annual Message to Congress. James D. Richardson (U.S. Representative from Tennessee), ed., A Compilation of the Messages and Papers of the Presidents 1789-1897, 10 vols. (Washington, D.C.: U.S. Government Printing Office, published by Authority of Congress, 1897, 1899; Washington, D.C.: Bureau of National Literature and Art, 1789-1902, 11 vols., 1907, 1910), Vol. IX, pp. 635, 637-638.

[125] Wilson, (Thomas) Woodrow. July 10, 1919, in an address to the Senate regarding the Treaty of Peace with Germany which was signed at Versailles, France, June 28, 1919. A Compilation of the Messages and Papers of the Presidents 20 vols. (New York: Bureau of National Literature, Inc., prepared under the direction of the Joint Committee on Printing, of the House and Senate, pursuant to an Act of the 52nd Congress of the United States, 1893, 1923), Vol. XVII, p. 8737.

[126] Harding, Warren Gamaliel. December 23, 1921, in a statement issued from the White House expressing his support of the American delegation at the Conference drawing up the Four-Power Treaty. A Compilation of the Messages and Papers of the Presidents 20 vols. (New York: Bureau of National Literature, Inc., prepared under the direction of the Joint Committee on Printing, of the House and Senate, pursuant to an Act of the 52nd Congress of the United States, 1893, 1923), Vol. XVIII, p. 9059.

[127] Mother Teresa of Calcutta. Bless Your Heart (series II) (Eden Prairie, MN: Heartland Sampler, Inc., 1990), 10.15.

[128] South Carolina Supreme Court. 1846, City of Charleston v. S.A. Benjamin, 2 Strob. 521-524 (1846).

[129,130] Madison, James. June 20, 1785. James Madison, Memorial & Remonstrance (Wash, D.C.: Library of Congress, Rare Book Collection, delivered to General Assembly of State of Virginia, 1785; Massachusetts: Isaiah Thomas, 1786), (Boston: Lincoln & Edmands, 1819), p. 7. Norman Cousins, "In God We Trust" (NY: Harper & Bros, 1958), p. 309.

[131] Williams, Roger. 1644, *Plea for Religious Liberty*. Roger Williams, *The Bloudy Tenent of Persecution* ("Publications of the Narragansett Club" [Providence, R.I.], Vol. III [1867]), pp. 3-4, 63, 58-9, 138-39, 148, 170-71, 201, 247-50, 372-73, 424-25.

[132] Madison, James. July 9, 1812, Proclamation of Day of Public Humiliation & Prayer. James D. Richardson, ed., A Compilation of the Messages & Papers of the Presidents 1789-1897, 10 vols. (Wash., D.C.: U.S. Gov. Printing Office; Wash., D.C.: Bureau of Nat. Literature & Art, 1789-1902, 11 vols., 1907-10), Vol. I, p. 513. Benjamin Franklin Morris, The Christian Life & Character of the Civil Institutions of the U.S. (Philadelphia: George W. Childs, 1864), p. 549.

[133] Morris, Gouverneur. 1785, in An Address on the Bank of North America given in the Pennsylvania State Assembly. Jared Sparks, ed., The Life of Gouverneur Morris, with Selections from His Correspondence and Miscellaneous Papers, 3 vols. (Boston: Gray and Bowen, 1832), Vol. III, p. 465. Stephen McDowell and Mark Beliles, "The Providential Perspective" (Charlottesville, VA: The Providence Foundation, P.O. Box 6759, Charlottesville, Va. 22906, January 1994), Vol. 9, No. 1, p. 5. John Eidsmoe, Christianity and The Constitution - The Faith of Our Founding Fathers (Baker Book House, 1987), pp. 183-84.

[134] Jackson, Andrew. December 8, 1831, in his Third Annual Message to Congress. James D. Richardson (U.S. Representative from Tennessee), ed., A Compilation of the Messages and Papers of the Presidents 1789-1897, 10 vols. (Washington, D.C.: U.S. Government Printing Office, published by Authority of Congress, 1897, 1899; Washington, D.C.: Bureau of National Literature and Art, 1789-1902, 11 vols., 1907, 1910), Vol. II, pp. 544-549, 555-558.

[135] Adams, Samuel. Nov. 20, 1772, report for the Committees of Correspondence, titled, *The Rights of the Colonists*, in the section: "The Rights of the Colonist as Men." Old South Leaflets. David C. Whitney, Signers of the Declaration of Independence Founders of Freedom (1964), p. 49. Annals of America, 20 vols. (Chicago, IL: Encyclopedia Britannica, 1968), Vol. 2, p. 217. Lucille Johnston, Celebrations of a Nation (Arlington, VA: The Year of Thanksgiving Foundation, 1987), p. 79.

[136] Mason, George. June 12, 1776, Virginia Bill of Rights, Article XVI. Frances Newton Thorpe, ed., Federal & State Constitutions, Colonial Charters, & Other Organic Laws of the States, Territories, & Colonies now or heretofore forming the United States, 7 vols. (Wash.: Gov. Printing Office, 1905-9; St. Clair Shores, MI: Scholarly Press, 1968), Vol. VII, p. 3814. Henry Steele Commager, ed., Documents of American History, 2 vols. (NY: F.S. Crofts & Co., 1934; Appleton Century Crofts, Inc., 1948, 6th ed., 1958; Englewood Cliffs, NJ: Prentice Hall, Inc., 9th ed., 1973), pp. 103-4. Anson Phelps Stokes & Leo Pfeffer, Church & State in United States (NY: Harper & Row, Pub., 1950, revised one vol ed, 1964), p. 42. Annals of America, 20 vols. (Chicago, IL: Encyclopedia Britannica, 1968), Vol. 2, p. 433. Charles Fadiman, ed., The American Treasury (NY: Harper & Brothers, Pub., 1955), p. 121.

[137] Henry, Patrick. William Wirt Henry (grandson of Patrick Henry), editor, Patrick Henry: Life, Correspondence & Speeches (NY: Charles Scribner's Sons, 1891), Vol. III, pp. 606-607.

[138] Henry, Patrick. Attributed. M.E. Bradford, The Trumpet Voice of Freedom: Patrick Henry of Virginia (Marlborough, NH: Plymouth Rock Foundation, 1991), p. iii. Steve C. Dawson, God's Providence in America's History (Rancho Cordova, CA: Steve C. Dawson, 1988), Vol. I, p. 5. "The Voice of America's Past," Torch (Dallas, TX: Texas Eagle Forum, Feb. 1994), Vol. 1, No. 7, p. 5. John Eidsmoe, "Institute on the Constitution" tape series, Lecture #3 (Pub. by Virginia Freeman Pub., Stuarts Draft, VA). D. James Kennedy & Jerry Newcombe, What if Jesus had never been born? (Nashville, TN: Thomas Nelson Inc., 1994), p. 67. Billy Falling, The Political Mission of the Church (Valley Center, CA: Billy Falling Pub., 1990), p. 43.

[139] Madison, James. July 23, 1813, Proclamation of a National Day of Public Humiliation & Prayer. James D. Richardson (U.S. Rep.-TN), ed., A Compilation of the Messages & Papers of the Presidents 1789-1897, 10 vols. (Washington, D.C.: U.S. Gov. Printing Office, 1897, 1899; Wash., D.C.: Bureau of National Literature & Art, 1789-1902, 11 vols., 1907, 1910), Vol. I, pp. 532-3.

[140] Jefferson, Thomas. July 4, 1826, epitaph inscribed on his tombstone, which he authored himself.

[141] Jefferson, Thomas. Jan. 16, 1786, bill written by the Committee on Religion, Virginia Assembly; inscribed on the Jefferson Memorial, Washington D.C. H.A. Washington, ed., The Writings of Thomas Jefferson Being His Autobiography, Correspondence, Reports, Messages, Addresses, & Other Writings, Official & Private, 9 vols. (Jackson: 1859); (Washington: 1853-54); (Philadelphia: 1871), Vol. 8; (NY: Derby), Vol. VIII, p. 45456. William Taylor Thom, The Struggle for Religious Freedom in Virginia: The Baptists, Johns Hopkins Studies in Historical & Political Science, Herbert B. Adams, ed., (Baltimore: Johns Hopkins, 1900), p. 79. Annals of America, 20 vols. (Chicago, IL: Encyclopedia Britannica, 1968), Vol. 3, p. 53. Norman Cousins, In God We Trust The Religious Beliefs & Ideas of the American Founding Fathers (NY: Harper & Brothers, 1958), p. 124.

[142] Washington, George. June 8, 1783, original source of prayer is concluding paragraph Washington's farewell circular sent to governors of states from headquarters, Newburgh, NY. This version is of Pohick Church, Fairfax County, VA, where Washington was a vestryman 1762-1784. It also appears on a plaque in St. Paul's Chapel in New York City. John F. Schroeder, ed., Maxims of Washington (Mt. Vernon: Mt. Vernon Ladies' Assoc., 1942), p. 299.

[143] Mather, Cotton. 1702, in Magnalia Christi Americana, (The Great Achievement of Christ in America), introduction. John Bartlett, Bartlett's Familiar Quotations (Boston: Little, Brown & Co., 1855, 1980), pp. 319-320.

[144] Pennsylvania, Frame of Government of. Apr. 25, 1682, in the preface of his Frame of Government of Pennsylvania. A Collection of Charters & Other Public Acts Relating to the Province of Pennsylvania (Philadelphia: B. Franklin, 1740), pp. 10-12. Thomas Clarkson, Memoirs of the

Private & Public Life of William Penn (London: Longman, Hurst, Orme, & Grown, 1813; Richard Taylor & Co., 1813), Vol. I, pp. 299-305. William Wistar Comfort, William Penn & Our Liberties (Pub. in Penn Mutual's Centennial Year in honor of the man whose name the company adopted at its founding in 1847.) Philadelphia: The Penn Mutual Life Insurance Co., 1947, n.p. Benjamin Franklin Morris, The Christian Life & Character of the Civil Institutions of the United States (Philadelphia: George W. Childs, 1864), pp. 82-83. Frances Newton Thorpe, ed., Federal and State Constitutions, Colonial Charters, & Other Organic Laws of States, Territories, & Colonies now or heretofore forming United States, 7 vols. (Washington: Government Printing Office, 1905; 1909; St. Clair Shores, MI: Scholarly Press, 1968), Vol. V, pp. 3052-3059.

[145] Jefferson, Thomas. Jan. 16, 1786, bill written by the Committee on Religion, Virginia Assembly; inscribed on the Jefferson Memorial, Washington D.C. H.A. Washington, ed., The Writings of Thomas Jefferson Being His Autobiography, Correspondence, Reports, Messages, Addresses, & Other Writings, Official & Private, 9 vols. (Jackson: 1859); (Wash.: 1853-4); (Philadelphia: 1871), Vol. 8; (NY: Derby), Vol. VIII, p. 454-6. William Taylor Thom, The Struggle for Religious Freedom in Virginia: The Baptists, Johns Hopkins Studies in Historical & Political Science, Herbert B. Adams, ed., (Baltimore: Johns Hopkins, 1900), p. 79. Annals of America, 20 vols. (Chicago, IL: Encyclopedia Britannica, 1968), Vol. 3, p. 53.

[146] Williams, Roger. 1644, *Plea for Religious Liberty*. Roger Williams, *The Bloudy Tenent of Persecution* ("Publications of the Narragansett Club" [Providence, R.I.], Vol. III [1867]), pp. 3-4, 63, 58-9, 138-39, 148, 170-71, 201, 247-50, 372-73, 424-25.

[147] U.S. Supreme Court. Feb. 29, 1892, Church of the Holy Trinity v. United States, 143 US 457-458, 465-471, 36 L ed 226, (submitted & argued Jan. 7, 1892), Justice David Josiah Brewer delivering the court's opinion. David Josiah Brewer, The United States: A Christian Nation, (Pub. by John D. Winston Co., Philadelphia, PA, 1905) reprinted by Gary DeMar, American Vision, Inc., 2512 Cobb Parkway, Smyrna, Georgia 30080, 1996), p. 87.

[148] Tocqueville, Alexis de. The Republic of the United States of America & Its Political Institutions, Reviewed & Examined, Henry Reeves, trans., (Garden City, NY: A.S. Barnes & Co., 1851), Vol. I, p. 335, 328.

[149] Winthrop, John. 1630, "A Model of Christian Charity." Stewart Mitchell, editor, The Winthrop Papers, 1623-1630 (Boston: Massachusetts Historical Society, 1931), Vol. II, pp. 292-295.

[150] New England Primer. 1737. Alphabet of Religious Jingles, Dover Pub., Inc., NY, N.Y., Gary DeMar, God & Government, A Biblical & Historical Study (Atlanta, GA: American Vision Press, 1984), p. 19.

[151] Boston Tea Party. 1773, unanimous declaration by the men of Marlborough, Massachusetts. Charles E. Kistler, This Nation Under God (Boston: Richard G. Badger, The Gorham Press, 1924), p. 56.

[152] Adams, Abigail. June 18, 1775, in writing to her husband John Adams, in the midst of the conflict with Britain. Charles Francis Adams (son of John Quincy Adams & grandson of John Adams), Familiar Letters of John Adams with his wife Abigail Adams-during the Revolution (NY: Hurd & Houghton, 1876), Vol. XXVI, pp. 3-4.

[153] Trumbull, Jonathan. July 13, 1775, to General Washington. Jared Sparks, ed., Correspondence of the American Revolution-being Letters of Eminent Men to George Washington from the time of his Taking Command of the Army to the End of his Presidency, 4 vols. (Boston: Little, Brown & Co., 1853), Vol. I, pp. 2-3. Douglas Southall Freeman, George Washington, 6 vols. (NY: Charles Scribner's Sons, 1948-54), Vol. III, pp. 503-4.

[154] Jefferson, Thomas. July 3, 1776, proposition for a national seal. Journals of the Continental Congress, 1776, Vol. V, p. 530. Charles Francis Adams (son of John Quincy Adams & grandson of John Adams), ed., Letters of John Adams, Addressed to His Wife (Boston: Charles C. Little & James Brown, 1841), Vol. I, p. 152.

[155] Adams, Abigail. June 20, 1776, to her husband, John Adams, in Philadelphia. L.H. Butterfield, ed., Adams Family Correspondence (Cambridge, MA: The Belknap Press of Harvard Univ. Press, 1963), Vol. II, p. 16.

[156] Jefferson, Thomas. Mar. 4, 1805, Second Inaugural Address. James D. Richardson (U.S. Rep-TN), ed., A Compilation of the Messages & Papers of the Presidents 1789-1897, 10 vols. (Washington, D.C.: U.S. Government Printing Office, pub. by Authority of Congress, 1897, 1899; Wash., D.C.: Bureau of National Literature & Art, 1789-1902, 11 vols., 1907, 1910), Vol. I, p. 378-82.

[157] Adams, John. Feb. 16, 1809, to Judge F.A. Van der Kemp. Norman Cousins, ed., 'In God We Trust': The Religious Beliefs & Ideas of the American Founding Fathers (NY: Harper & Brothers, 1958), pp. 102-103.

[158] Grund, Francis J. 1837. Francis J. Grund, The Americans in Their Moral, Social & Political Relations, (1837), Vol. I, pp. 281-94. Anson Phelps Stokes & Leo Pfeffer, Church & State in the United States (NY: Harper & Row, Pub., 1950, one vol., 1964), p. 210.

[159] Maryland, State of. Aug. 14, 1776, Constitution, Article XXXV. The Constitutions of All the United States According to the Latest Amendments (Lexington, KY: Thomas T. Skillman, 1817), p. 188. Benjamin Franklin Morris, The Christian Life & Character of the Civil Institutions of the United States (Philadelphia, PA: L. Johnson & Co., 1863; George W. Childs, 1864), p. 233. Frances Newton Thorpe, ed., Federal & State Constitutions, Colonial Charters, & Other Organic Laws of the States, Territories, & Colonies now or heretofore forming the United States, 7 vols. (Washington: Government Printing Office, 1905; 1909; St. Clair Shores, MI: Scholarly Press, 1968), Vol. III. Federal & State Constitutions, Colonial Charters, & Other Organic Laws of the States, Territories, & Colonies now or heretofore forming the United States, 7 vols. (Washington: Government Printing Office, 1909).

[160] Maryland, State of. 1851, Constitution. Supreme Court Justice David Josiah Brewer, who served 1890-1910, in his work, The United States A Christian Nation (Philadelphia: John C. Winston Co., 1905, Supreme Court Collection).

[161] Rush, Benjamin. July 9, 1788, to Elias Boudinot regarding a parade in Philadelphia. L.H. Butterfield, editor, Letters of Benjamin Rush (Princeton, New Jersey: American Philosophical Society, 1951), Vol. I, p. 474.

[162] Washington, George. Jan. 1790, to the Hebrew Congregations of Philadelphia, Newport, Charlestown & Richmond. William Barclay Allen, ed., George Washington-A Collection (Indianapolis: Liberty Classics, Liberty Fund, Inc., 7440 N. Shadeland, Indianapolis, IN 46250, 1988; based almost entirely on materials reproduced from The Writings of George Washington from the original manuscript sources, 1745-1799/John Clement Fitzpatrick, editor), pp. 545-546. John Clement Fitzpatrick, ed., The Writings of George Washington, from the Original Manuscript Sources 1749-99, 39 vols. (Wash., D.C.: U.S. Gov. Printing Office, 1931-1944).

[163] Washington, George. Aug. 17, 1790, in an address to the Hebrew Congregation in Newport, Rhode Island. William Barclay Allen, ed., George

ENDNOTES

Washington-A Collection (Indianapolis: Liberty Classics, Liberty Fund, Inc., 7440 N. Shadeland, Indianapolis, IN 46250, 1988; based almost entirely on materials reproduced from The Writings of George Washington from the original manuscript sources, 1745-1799/John Clement Fitzpatrick, editor), pp. 547-548. John Clement Fitzpatrick, ed., The Writings of George Washington, from the Original Manuscript Sources 1749-1799, 39 vols. (Washington, D.C.: U.S. Government Printing Office, 1931-1944).

[164] Washington, George. Writing to the Hebrew Congregations, Savannah, Georgia. William Barclay Allen, ed., George Washington-A Collection (Indianapolis: Liberty Classics, Liberty Fund, Inc., 7440 N. Shadeland, Indianapolis, IN 46250, 1988; from The Writings of George Washington original manuscript sources, 1745-99/John Clement Fitzpatrick, ed.), p. 549. John Clement Fitzpatrick, ed., The Writings of George Washington, from the Original Manuscript Sources 1749-99, 39 vols. (Wash., D.C.: U.S. Government Printing Office, 1931-1944). John F. Schroeder, ed., Maxims of Washington (Mt. Vernon Ladies' Assoc., 1942), p. 303.

[165] Buchanan, James. Apr. 24, 1860, in writing to the House of Representatives. James D. Richardson (U.S. Rep.-TN), ed., A Compilation of the Messages & Papers of the Presidents 1789-1897, 10 vols. (Wash., D.C.: U.S. Gov. Printing Office,,1897, 1899; Washington, D.C.: Bureau of National Literature & Art, 1789-1902, 11 vols, 1907, 1910), Vol. 5, p. 592.

[166] U.S. Congress. May 1, 1789, in the U.S. House of Representatives. "Our Christian Heritage," Letter from Plymouth Rock (Marlborough, NH: The Plymouth Rock Foundation), p. 4. Gary DeMar, America's Christian History: The Untold Story (Atlanta, GA: American Vision Pub., Inc., 1993), p. 51.

[167] Lincoln, Abraham. July 12, 1862, due to lack of chaplains for Jewish soldiers, new wording written to include Hebrew faith. Anson Phelps Stokes & Leo Pfeffer, Church & State in the United States (NY: Harper & Row, Pub., 1950, 1964), p. 473.

[168] Grant, Ulysses Simpson. May 14, 1872, in writing to the U.S. Senate. James D. Richardson (U.S. Rep.-TN), ed., A Compilation of the Messages & Papers of the Presidents 1789-1897, 10 vols. (Washington, D.C.: U.S. Government Printing Office, 1897, 1899; Wash, D.C.: Bureau of National Literature & Art, 1789-1902, 11 vols., 1907, 1910), Vol. 7, pp. 167-8.

[169] Grant, Ulysses Simpson. May 22, 1872, in writing to the House of Representatives. James D. Richardson (U.S. Rep.-TN), ed., A Compilation of the Messages & Papers of the Presidents 1789-1897, 10 vols. (Wash., D.C.: U.S. Government Printing Office 1897, 1899; Wash., D.C.: Bureau of National Literature & Art, 1789-1902, 11 vols., 1907, 1910), Vol. 7, p. 168.

[170] Arthur, Chester Alan. Dec. 6, 1881, in his First Annual Message. James D. Richardson, ed., A Compilation of the Messages & Papers of the Presidents 1789-1897, 10 vols. (Wash., D.C.: U.S. Gov. Printing Office, 1897, 1899; Washington, D.C.: Bureau of National Literature & Art, 1789-1902, 11 vols, 1907, 1910), Vol. 8, pp. 25-26, 37, 39, 40, 42, 57.

[171] Arthur, Chester Alan. May 2, 1882, in correspondence with the U.S. House of Representatives, written from his Executive Mansion in Washington, D.C. James D. Richardson (U.S. Rep.-TN), ed., A Compilation of the Messages & Papers of the Presidents 1789-1897, 10 vols. (Washington, D.C.: U.S. Gov. Printing Office, pub. by Authority of Congress, 1897, 1899; Washington, D.C.: Bureau of Nat. Lit. & Art, 1789-1902, 11 vols, 1907, 1910), Vol. 8, p. 103.

[172] Arthur, Chester Alan. Dec. 4, 1882, in his Second Annual Message to Congress. James D. Richardson (U.S. Rep.-TN), ed., A Compilation of the Messages & Papers of the Presidents 1789-1897, 10 vols. (Wash., D.C.: U.S. Gov. Printing Office, 1897, 1899; Wash., D.C.: Bureau of National Literature & Art, 1789-1902, 11 vols, 1907, 1910), Vol. 8, pp. 127, 148.

[173] Harrison, Benjamin. Apr. 4, 1889, Proclamation of Prayer & Thanksgiving. James D. Richardson, ed., A Compilation of the Messages & Papers of the Presidents 1789-1897, 10 vols. (Wash., D.C.: U.S. Gov. Printing Office, 1897, 1899; Washington, D.C.: Bureau of National Literature & Art, 1789-1902, 11 vols, 1907, 1910), Vol. IX, pp. 18-19.

[174] Harrison, Benjamin. Dec. 9, 1891, in his Third Annual Message. James D. Richardson, ed., A Compilation of the Messages & Papers of the Presidents 1789-1897, 10 vols. (Wash, D.C.: U.S. Gov. Printing Office, pub. by Authority of Congress, 1897, 1899; Washington, D.C.: Bureau of National Literature & Art, 1789-1902, 11 vols., 1907, 1910), Vol. IX, pp. 188, 198.

[175] Cleveland, (Stephen) Grover. Dec. 2, 1895, in his Third Annual Message. James D. Richardson, ed., A Compilation of the Messages & Papers of the Presidents 1789-1897, 10 vols. (Wash., D.C.: U.S. Gov. Printing Office, 1897, 1899; Wash., D.C.: Bureau of National Literature & Art, 1789-1902, 11 vols, 1907, 1910), Vol. IX, pp. 635, 637-8.

[176] Roosevelt, Theodore. Dec. 6, 1904, in his Fourth Annual Message to Congress. A Compilation of the Messages & Papers of the Presidents 20 vols. (NY: Bureau of National Literature, Inc., prepared under the direction of the Joint Committee on Printing, of the House & Senate, 1893, 1923), Vol. XIV, p. 6903, 6915-6, 6921-6922, 6924-6925, 6928-6929.

[177] Roosevelt, Theodore. Dec. 5, 1905, in his Fifth Annual Message to Congress. A Compilation of the Messages & Papers of the Presidents 20 vols. (NY: Bureau of National Literature, Inc., prepared under the direction of the Joint Committee on Printing, of the House & Senate, 1893, 1923), Vol. XIV, pp. 6973, 6975-6, 6980, 6984-6, 6992-4, 7003, 7008, 7015-6.

[178] Roosevelt, Theodore. Dec. 3, 1906, in his Sixth Annual Message to Congress. A Compilation of the Messages & Papers of the Presidents 20 vols. (NY: Bureau of National Literature, Inc., prepared under the direction of the Joint Committee on Printing, of the House & Senate, Act of 52nd Congress, 1893, 1923), Vol. XIV, pp. 7030-2, 7046-8,

[179] Wilson, (Thomas) Woodrow. Jan. 11, 1916, Proclamation of a Contribution Day for the aid of stricken Jewish people. A Compilation of the Messages & Papers of the Presidents 20 vols. (NY: Bureau of National Literature, Inc., prepared under the direction of the Joint Committee on Printing, of the House & Senate, 1893, 1923), Vol. XVII, p. 8174-8175.

[180] Wilson, (Thomas) Woodrow. Sept. 1, 1918, to Rabbi Stephen S. Wise in New York City, endorsing Zionist Movement. A Compilation of the Messages & Papers of the Presidents 20 vols. (NY: Bureau of National Literature, Inc., prepared under the direction of the Joint Committee on Printing, of the House & Senate, 1893, 1923), Vol. XVII, p. 8575.

[181] Coolidge, (John) Calvin. Oct. 26, 1924, address delivered via telephone from the White House to the Federation of Jewish Philanthropic Societies of New York City, assembled at the Hotel Pennsylvania. Calvin Coolidge, Foundations of the Republic-Speeches & Addresses (NY: Charles Scribner's Sons, 1926), pp. 169-172.

[182] Coolidge, (John) Calvin. May 3, 1925, laying cornerstone of Jewish Community Center, Washington, D.C. Calvin Coolidge, Foundations of the Republic-Speeches & Addresses (NY: Charles Scribner's Sons, 1926), pp. 209-218.

[183] Truman, Harry S. Apr. 12, 1945, first Address to Congress. Merle Miller, Plain Speaking-An Oral Biography of Harry S. Truman (Berkley, 1982).

Charles E. Jones, The Books You Read (Harrisburg, PA: Executive Books, 1985), p. 197. Edmund Fuller & David E. Green, God in the White House-The Faiths of American Presidents (NY: Crown Pub., 1968), p. 210.

[184] Truman, Harry S. Harry S. Truman, Memoirs by Harry S. Truman-Volume Two: Years of Trial & Hope (Garden City, NY: Doubleday & Co., Inc., 1956), p. 134.

[185] Truman, Harry S. July 24, 1945, memorandum to Winston Churchill. Harry S. Truman, Memoirs by Harry S. Truman-Volume Two: Years of Trial & Hope (Garden City, NY: Doubleday & Co. 1956), p. 135.

[186] Truman, Harry S. 1945, statement to press. Harry S. Truman, Memoirs by Harry S. Truman-Volume Two: Years of Trial & Hope (Garden City, NY: Doubleday & Co., 1956), p. 136.

[187] Truman, Harry S. Harry S. Truman, Memoirs by Harry S. Truman-Volume Two: Years of Trial & Hope (Garden City, NY: Doubleday & Co., 1956), p. 157.

[188] Truman, Harry. 1946. Anson Phelps Stokes, Church & State in U.S. (NY: Harper & Bros., 1950), Vol. III, p. 712-3

[189] Truman, Harry S. Dec. 6, 1947, dedication of Everglades National Park. T.S. Settel, & the staff of Quote, ed., The Quotable Harry Truman intro. by Merle Miller (NY: Droke House Pub., Inc., Berkley Pub. Corp., 1967), pp. 113-114.

[190] http://www.fourchaplains.org, Dwight David Eisenhower, Feb. 7, 1954, Remarks from White House, 2:30 P.M., part of American Legion "BACK-TO-GOD" Program. Public Papers of the Presidents (Wash., D.C., U.S. Gov. Printing Office).

[191] U.S. Corp of Cadets. July 24, 1949, New York Times. Anson Phelps Stokes & Leo Pfeffer, Church & State in the United States (NY: Harper & Row, Pub., 1950, revised one-volume edition, 1964), p. 473-474.

[192] Kennedy, John Fitzgerald. Jan. 20, 1961, Inaugural Address. Inaugural Addresses of the Presidents of the United States From 1789 to 1969 (Washington, D.C.: U.S. Government Printing Office; 91st Congress, 1st Session, House Document 91142, 1969), pp. 267-270. Department of State Bulletin (Office of Public Services, Bureau of Public Affairs, Feb. 6, 1961). Davis Newton Lott, The Inaugural Addresses of the American Presidents (NY: Holt, Rinehart & Winston, 1961), p. 269.

[193] King, Martin Luther, Jr. Apr. 16, 1963, message written from jail cell in Birmingham, Alabama. Christian Century, June 12, 1963. Annals of America, 20 vols. (Chicago, IL: Encyclopedia Britannica, 1968), Vol. 18, pp. 143-149.

[194] King, Martin Luther, Jr. Aug. 28, 1963, at Civil Rights March, Washington. The SCLC Story in Words & Pictures, 1964, pp. 50-51. Annals of America, 20 vols. (Chicago, IL: Encyclopedia Britannica, Inc., 1976), Vol. 18, pp. 156-159. John Bartlett, Bartlett's Familiar Quotations (Boston: Little, Brown & Co., 1855, 1980), p. 909.

[195] Johnson, Lyndon. Dec. 30, 1963, dedicated Agudas Achim Congregation synagogue, Austin, TX. Public Papers of the Presidents.

[196] Reagan, Ronald Wilson. Mar. 23, 1982, Nat. Conference of Christians & Jews, NY. Frederick J. Ryan, Jr., ed., Ronald Reagan-The Wisdom & Humor of the Great Communicator (San Francisco: Harper Collins Pub., 1995), p. 64.

[197] Reagan, Ronald Wilson. Jan. 31, 1983, annual convention of National Religious Broadcasters. David R. Shepherd, ed., Ronald Reagan: In God I Trust (Wheaton, IL: Tyndale House Pub., Inc., 1984), pp. 33-34, 83-84, 105-106.

[198] Reagan, Ronald Wilson. Apr. 2, 1983, Radio Address to the Nation. David R. Shepherd, ed., Ronald Reagan: In God I Trust (Wheaton, IL: Tyndale House Pub., Inc., 1984), pp. 38-40.

[199] Reagan, Ronald. Dec. 21, 1984, Hanukkah Message. Public Papers of the Presidents.

[200] Bush, George H.W. Dec. 21, 1989, Hanukkah Message. Public Papers of the Presidents.

[201] Reagan, Ronald Wilson. Aug. 17, 1992, Rep. Nat. Con., Houston, TX. Frederick J. Ryan, Jr., ed., Ronald Reagan-The Wisdom & Humor of the Great Communicator (San Francisco: Harper Collins Pub., 1995), pp. 153-5.

[202] Bush, George W. Dec. 10, 2001, historic first lighting of menorah at White House. Public Papers.

[203] Limbaugh, Rush H. in his book, *See, I Told You So* (NY: Pocket Books, div. Simon & Schuster Inc., 1993), p. 69-72.

[204,205] Thatcher, Margaret Hilda. Feb. 5, 1996, in New York City, prior to her trip to Utah where she addressed the UK -Utah Festival, in an interview with Joseph A. Cannon, titled "The Conservative Vision of Margaret Thatcher," pub. in Human Events-The National Conservative Weekly, (Potomac, MD: Human Events Pub., Inc., 7811 Montrose Rd, Potomac, MD, 20854, 1-800-787-7557; Eagle Pub., Inc.), Mar. 29, 1996, Vol. 52, No. 12, pp. 12-14.

[206] Madison, James. June 20, 1785. Memorial & Remonstrance (Wash., D.C.: Library of Congress, Rare Book Collection, to General Assembly of State of Virginia, 1785; Massachusetts: Isaiah Thomas, 1786). Robert Rutland, ed., The Papers of James Madison (IL: Univ. of Chicago Press, 1973), Vol. VIII, pp. 299, 304. Stephen McDowell & Mark Beliles, "The Providential Perspective" (Charlottesville, VA: The Providence Foundation, P.O. Box 6759, Charlottesville, Va. 22906, Jan. 1994), Vol. 9, No. 1, p. 5.

[207] Key, Francis Scott. Charles Wallis, ed., Our American Heritage (NY: Harper & Row, Pub., Inc., 1970), p. 144.

[208] U.S. Supreme Court. 1789, Robert Byrd, U.S. Senator-W.VA, July 27, 1962, message to Congress two days after the Supreme Court declared prayer in schools unconstitutional. Robert Flood, The Rebirth of America (Philadelphia: Arthur S. DeMoss Foundation, 1986), pp. 66-69.

[209] Truman, Harry S. Nov. 11, 1949, National Conference of Christians & Jews in Washington, D.C. T.S. Settel, & the staff of Quote, ed., The Quotable Harry Truman (NY: Droke House Pub., Inc., Berkley Pub. Corp., 1967), p. 37.

[210] Franklin, Benjamin. 1754. Benjamin Franklin, Information on Those Who Would Remove to America (London: M. Gurney, 1754), pp. 22-3. Benjamin Franklin, Works of the Late Doctor Benjamin Franklin Consisting of His Life, Written by Himself, Together with Essays, Humorous, Moral & Literary, Chiefly in the Manner of the Spectator, Richard Price, ed., (Dublin: P. Wogan, P. Byrne, J. Moore, & W. Jones, 1793), p. 289.

[211] Tocqueville, Alexis de. Aug. 1831. de Tocqueville, The Republic of the United States of America & Its Political Institutions-Reviewed & Examined, Henry Reeves, trans., (Garden City, NY: A.S. Barnes & Co., 1851), Vol. I, p. 334. de Tocqueville, Democracy in America, 2 vols. (NY: Alfred A. Knopf, 1945), Vol. I, pp. 311, 319-20. de Tocqueville, Democracy in America, George Lawrence, trans, (NY: Harper & Row, 1988) p. 47. Tryon Edwards, D.D., The New Dictionary of Thoughts-A Cyclopedia of Quotations (Garden City, NY: Hanover House, 1852; revised C.H. Catrevas, Ralph Emerson Browns & Jonathan Edwards, 1891; Standard Book Co., 1955, 1963), p. 337. Annals of America, 20 vols. (Chicago, IL: Encyclopedia Britannica, 1968, 1977), Vol. 5, p. 486-97.

[212] Maryland, State of. Aug. 14, 1776, Constitution, Article XXXV. The Constitutions of All the United States According to the Latest

Amendments (Lexington, KY: Thomas T. Skillman, 1817), p. 188. Benjamin Franklin Morris, The Christian Life & Character of the Civil Institutions of the United States (Philadelphia, PA: L. Johnson & Co., 1863; George W. Childs, 1864), p. 233. Frances Newton Thorpe, ed., Federal & State Constitutions, Colonial Charters, & Other Organic Laws of the States, Territories, & Colonies now or heretofore forming the United States, 7 vols. (Washington: Government Printing Office, 1905; 1909; St. Clair Shores, MI: Scholarly Press, 1968), Vol. III. Federal & State Constitutions, Colonial Charters, & Other Organic Laws of the States, Territories, & Colonies now or heretofore forming the United States, 7 vols. (Washington: Government Printing Office, 1909).

[213] Maryland, State of. 1851, Constitution. Supreme Court Justice David Josiah Brewer, who served 1890-1910, in his work, The United States A Christian Nation (Philadelphia: John C. Winston Co., 1905, Supreme Court Collection).

[214] Maryland, State of. 1864, Constitution. Benjamin Franklin Morris, The Christian Life & Character of the Civil Institutions of the United States (Philadelphia: George W. Childs, 1864). Supr. Ct. Justice David Josiah Brewer, 1890-1910, in The United States Christian Nation (Philadelphia: John C. Winston Co., 1905, Supreme Court Collection).

[215] U.S. Constitution of the. Sept. 17, 1787. Oath of Office for U.S. Senators & Representatives. Donald A. Ritchie, The Young Oxford Companion to the Congress of the United States (NY: Oxford Univ. Press, 1993), p. 137.

[216] Inaugural Addresses of Presidents. Messages & Papers of the Presidents. Public Papers of Presidents. William J. Federer, Ten Commandments & their Influence on American Law (Amerisearch: St. Louis, MO), pp. 49-51.

[217] William J. Federer, The Ten Commandments & their Influence on American Law (Amerisearch, Inc.: St. Louis, MO), p. 52-7.

[218] Ford, Gerald Rudolph. December 5, 1974, Thursday, National Day of Prayer, 1974, Proclamation 4338, in quoting a 1955 speech of Dwight David Eisenhower. Mrs. James Dobson (Shirley), chairman, The National Day of Prayer Information Packet (Colorado Springs, CO: National Day of Prayer Tack Force, May 6, 1993).

[219] Eisenhower, Dwight David. In the magazine, Episcopal Churchnews. Edmund Fuller and David E. Green, God in the White House - The Faiths of American Presidents (NY: Crown Publishers, Inc., 1968), pp. 215-216.

[220] Eisenhower, Dwight David. July 9, 1953, to National Chairmen of Commission on Religious Organizations, Nat. Conference of Christians & Jews; Public Papers of the Presidents-Dwight D. Eisenhower, 1953-Containing Public Messages of the President, Jan. 20-Dec. 31, 1953 (Wash., DC: U.S. Gov. Printing Off., 1960), Item 132, p. 489-90.

[221] Reagan, Ronald Wilson. Jan. 31, 1983, annual convention National Religious Broadcasters. David R. Shepherd, ed., Ronald Reagan: In God I Trust (Wheaton, IL: Tyndale House Pub., Inc., 1984), pp. 33-34, 83-84, 105-106.

[222] Truman, Harry S. Mar. 6, 1946, Conference of Federal Council of Churches, Columbus, Ohio. T.S. Settel, & staff of Quote, The Quotable Harry Truman intro by Merle Miller (NY: Droke House Pub., Inc., Berkley Pub. Corp., 1967), pp. 84, 162.

[223] New Jersey State Court. 1950, Doremus v. Board of Ed. Borough of Hawthorne, 5 NJ 435, 75 A. 880 (NJ 1950).

[224] Jefferson, Thomas. Mar. 4, 1801, First Inaugural Address. James D. Richardson (U.S. Rep.-TN), ed., A Compilation of the Messages & Papers of the Presidents 1789-1897, 10 vols. (Wash., D.C.: U.S. Government Printing Office, 1897, 1899; Wash., D.C.: Bureau of National Literature & Art, 1789-1902, 11 vols., 1907, 1910), Vol. I, p. 322-324.

[225, 226, 227] New Jersey State Court. 1950, Doremus v. Bd. of Ed. Borough of Hawthorne, 5 NJ 435, 75 A. 880 (NJ 1950).

[228] Rush, Benjamin. 1798. 1786, in "Thoughts upon the Mode of Education Proper in a Republic," pub. in Early American Imprints. Benjamin Rush, Essays, Literary, Moral & Philosophical (Philadelphia: Thomas & Samuel F. Bradford, 1798), p. 8, "Of the Mode of Education Proper in a Republic." Annals of America, 20 vols. (Chicago, IL: Encyclopedia Britannica, 1968), Vol. 4, pp. 28-29.

[229] Pierce, Franklin. Dec. 4, 1854, Second Annual Message. James D. Richardson, ed., A Compilation of the Messages & Papers of the Presidents 1789-1897, 10 vols. (Washington, D.C.: U.S. Government Printing Office, 1897, 1899; Washington, D.C.: Bureau of National Literature & Art, 1789-1902, 11 vols., 1907, 1910), Vol. 5, pp. 273, 292-293.

[230] Grant, Ulysses Simpson. Mar. 4, 1869, First Inaugural Address. James D. Richardson (U.S. Rep.-TN), ed., A Compilation of the Messages & Papers of the Presidents 1789-1897, 10 vols. (Wash., D.C.: U.S. Government Printing Office, 1897, 1899; Wash., D.C.: Bureau of National Literature & Art, 1789-1902, 11 vols., 1907, 1910), Vol. 7, pp. 78.

[231] Roosevelt, Theodore. Dec. 5, 1905, Fifth Annual Message. A Compilation of the Messages & Papers of the Presidents 20 vols. (NY: Bureau of National Literature, Inc., under the direction of the Joint Committee on Printing, of the House & Senate, 1893, 1923), Vol. XIV, pp. 6973, 6975-6976, 6980, 6984-6986, 6992-6994, 7003, 7008, 7015-7016.

[232] Roosevelt, Theodore. Dec. 3, 1906, 6th Annual Message. A Compilation of the Messages & Papers of the Presidents 20 vols. (NY: Bureau of National Literature.), Vol. XIV, pp. 7030-2, 7046-8.

[233] U.S. Supreme Court. 1948, Justice Frankfurter, McCollum v. Board of Ed. District No. 71, 333 U.S. 203, 206 , 236

[234] New Jersey State Court. 1950, Doremus v. Board of Ed. of Borough of Hawthorne, 5 NJ 435, 75 A. 880 (NJ 1950).

[235, 236] Massachusetts Supreme Court. 1838, Commonwealth v. Abner Kneeland, 37 Mass. (20 Pick) 206, 216-217 (1838).

[237] New York State Court. 1935, Lewis v. Board of Education of City of New York, 157 Misc. 520, 285 N.Y.S. 164 (Sup.Ct. 1935), aff'd per curiam, 247 App.Div. 106, 286, N.Y.S. 174 (App.Div 1936), pp. 169-170.

[238] U.S. Supreme Court. 1963, School District of Abington Township v. Schempp, 374 U.S. 203, 212, 225, 83 S. Ct. 1560, 10 L. Ed. 2d 844 (1963), pp. 21, 71.

[239] Minnesota State Court. 1927, Kaplan v. Independent School Dist. of Virginia, 214 N.W. 18 (Minn. 1927), pp. 18 20.

[240] U.S. Supreme Court. 1992, Lee v. Weisman; 120 L. Ed. 2d 467, 519 (1992), dissenting opinion given by Justice Antonin Scalia, joined by Chief Justice William Rehnquist, Justice Byron White & Justice Clarence Thomas.

[241] Bacon, Sir Francis. *Of Atheism.* Bartlett's Familiar Quotations (Boston: Little, Brown & Co., 1855, 1980), p. 180.

[242] Franklin, Benjamin. Leonard Labaree, ed., Papers of Benjamin Franklin (New Haven: Yale Press, 1959), V. I, p. 108.

[243] Franklin, Benjamin. 1754. Benjamin Franklin, Information on Those Who Would Remove to America (London: M. Gurney, 1754), pp. 22, 23. Benjamin Franklin, Works of the Late Doctor Benjamin Franklin Consisting of His Life, Written by Himself, Together with Essays, Humorous, Moral & Literary, Chiefly in the Manner of the Spectator, Richard Price, ed., (Dublin: P. Wogan, P. Byrne, J. Moore, & W. Jones, 1793), p. 289.

[244] Burke, Edmund. Mar. 22, 1775, to Parliament-*Second Speech on the Conciliation with America-The Thirteen Resolutions*. Sidney Carelton Newsom, ed., Burke's Speech on Conciliation with America (NY: Macmillan Co., 1899; 1913).

[245] Dwight, Timothy. July 4, 1798, as president of Yale College, address delivered at New Haven, titled, "The Duty of Americans, at the Present Crisis, Illustrated in a Discourse, Preached on the Fourth of July, 1798. (#Ital original). Annals of America, 20 vols. (Chicago, IL: Encyclopedia Britannica, 1968, 1977), Vol. 4, pp. 33-9.

[246] Fabre, Henri. Henry M. Morris, Men of Science-Men of God (El Cajon, CA: Master Books, Creation Life Pub., 1990), p. 62-3.

[247] Fosdick, Henry Emerson. Perry Tanksley, To Love is to Give (Jackson, MS: Allgood Books, Box 1329; Parthenon Press, 201 8th Ave., South, Nashville, TN, 1972), p. 65.

[248] Mather, Cotton. Magnalia Christi Americana. Stephen Foster, Their Solitary Way (New Haven: Yale Univ. Press, 1971), p. 121.

[249] Coolidge, (John) Calvin. Oct. 6, 1925, American Legion Convention, Omaha, Nebraska. Calvin Coolidge, Foundations of the Republic Speeches & Addresses (NY: Charles Scribner's Sons, 1926), pp. 287-301.

[250] Colorado State Court. 1927, Vollmar v. Stanley, 255 Pac. 610 (Col. 1927), pp. 617-618.

[251] Burger, Warren Earl. 1985, U.S. Supreme Court, Lynch v. Donnelly, 465 U.S. 668, 673 (1985). John Whitehead, The Rights of Religious Persons in Public Education (Wheaton, IL: Crossway Books, Good News Pub., 1991), pp. 49, 52. Tracy Everbach, Dallas Morning News, 3/16/93, pp. 1A, 8A.

[252] Reagan, Ronald Wilson. May 6, 1982, Nat. Day of Prayer Ceremony. David R. Shepherd, ed., Ronald Reagan: In God I Trust (Wheaton, IL: Tyndale House, 1984), pp. 5961, 131-2. Frederick J. Ryan, Jr., ed., Ronald Reagan The Wisdom & Humor of the Great Communicator (San Francisco: Collins Pub., Div. Harper Collins, 1995), p. 119.

[253] Watts, J.C. Feb. 4, 1997, Library of Congress, Wash., D.C., Republican response to Clinton's State of Union

[254] Pennsylvania, Frame of Government of. Apr. 25, 1682, Fundamental Constitutions written by William Penn. The Historical Society of Pennsylvania Collection, Philadelphia.

[255] South Carolina Supreme Court. 1846, City of Charleston v. S.A. Benjamin, 2 Strob. 521-524 (1846).

[256] U.S. Supreme Court. 1889, Davis v. Beason, 133 U.S. 333, 341-343, 348 (1890).

[257] Garfield, James Abram. 1876, commemorating centennial of Declaration of Independence. "A Century of Congress," by James A. Garfield, pub. in Atlantic, July 1877. John M. Taylor, Garfield of Ohio The Available Man (NY: W.W. Norton & Co.), p. 180.

[258] Hodge, Charles. 1871. Charles Hodge, Systematic Theology, 1871 (reprinted Grand Rapids, MI: William B. Eerdmans Publ. Co., 1975), pp. 343-346. Verna M. Hall, Christian History of the American Revolution-Consider & Ponder (San Francisco: Foundation for American Christian Education, 1976), p. 156.

[259] Jim Burns, Media Research Center, Bev/T.O. Donovan, 10/31/2001. Matt Staver, The Liberty Alert (Orlando, FL: The Liberty Counsel, 9/25/2001, 3:42:07 PM Central Daylight Time, www.lc.org. Ryan McCarthy, The Sacramento Bee, "ACLU demand fuels controversy over patriotism," www.fresnobee.com/local/v-print/story/955799p-1017055c.html, Oct. 7, 2001.

[260] Howard Fineman, Newsweek Magazine, Jan. 2002, Ken Connor, Family Research Council, 801 G Street, N.W., Washington, D.C. 20001, 202-393-2134, www.frc.org, Washington Update, Jan. 2, 2002.

[261] Reagan, Ronald Wilson. Feb. 25, 1984, radio address. David R. Shepherd, ed., Ronald Reagan: In God I Trust (Wheaton, IL: Tyndale House Pub., Inc., 1984), pp. 77-79.

[262] Williams, Roger. 1644, *Plea for Religious Liberty*. Roger Williams, *The Bloudy Tenent of Persecution* ("Publications of the Narragansett Club" [Providence, R.I.], Vol. III [1867]), pp. 3-4,, 58-63, 138-39, 148, 170-71, 201, 247-50, 372-73, 424-25.

[263] Reagan, Ronald Wilson. Aug. 23, 1984, Ecumenical Prayer Breakfast in Dallas, TX. "Remarks by President at Prayer Breakfast," New York Times, Aug. 24, 1984, p. A11. Jeffrey K. Hadden and Anson Shupe, Televangelist: Power & Politics on God's Frontier (NY: Henry Holt & Co., 1988), p. 36.

[264] *The Daily Nebraskan*, Apr. 13, 2002.

[265] Rabbi Daniel Lapin, *America's Real War* (Multnomah Pub., Inc., Sisters, OR, 1999), pp. 56-57.

[266] Reagan, Ronald. Mar. 15, 1982, to Alabama State Legislature. David R. Shepherd, ed., Ronald Reagan: In God I Trust (Wheaton, IL: Tyndale House Pub., Inc., 1984), p. 131.

[267] George Orwell, 1984 (London: Martin Secker & Warburg, 1949).

[268,269,270,271,272,273,274] U.S. Supreme Court. 1992, Lee v. Weisman; 120 L.Ed. 2d 467, 509, 510-511, 514, 516, 519 (1992), Lee v. Weisman, 112 S.Ct. 2649 (1992). Dissenting opinion given by Justice Scalia, joined by Justices Rehnquist, White and Thomas.

[275] Reagan, Ronald Wilson. Mar. 8, 1983, National Assoc. of Evangelicals. William Safire, ed., Lend Me Your Ears-Great Speeches in History (NY: W.W. Norton & Co., 1992), p. 464. David R. Shepherd, ed., Ronald Reagan: In God I Trust (Wheaton, IL: Tyndale House, 1984), pp. 35-8, 133-4. Frederick J. Ryan, Jr., ed., Ronald Reagan-The Wisdom & Humor of The Great Communicator (San Francisco: Collins Pub., Div. of Harper Collins Pub., 1995), p. 42.

[276,277] Rees Lloyd, "Legion Stands Up for Scouts after ACLU-DoD Settlement." The American Legion, Feb. 2005 issue, 700 N. Pennsylvania St., P.O. Box 1055, Indianapolis, IN 46206, pg. 18.

[278] Reagan, Ronald Wilson. Sept. 18, 1982, Radio Address. David R. Shepherd, ed., Ronald Reagan: In God I Trust (Wheaton, IL: Tyndale House Pub., Inc., 1984), pp. 65-67. Frederick J. Ryan, Jr., ed., Ronald Reagan-The Wisdom & Humor of the Great Communicator (San Francisco: Collins Pub., Division of Harper Collins Pub., 1995), p. 117.

[279] "White House Decries ACLU Assault on Christmas" Wash., D.C. Talon News, 12/24/04, reporter Jeff Gannon.

[280,281,282,283,284] Williams, Roger. 1644, *Plea for Religious Liberty*. Roger Williams, *The Bloudy Tenent of Persecution* ("Publications of the Narragansett Club" [Providence, R.I.], Vol. III [1867]), pp. 3-4, 58-63, 138-39, 148, 170-71, 201, 247-50, 372-73, 424-25.

[285] Reagan, Ronald Wilson. Sept. 25, 1982, candle-lighting ceremony for prayer in schools. David R. Shepherd, ed., Ronald Reagan: In God I Trust (Wheaton, IL: Tyndale House Pub., Inc., 1984), pp. 67-68. Frederick J. Ryan, Jr., ed., Ronald Reagan-The Wisdom & Humor of the Great Communicator (San Francisco: Collins Pub., Division of Harper Collins Pub., 1995), p. 119.

[286] Oct. 2nd. Toynbee, Arnold Joseph. Mar. 30, 1956, comment recorded in Collier's. James Beasely Simpson. Best Quotes of '54, '55, '56 (NY:

Thomas Y. Crowell Co., 1957), p. 352.

[287] Arthur, Chester Alan. Dec. 6, 1881, First Annual Message. James D. Richardson, ed., A Compilation of the Messages & Papers of the Presidents 1789-1897, 10 vols. (Wash., D.C.: U.S. Government Printing Office, pub. by Authority of Congress, 1897, 1899; Washington, D.C.: Bureau of National Literature & Art, 1789-1902, 11 vols., 1907, 1910), Vol. 8, pp. 25-26, 37, 39, 40, 42, 57.

[288] Cleveland, (Stephen) Grover. Dec. 11, 1894, to the Senate. James D. Richardson (U.S. Rep.-TN), ed., A Compilation of the Messages & Papers of the Presidents 1789-1897, 10 vols. (Washington, D.C.: U.S. Gov. Printing Office, 1897, 1899; Washington, D.C.: Bureau of Nat. Lit. & Art, 1789-1902, 11 vols., 1907, 1910), Vol. IX, p. 557.

[289] Cleveland, (Stephen) Grover. Dec. 2, 1895, Third Annual Message to Congress. James D. Richardson (U.S. Rep.-TN), ed., A Compilation of the Messages & Papers of the Presidents 1789-1897, 10 vols. (Washington, D.C.: U.S. Government Printing Office, 1897, 1899; Wash., D.C.: Bureau of National Literature & Art, 1789-1902, 11 vols., 1907, 1910), Vol. IX, pp. 635-8.

[290] Cleveland, (Stephen) Grover. Dec. 7, 1896, Fourth Annual Message. James D. Richardson, ed., A Compilation of the Messages & Papers of the Presidents 1789-1897, 10 vols. (Wash., D.C.: U.S. Government Printing Office, pub. by Authority of Congress, 1897, 1899; Washington, D.C.: Bureau of National Literature & Art, 1789-1902, 11 vols., 1907, 1910), Vol. IX, pp. 715-716.

[291] McKinley, William. Dec. 5, 1898, Second Annual Message. James D. Richardson, ed., A Compilation of the Messages & Papers of the Presidents 1789-1897, 10 vols. (Washington, D.C.: U.S. Government Printing Office, pub. by Authority of Congress, 1897, 1899; Washington, D.C.: Bureau of National Literature & Art, 1789-1902, 11 vols., 1907, 1910), Vol. X, pp. 173, 189-190.

[292] Roosevelt, Theodore. Dec. 6, 1904, Fourth Annual Message. A Compilation of the Messages & Papers of the Presidents 20 vols. (NY: Bureau of National Literature, Inc., prepared under the direction of Joint Committee on Printing, of the House & Senate, pursuant to an Act of the 52nd U.S. Congress, 1893, 1923), Vol. XIV, p. 6903, 6915-6916, 6921-6922, 6924-6925, 6928-6929.

[293] Wilson, (Thomas) Woodrow. May 24, 1920, special message to Congress asking permission to assume the mandate for Armenia under the League of Nations. A Compilation of the Messages & Papers of the Presidents 20 vols. (NY: Bureau of National Literature, Inc., 1893, 1923), Vol. XVIII, pp. 8853-5.

[294] Harding, Warren Gamaliel. July 31, 1923, speech he was unable to deliver due to illness, released for publication in San Francisco. A Compilation of the Messages & Papers of the Presidents 20 vols. (NY: Bureau of Nat. Lit., 1893, 1923), Vol. 18, p. 9311-2.

[295] Opinion Journal, Wall Street Journal Editorial Page, May 20, 2005, Ali Al-Ahmed, director of the Saudi Institute in Washington, D.C., article titled: "Hypocrisy Most Holy-Muslims should show some respect to others' religions," posted Friday, May 20, 2005 12:01 a.m. http://www.opinionjournal.com/editorial/feature.html?id=110006712

[296] Williams, Roger. 1644, *Plea for Religious Liberty*. Roger Williams, *The Bloudy Tenent of Persecution* ("Publications of the Narragansett Club" [Providence, R.I.], Vol. III [1867]), pp. 3-4, 58-63, 138-39, 148, 170-71, 201, 247-50, 372-73, 424-25.

[297] Washington, George. Paul F. Boller, Jr., George Washington & Religion (Dallas: S. Methodist Univ. Press, 1963), pp. 24-30.

[298] Washington, George. May 10, 1789, to General Committee of United Baptist Churches of VA. Jared Sparks, ed., The Writings of George Washington 12 vols. (Boston: American Stationer's Co., 1837; NY: F. Andrew's, 1834-47), Vol. XII, p. 154. Charles F. James, Documentary History of Struggle for Religious Liberty in Virginia (1899, reprint, NY: Da Capo, 1971), p. 173. John Clement Fitzpatrick, ed., The Writings of George Washington, from Original Manuscript Sources 1749-99, 39 vols. (Washington, D.C.: U.S. Gov. Printing Office, 1931-1944), Vol. 30, p. 321.

[299] Washington, George. May 26, 1789, letter received from General Assembly of the Presbyterian Church in the U.S.A. Jedediah Morse, D.D., Biographical Sketch of General George Washington, Dec. 31, 1799. William S. Baker, Character Portraits of Washington, 1887, p. 77. William J. Johnson, George Washington-The Christian (St. Paul, MN: William J. Johnson, Merriam Park, 1919; Nashville, TN: Abingdon Press, 1919; reprinted Milford, MI: Mott Media, 1976; reprinted Christian Liberty Press, 502 W. Euclid., Arlington Heights, IL., 60004, 1992), pp. 166-7.

[300] Washington, George. 1789, to General Assembly of Presbyterian Churches in US. Jared Sparks, ed., The Writings of George Washington 12 vols. (Boston: American Stationer's Co., 1837; NY: F. Andrew's, 1834-47), Vol. XII, p. 152. William Barclay Allen, ed., George Washington-A Collection (Indianapolis: Liberty Classics, Liberty Fund, Inc., 7440 N. Shadeland, Indianapolis, IN 46250, 1988; based on Writings of George Washington from original manuscripts, 1745-99, p. 533. John Clement Fitzpatrick, ed., The Writings of George Washington, from Original Manuscripts 1749-99, 39 vols. (Wash., D.C.: U.S. Gov. Printing Office, 1931-44).

[301] Washington, George. May 29, 1789, to Methodist Episcopal Bishop of New York. Jared Sparks, ed., The Writings of George Washington 12 vols. (Boston: American Stationer's Co., 1837; NY: F. Andrew's, 1834-1847), Vol. XII, p. 153.

[302] Washington, George. To Directors of Society of United Brethren for Propagating Gospel among Heathen. Jared Sparks, ed., The Writings of George Washington 12 vols. (Boston: American Stationer's Co., 1837; NY: F. Andrew's, 1834-47), Vol. XII, p. 160.

[303] Washington, George. Aug. 19, 1789, to General Convention of Bishops, Clergy & the Laity of the Protestant Episcopal Church of NY, NJ, PA, Del, MD, VA & NC. Jared Sparks, ed., The Writings of George Washington 12 vols. (Boston: American Stationer's Co., 1837; NY: F. Andrew's, 1834-1847), Vol. XII, pp. 162-163.

[304] Washington, George. Oct. 9, 1789, to Synod of the Dutch Reformed Church in North America. Old South Leaflets. John Clement Fitzpatrick, ed., The Writings of George Washington, from the Original Manuscript Sources 1749-1799, 39 vols. (Wash., D.C.: U.S. Gov. Printing Office, 1931-1944), Vol. XXX, p. 432.

[305] Washington, George. Oct. 1789, to the Quakers at their annual meeting for Pennsylvania, New Jersey, Delaware, & the western part of Virginia & Maryland. Old South Leaflets. William Barclay Allen, ed., George Washington-A Collection (Indianapolis: Liberty Classics, Liberty Fund, Inc., 7440 N. Shadeland, Indianapolis, IN 46250, 1988; from The Writings of George Washington from the original manuscript sources, 1745-99, pp. 533-4. John Clement Fitzpatrick, ed., The Writings of George Washington, from the Original Manuscript Sources 1749-99, 39 vols. (Wash., D.C.: U.S. Gov. Printing Office, 1931-44).

[306] Washington, George. Oct. 28, 1789, to Massachusetts & New Hampshire churches of the First Presbytery of the Eastward, Newburyport. The Massachusetts Centinel, Dec. 5, 1789. Norman Cousins, In God We Trust-The Religious Beliefs & Ideas of the Founding Fathers (NY: Harper & Brothers, 1958), p. 60. Anson Phelps Stokes & Leo Pfeffer, Church & State in the U.S. (NY: Harper & Row, Pub., 1950, revised one-volume edition, 1964), p. 92.

[307] Washington, George. Jan. 1790, to Hebrew Congregations of Philadelphia, Newport, Charlestown & Richmond. William Barclay Allen, ed.,

George Washington-A Collection (Indianapolis: Liberty Classics, Liberty Fund., 7440 N. Shadeland, Indianapolis, IN 46250, 1988; from The Writings of George Washington original sources, 1745-99, pp. 545-6. John Clement Fitzpatrick, ed., The Writings of George Washington, from Original Manuscripts 1749-99, 39 vols. (Wash., D.C.: U.S. Gov. Printing Office, 1931-44).

[308] Washington, George. Aug. 17, 1790, to Hebrew Congregation, Newport, Rhode Island. William Barclay Allen, ed., George Washington-A Collection (Indianapolis: Liberty Classics, Liberty Fund, Inc., 7440 N. Shadeland, Indianapolis, IN 46250, 1988; from The Writings of George Washington from original manuscript sources, 1745-99, pp. 547-8. John Clement Fitzpatrick, ed., The Writings of George Washington, from Original Sources 1749-99, 39 vols. (Wash., D.C.: U.S. Gov. Printing Office, 1931-44).

[309] Washington, George. To Hebrew Congregations, Savannah, Georgia. William Barclay Allen, ed., George Washington-A Collection (Indianapolis: Liberty Classics, Liberty Fund, Inc., 7440 N. Shadeland, Indianapolis, IN 46250, 1988; based on materials reproduced from The Writings of George Washington from the original manuscript sources, 1745-99, p. 549. John Clement Fitzpatrick, ed., The Writings of George Washington, from Original Manuscripts 1749-99, 39 vols. (Wash., D.C.: U.S. Gov. Printing Office, 1931-44).

[310] Washington, George. Mar.15, 1790, to Roman Catholic Churches in America. William Barclay Allen, ed., George Washington-A Collection (Indianapolis: Liberty Classics, Liberty Fund, Inc., 7440 N. Shadeland, Indianapolis, IN 46250, 1988; based almost entirely on materials reproduced from The Writings of George Washington from original manuscript, 1745-1799/pp. 546-547. John Clement Fitzpatrick, ed., The Writings of George Washington, from the Original Manuscript Sources 1749-1799, 39 vols. (Washington, D.C.: U.S. Gov Printing Office, 1931-1944).

[311] Washington, George. Jan. 27, 1793, to congregation of New Church in Baltimore, Washington. Norman Cousins, In God We Trust-The Religious Beliefs & Ideas of the Founding Fathers (NY: Harper & Brothers, 1958), pp. 48, 62. John F. Schroeder, ed., Maxims of Washington (Mt. Vernon Ladies' Assoc., 1942), pp. 301-302.

[312] Washington, George. To Episcopal Church. Paul F. Boller, Jr., George Washington & Religion (Dallas: Southern Methodist Univ. Press, 1963), pp. 163-194. John Eidsmoe, Christianity & the Constitution-The Faith of Our Founding Fathers (Grand Rapids, MI: Baker Book House, A Mott Media Book, 1987, 6th printing 1993), p. 121.

[313] Jefferson, Thomas. Jan. 1, 1802, to Nehemiah Dodge, Ephraim Robbins, & Stephen Nelson of the Danbury Baptist Assoc., Danbury, Connecticut. Reynolds v. U.S., 98 U.S. 164 (1878). A.A. Lipscomb & Albert Bergh, eds., The Writings of Thomas Jefferson 20 vols. (Wash., D.C.: Thomas Jefferson Memorial Assoc., 1903-1904). Norman Cousins, In God We Trust-The Religious Beliefs & Ideas of the American Founding Fathers (NY: Harper & Bros, 1958), p. 135. Arthur Frommer, Bible in the Public Schools (NY: Liberal Press, 1963), p. 19. Charles E. Rice, The Supreme Court & Public Prayer: The Need for Restraint (NY: Fordham Univ. Press, 1964), p. 63. Merrill D. Peterson, Jefferson Writings, Merrill D. Peterson, ed., (NY: Literary Classics of US, 1984), p. 510. Henry Steele Commager, ed., Freedom of Religion & Separation of Church & State (Mount Vernon, NY: A. Colish, Inc., 1985), pp. 28-9.

[314] Jefferson, Thomas. Mar. 4, 1805, Second Inaugural Address. James D. Richardson, ed., Compilation of the Messages & Papers of the Presidents 1789-1897, 10 vols. (Washington, D.C.: Gov. Printing Office, 1897, 1899; Washington, D.C.: Bureau of National Literature & Art, 1789-1902, 11 vols., 1907, 1910), Vol. I, p. 378-382.

[315] Jefferson, Thomas. Jan. 23, 1808, to Samuel Miller. Jefferson Writings, Merrill D. Peterson, ed., (NY: Literary Classics of U.S., 1984), p. 1186-7. Thomas Jefferson Randolph, editor, Memoirs, Correspondence, & Private Papers of Thomas Jefferson, 4 vols. (London & Charlottesville, VA: 1829), Vol. IV, p. 106. Thomas Jefferson, Memoir, Correspondence, & Miscellanies, From the Papers of Thomas Jefferson, Thomas Jefferson Randolph, ed. (Boston: Gray & Bowen, 1830), Vol. IV, pp. 103-4. Paul Leicester Ford, ed., The Writings of Thomas Jefferson, 10 vols. (NY: G.P. Putnam's Sons, 1892-9), Vol. IX, pp. 174-5. A.A. Lipscomb & Albert Bergh, eds., The Writings of Thomas Jefferson 20 vols. (Wash., D.C.: T. Jefferson Memorial Assoc., 1903-4), Vol. XI, p. 428.

[316] Madison, James. June 12, 1788, journal entry. Gaillard Hunt, ed., Writings of James Madison, comprising public papers & private correspondence, first time printed, 9 vols. (NY: G.P. Putnam's Sons, 1900-1910), Vol. 5, pp. 132, 176.

[317] Williams, Roger. 1644, *Plea for Religious Liberty*. Roger Williams, *The Bloudy Tenent of Persecution* ("Publications of the Narragansett Club" [Providence, R.I.], Vol. III [1867]), pp. 3-4, 63, 58-9, 138-39, 148, 170-71, 201, 247-50, 372-73, 424-25.

[318] Cooley, Thomas. Treatise on Constitutional Limitations, 8th Edition, Vol. 2, pp. 966, 974.

[319] Reagan, Ronald Wilson. May 10, 1982, Briefing with Editors from the Midwest. David R. Shepherd, ed., Ronald Reagan: In God I Trust (Wheaton, IL: Tyndale House Pub., Inc., 1984), pp. 62-63.

[320] Madison, James. June 7, 1789, proposal in the U.S. Congress for an amendment with wording: John Eidsmoe, Christianity & the Constitution-The Faith of Our Founding Fathers (Grand Rapids, MI: Baker Book House, Mott Media Book, 1987, 1993), p. 109.

[321] Madison, James. Oct. 31, 1785, "Punishing Disturbers of Religious Worship & Sabbath Breakers" & "Appointing Days of Public Fasting & Thanksgiving." Edmund Fuller & David E. Green, God in the White House-Faiths of American Presidents (NY: Crown Pub., Inc., 1968), p. 41. Daniel L. Driesbach, Real Threat & Mere Shadow: Religious Liberty & First Amendment (Westchester, IL: Crossway Books, 1987), pp. 120-122. John Whitehead, The Rights of Religious Persons in Public Schools (Wheaton, IL: Crossway Books, Good News Pub., 1991), pp. 41, 235.

[322] Madison, James. Nov. 1784, notes on bill for government support of religion. Gaillard Hunt, ed., Writings of James Madison, comprising his public papers & his private correspondence, 9 vols. (NY: G.P. Putnam's Sons, 1900-10). Norman Cousins, In God We Trust-The Religious Beliefs & Ideas of the American Founding Fathers (NY: Harper & Brothers, 1958). p. 303-4.

[323] Madison, James. June 20, 1785. James Madison, Memorial & Remonstrance (Washington, D.C.: Library of Congress, Rare Book Collection, to General Assembly of Virginia, 1785; Massachusetts: Isaiah Thomas, 1786).

[324] Madison, James. July 23, 1813, Proclamation of a National Day of Public Humiliation & Prayer. James D. Richardson, ed., A Compilation of the Messages & Papers of the Presidents 1789-1897, 10 vols. (Washington, D.C.: U.S. Government Printing Office, 1897, 1899; Washington, D.C.: Bureau of National Literature & Art, 1789-1902, 11 vols., 1907, 1910), Vol. I, pp. 532-533.

[325] Madison, James. Nov. 16, 1814, National Day of Public Humiliation, Fasting & Prayer Proclamation. James D. Richardson (U.S. Rep.-TN), ed., A Compilation of the Messages & Papers of the Presidents 1789-1897, 10 vols. (Wash., D.C.: U.S. Government Printing Office, 1897, 1899; Wash., D.C.: Bureau of National Literature & Art, 1789-1902, 11 vols., 1907, 1910), Vol. I, p. 558.

[326] Madison, James. 1815, Presidential Proclamation. James D. Richardson (U.S. Rep.-TN), ed., A Compilation of the Messages & Papers of the

Presidents 1789-1897, 10 vols. (Washington, D.C.: U.S. Government Printing Office, 1897, 1899; Washington, D.C.: Bureau of National Literature & Art, 1789-1902, 11 vols., 1907, 1910).

[327] Madison, James. July 9, 1812, Proclamation of a National Day of Public Humiliation & Prayer. James D. Richardson, ed., A Compilation of the Messages & Papers of the Presidents 1789-1897, 10 vols. (Wash., D.C.: U.S. Gov. Printing Office, Authority of Congress, 1897, 1899; Washington, D.C.: Bureau of National Literature & Art, 1789-1902, 11 vols., 1907, 1910), Vol. I, p. 513.

[328, 329] Story, Joseph. 1833. Joseph Story, Commentaries on the Constitution, 1833 (Boston: Hilliard, Gray, & Co., 1833; reprinted NY: Da Capo Press, 1970), Vol. III, p. 726, Sec. 1868, & p. 727, Sec. 1869. Joseph Story, A Familiar Exposition of the Constitution of the United States (MA: Marsh, Capen Lyon, & Webb, 1840; reprinted NY: Harper & Brothers, 1854; reprinted Washington, D.C.; Regnery Gateway, 1986), pp. 259-261, p. 314, Sec. 441, p. 316, Sec. 444. Joseph Story, Commentaries on the Constitution of the United States (1891), Secs. 1874, 1876, 1877.

[330] U.S. Congress. June 8, 1789, James Madison introducing the initial version of the First Amendment. Annals of the Congress of the United States-First Congress, The Debates & Proceedings in the Congress of the United States with an Appendix Containing Important State Papers & Public Documents & All the Laws of a Public Nature-with a Copious Index 42 vols. (Washington, D.C.: Gales & Seaton, 1834-56), Vol. I, p. 434. Gaillard Hunt, ed., Writings of James Madison, comprising his public papers & his private correspondence, for the first time printed, 9 vols. (NY: G.P. Putnam's Sons, 1900-1910). Norman Cousins, In God We Trust-The Religious Beliefs & Ideas of the American Founding Fathers (NY: Harper & Brothers, 1958), pp. 316-317.

[331] U.S. Congress. George Mason's previously proposed wording for the First Amendment. Kate Mason Rowland, The Life of George Mason (NY: G.P. Putnam's Sons, 1892), Vol. I, p. 244.

[332] U.S. Congress. Aug. 15, 1789, the House Select version of the First Amendment. Annals of the Congress of the United States-First Congress (Washington, D.C.: Gales & Seaton, 1834), Vol. I, p. 434. Wells Bradley, "Religion & Government: The Early Days" (Tulsa, OK: Tulsa Christian Times, Oct. 1992), p. 7. Edwin S. Gaustad, Neither King nor Prelate-Religion & the New Nation, 1776-1826 (Grand Rapids, MI: William B. Eerdmans Pub. Co., 1993), p. 157.

[333] U.S. Congress. Aug. 15, 1789, Peter Sylvester of New York debating the First Amendment. The Debates & Proceedings in the Congress of the United States (Washington, D.C.: Gales & Seaton, 1834), Vol. I, p. 757-759. M.E. Bradford, Religion & The Framers: The Biographical Evidence (Marlborough, NH: Plymouth Rock Fnd, 1991), p. 11. Wells Bradley, "Religion & Government: The Early Days" (Tulsa, OK: Tulsa Christian Times, 10/1992), p. 7.

[334] U.S. Congress. Aug. 15, 1789, statement by Mr. Elbridge Gerry, Massachusetts, regarding wording of proposed First Amendment. The Debates & Proceedings in the Congress of the United States (Wash., D.C.: Gales & Seaton, 1834), Vol. I, p. 757-9.

[335] U.S. Congress. Aug. 15, 1789, James Madison's notes on debates of First Amendment. The Debates & Proceedings in the Congress of the United States (Washington, DC: Gales & Seaton, 1834), Vol. I, p. 757-759. Philip B. Kurland & Ralph Lerner, eds., The Founders' Constitution, 5 vols. (IL: Univ. of Chicago Press, 1987), Vol. V, p. 93. M.E. Bradford, Religion & The Framers-The Biographical Evidence (Marlborough, NH: Plymouth Rock Fnd, 1991), p. 12. Wells Bradley, "Religion & Government: The Early Days" (Tulsa, OK: Tulsa Christian Times, 10/92), p. 7.

[336, 337] U.S. Congress. Aug. 1789, Benjamin Huntington, in the debates on the First Amendment. M.E. Bradford, Religion & The Framers: The Biographical Evidence (Marlborough, NH: Plymouth Rock Foundation, 1991), p. 11. Wells Bradley, "Religion & Government: The Early Days" (Tulsa, OK: Tulsa Christian Times, Oct. 1992), p. 7.

[338] U.S. Congress. Aug. 1789, James Madison's response to Benjamin Huntington & Peter Sylvester regarding First Amendment. Philip B. Kurland & Ralph Lerner, eds., The Founders' Constitution, 5 vols. (IL: Univ. of Chicago Press, 1987), Vol. V, p. 93. M.E. Bradford, Religion & The Framers-The Biographical Evidence (Marlborough, NH: Plymouth Rock Fnd, 1991), p. 12.

[339] U.S. Congress. Aug. 1789, James Madison's notes on debates of First Amendment. The Debates & Proceedings in the Congress of the United States (Wash: D.C.: Gales & Seaton, 1834), Vol. I, p. 757-759. Philip B. Kurland & Ralph Lerner, eds., The Founders' Constitution, 5 vols. (IL: Univ. of Chicago Press, 1987), Vol. V, p. 93. M.E. Bradford, Religion & The Framers-The Biographical Evidence (Marlborough, NH: Plymouth Rock Fnd, Inc., 1991), p. 12. Wells Bradley, "Religion & Government: The Early Days" (Tulsa, OK: Tulsa Christian Times, Oct. 1992), p. 7.

[340] U.S. Congress. Aug. 15, 1789, Samuel Livermore of New Hampshire proposed wording of the First Amendment. Wells Bradley, "Religion & Government: The Early Days" (Tulsa, OK: Tulsa Christian Times, Oct. 1992), p. 7. Annals of the Congress of the United States-First Congress (Washington, D.C.: Gales & Seaton, 1834), Vol. I, pp. 729, 731. Edwin S. Gaustad, Neither King nor Prelate-Religion & the New Nation, 1776-1826 (Grand Rapids, MI: William B. Eerdmans Pub. Co., 1993), p. 157.

[341] U.S. Congress. Aug. 20, 1789, Fisher Ames of Massachusetts introduced language for the First Amendment. Wells Bradley, "Religion & Government: The Early Days" (Tulsa, OK: Tulsa Christian Times, Oct. 1992), p. 7. Annals of the Congress of the United States-First Congress (Washington, D.C.: Gales & Seaton, 1834), Vol. I, pp. 729, 731. Edwin S. Gaustad, Neither King nor Prelate- Religion & the New Nation, 1776-1826 (Grand Rapids, MI: William B. Eerdmans Pub. Co., 1993), p. 157.

[342] U.S. Congress. Sept. 3, 1789, Senate proposed several versions of First Amendment. Annals of the Congress of the United States-1st Congress (Washington, D.C.: Gales & Seaton, 1834), Vol. I, pp. 729-31.

[343, 344, 345] U.S. Congress. Sept. 3, 1789, Senate proposed several versions of First Amendment. Annals of the Congress of the United States-First Congress (Wash., D.C.: Gales & Seaton, 1834), Vol. I, pp. 729-31. S.E. Morrison, ed., Sources & Documents Illustrating the American Revolution, 1754-1788, & the Formation of the Federal Constitution (NY: Oxford Univ. Press, 1923), p. 158. Edwin S. Gaustad, Neither King nor Prelate-Religion & the New Nation, 1776-1826 (Grand Rapids, MI: Eerdmans Pub., 1993), p. 158.

[346] U.S. Congress. Sept. 9, 1789, Senate agreed on this version of First Amendment. Wells Bradley, "Religion & Government: The Early Days" (Tulsa, OK: Tulsa Christian Times, Oct. 1992), p. 7. Annals of the Congress of the United States-First Congress (Washington, D.C.: Gales & Seaton, 1834), Vol. I, p. 729-31. Edwin S. Gaustad, Neither King nor Prelate-Religion & the New Nation, 1776-1826 (Grand Rapids, MI: William B. Eerdmans Pub. Co., 1993), p. 158. S.E. Morrison, ed., Sources & Documents Illustrating the American Revolution, 1754-88, & Formation of the Federal Constitution (NY: Oxford Univ. Press, 1923), p. 158.

[347, 348] U.S. Congress. Sept. 25, 1789, wording agreed upon by a joint committee of the House & Senate. Wells Bradley, "Religion & Government: The Early Days" (Tulsa, OK: Tulsa Christian Times, Oct. 1992), p. 7. Annals of the Congress of the United States-1st Congress (Washington,

D.C.: Gales & Seaton, 1834), Vol. I, pp. 729, 731. S.E. Morrison, ed., Sources & Documents Illustrating the American Revolution, 1754-1788, & Formation of Federal Constitution (NY: Oxford Univ. Press, 1923), p. 158. Edwin S. Gaustad, Neither King nor Prelate-Religion & New Nation, 1776-1826 (Grand Rapids, MI: Eerdmans Pub., 1993), p. 158.

[349] Reagan, Ronald Wilson. Mar. 8, 1983, to National Assoc. of Evangelicals. William Safire, ed., Lend Me Your Ears-Great Speeches in History (NY: W.W. Norton & Co. 1992), p. 464.

[350] Clinton, William Jefferson "Bill". July 12, 1995, address at James Madison High School, Vienna, VA. Kathy Lewis & Cara Tanamachi, Washington Bureau of the Dallas Morning News, "Clinton orders guidelines on school religious issues-President wants to head off GOP prayer amendment" (Dallas, TX: Dallas Morning News, Inc., A.H. Belo Corporation, 7/13/95), pp. 1A, 10A.

[351] U.S. Congress. Jan. 19, 1853, Mr. Badger, report of Congressional investigations in U.S. Senate. Reports of Committees of U.S. Senate, 2nd Session of 32nd Congress, 1852-53 (Washington: Robert Armstrong, 1853), pp. 1, 6, 8-9. Benjamin Franklin Morris, The Christian Life & Character of the Civil Institutions of the United States (Philadelphia: George W. Childs, 1864), pp. 324-327.

[352] U.S. Congress. Mar. 27, 1854, Mr. Meacham, report of House Committee on Judiciary. Reports of Committees of House of Representatives made during 1st Session, 33rd Congress (Wash.: A.O.P. Nicholson, 1854), pp. 1, 6, 8-9. Benjamin Franklin Morris, The Christian Life & Character of the Civil Institutions of the United States (Philadelphia, PA: L. Johnson & Co., entered, in Clerk's Office of Dist. Court of U.S. for Eastern Dist. of PA, 1863; George W. Childs, 1864), pp. 317-24.

[353] U.S. Supreme Court. 1963, School District of Abington Township v. Schempp, 374 U.S. 203, 212, 225, 83 S. Ct. 1560, 10 L. Ed. 2d 844 (1963), pp. 21, 71.

[354] Ronald Reagan, radio address, Feb. 25, 1984, David R. Shepherd, ed., Ronald Reagan: In God I Trust (Wheaton, IL: Tyndale House Pub., Inc., 1984), pp. 77-79.

[355] U.S. District Court. 1983, W. District of Virginia, Crockett v. Sorenson, 568 F.Supp. 1422, 1425-1430

[356] Webster, Noah. 1828, American Dictionary of the English Language 1828 (reprinted San Francisco: Foundation for American Christian Education, 1967), definition of "secular."

[357] Adams, John. Mar. 6, 1799, *Proclamation of a National Day of Fasting & Prayer*. Public Papers.

[358] Taylor, Zachary. July 3, 1849, *Proclamation of National Day of Prayer* during epidemic. Public Papers.

[359] Johnson, Andrew. Oct. 26, 1867, *Proclamation of National Day of Thanksgiving & Praise*. Public Papers.

[360] Lincoln, Abraham. Mar. 30, 1863, *Proclamation of National Day of Fasting & Prayer*. Public Papers.

[361] Grant, Ulysses S. Oct. 27, 1875, *Proclamation of National Day of Thanksgiving*. Public Papers.

[362] Grant, Ulysses S. Oct. 26, 1876, *Proclamation of National Day of Thanksgiving*. Public Papers.

[363] Hayes, Rutherford. Oct. 29, 1877, *Proclamation of National Day of Thanksgiving & Prayer*. Public Papers.

[364] Hayes, Rutherford. Oct. 30, 1878, *Proclamation of National Day of Thanksgiving & Prayer*. Public Papers.

[365] Hayes, Rutherford. Nov. 3, 1879, *Proclamation of National Day of Thanksgiving & Prayer*. Public Papers.

[366] Arthur, Chester A. Nov. 4, 1881, *Proclamation of National Day of Thanksgiving & Prayer*. Public Papers.

[367] Cleveland, Grover. Nov. 2, 1885, *Proclamation of National Day of Thanksgiving & Prayer*. Public Papers.

[368] Cleveland, Grover. Oct. 25, 1887, *Proclamation of National Day of Thanksgiving & Prayer*. Public Papers.

[369] U.S. Supreme Court. 1963, *Abington Township v. Schempp*, 374 U.S. 203, 225, 300-301 (1963), Assoc. Justice Tom Clark writing the Court's opinion, Justice William Joseph Brennan, Jr. concurring.

[370] U.S. District Court. 1983, W. Dist. of Virginia, Crockett v. Sorenson, 568 F.Supp. 1422, 1425-1430.

[371] Reagan, Ronald. Oct. 13, 1983, Q & A w/women leaders of Christian organizations. David R. Shepherd, ed., Ronald Reagan: In God I Trust (Wheaton, IL: Tyndale House Pub., Inc., 1984), pp. 41-44, 70, 136-137.

[372] Jefferson, Thomas. Sept. 23, 1800, Benjamin Rush. Jefferson's Extracts from the Gospels, p. 320. John Bartlett, Bartlett's Familiar Quotations (Boston: Little, Brown & Co., 1855, 1980), p. 388.

[373] Reagan, Ronald Wilson. Jan. 26, 1984, Salute to Free Enterprise. David R. Shepherd, Ronald Reagan: In God We Trust (Wheaton, IL: Tyndale House Pub., Inc., 1984), pp. 138-139.

[374] U.S. Congress. Aug. 11, 1992, U.S. Rep. Nick Joe Rahall introduced legislation in 102nd Congress to declare Nov. 22-28, 1992, America's Christian Heritage Week. (103rd Cong. Res. H.J. 113), Cong. Record, Vol 138, No. 1, 8/12/92.

[375] Coolidge, Calvin. July 5, 1926, celebration of 150th anniversary of the Declaration of Independence, Philadelphia. Calvin Coolidge, Foundations of the Republic-Speeches & Addresses (NY: Charles Scribner's Sons, 1926), pp. 441-454. Charles Wallis, ed., Our American Heritage (NY: Harper & Row, Pub., 1970), p. 29.

[376] Reagan, Ronald Wilson. Feb. 25, 1984, radio address. David R. Shepherd, ed., Ronald Reagan: In God I Trust (Wheaton, IL: Tyndale House Pub., Inc., 1984), pp. 77-79.

[377] Coolidge, Calvin. July 5, 1926, 150th anniversary of Declaration of Independence, Philadelphia. Calvin Coolidge, Foundations of the Republic-Speeches & Addresses (NY: Charles Scribner's Sons, 1926), pp. 441-454.

[378] Jefferson, Thomas. 1781, Notes on the State of Virginia, Query XVIII, 1781, 1782, p. 237.

[379] Lowell, James Russell. Daniel Marsh, Unto The Generations (Buena Park, CA: ARC, 1970), p. 51. Edward L.R. Elson, D.D., Lit.D., LL.D., America's Spiritual Recovery (Westwood, NJ: Fleming H. Revell Co., 1954), p. 73.